Frameworks for Policy Analysis

Frameworks for Policy Analysis

Merging Text and Context

Raul P. Lejano

Routledge
Taylor & Francis Group
New York   London

Routledge is an imprint of the
Taylor & Francis Group, an informa business

Published in 2006 by
Routledge
Taylor & Francis Group
270 Madison Avenue
New York, NY 10016

Published in Great Britain by
Routledge
Taylor & Francis Group
2 Park Square
Milton Park, Abingdon
Oxon OX14 4RN

Printed in the United States of America on acid-free paper
10 9 8 7 6 5 4 3 2 1

International Standard Book Number-10: 0-415-95276-X (Softcover) 0-415-95275-1 (Hardcover)
International Standard Book Number-13: 978-0-415-95276-7 (Softcover) 978-0-415-95275-0 (Hardcover)
Library of Congress Card Number 2005025574

Library of Congress Cataloging-in-Publication Data

Lejano, Raul P., 1961-
 Frameworks for policy analysis: merging text and context / Raul P. Lejano.
  p. cm.
 Includes bibliographical references and index.
 ISBN 0-415-95275-1 (hb : alk. paper) -- ISBN 0-415-95276-X (pb : alk. paper)
 1. Policy sciences. 2. Public administration--Decision making. I. Title.

H97.L45 2005
320.6—dc22   2005025574

Taylor & Francis Group
is the Academic Division of Informa plc.

Visit the Taylor & Francis Web site at
http://www.taylorandfrancis.com

and the Routledge Web site at
http://www.routledge-ny.com

Contents

Dedication

To my mother, Alice, professor and humanitarian,
who is the most beautiful person I know,
who continues to teach me how to live
in faith and compassion.
And to my father, Rodolfo, engineer and runner,
who continues to teach me to work hard and well,
and to never, *never*, give up.

Acknowledgments

My gratitude goes out to my academic mentors. To Lloyd Shapley, whose enormous theoretical contributions are matched only by his generosity and Climis Davos, who taught me much about being original. I thank Helen Ingram for sharing with me her deep insight into institutions. I thank John Whiteley, who is a true intellectual and spiritual colleague. I thank Dan Stokols for his collaboration and guidance in developing a new line of research. I thank David McBride of Routledge for seeing something in this book to take it on and Angela Chnapko and Susan Fox-Greenberg for seeing it through the process.

I acknowledge the following for their permission to use their figures for the book:

Anna Carissa Lejano for Figures 1 and 2 and Figure 10.2.

Bahram Fazeli (Communities for a Better Environment) for Figure 7.1

Bebiano Mejino (Pawikan Conservation Project) for Figure 10.8

Elsevier for the use of Figures 6.1 to 6.5, which appear in Lejano, R.P. and H. Rei. Testing the assumptions behind emissions trading in non-market goods: The RECLAIM program in southern California, *Environmental Science & Policy* 8(2005):367–377; and Figures 10.1 and 10.3 to 10.7, which appear in Lejano, R.P. and A. Ocampo-Salvador. Context and differentiation: Comparative analysis of two community-based fishers' organizations, *Marine Policy* (forthcoming).

Introduction

In a sense, this book is an account of how we have mythologized policy. It is also a charting of directions that we can take policy analysis from this point onward. By "mythological," we simply mean the construction of self-contained symbolic systems to represent the policy field and the search for solutions within this same field.

Perhaps a useful place to begin is by noting our fondness for metaphors when speaking about policy. For example, we often refer to policy as if it were a prescription or some sort of social recipe that might be brought into any kitchen and employed to create the desired result. Yet another analogy is that of policy as a map that tells us, in the midst of a terrain of infinite possibilities, which one ideal path society should take. A modernist version of this class of metaphors is to liken policy to a telescope, with the policy expert, as Galileo, peering through the universe in search of its secret. Policy is the answer to the sphinx's riddle.

Running through all of these analogies is the notion that embedded in our concept of policy is the idea of analysis, the act of searching within the universe of possibilities for the true and eternal, hidden in all its complexity. In contrast to synthesis, which posits the creation of an altogether extraneous concept, analysis entails discernment within the opaque. But in its mythological state, this action amounts to nothing more than the confirmation of the *a priori* analytic — that is, the discovery of objects that we had already built into the system to begin with.

The common notion is not so much the asking of, "What does it mean to find an answer to a policy question?" or "How does policy reflect life as presently lived?" or "How might we go about the process of policy design?" The metaphor is, again, that of the telescope, not the looking

1

glass. The dominant concept is not self-reflection but that of analysis, the unearthing and revealing, as in panning for gold. We stop the world, examine it from a distance, and give it a shake or two until we divine its contents. And, so, policy analysis has, from the beginning, been wrought through and through with the process of searching and evaluating, comparing and choosing. This process, as we discuss in this book, has provided us with powerful methods for approaching policy problems, as well as profound limitations.

Let us illustrate these issues with a simple example. Beginning in the 1980s, development agencies began, in earnest, to make use of the classic metaphor of the market to diagnose the ills of modern-day governments. While subject to varying degrees of sophistication, the model remains a simple one: the ideal of undistorted communication of demands and costs through a pricing signal within a perfectly competitive market. Any elements in a market that prevent the perfect transmission of these values would be distortions to this ideal model. Now, the thing is that we institutionalize such models and fashion entire economies after them. Simple models lead to simple institutional recipes, however — in this case, a formula that, within international lending institutions, became known as the "structural adjustment package." This package consisted of a suite of measures that came directly out of the recondite model of the ideal market and so almost completely targeted those things that appeared as distortions to the model. These were solutions extracted from a self-contained symbolic field, which we called a "model," and were universal prescriptions meant to apply everywhere. So they were applied everywhere, in countries that ranged over an incredibly wide spectrum of wealth, demographics, histories, institutional experiences, and traditions. It is no wonder, then, that this common package of measures led to widely different results in different places (see Rapley, 1996 for a useful account).

There is a danger in the mythological approach to policy. The construction of self-contained symbolic systems, within which we pan for solutions that perhaps we unknowingly inserted to begin with, allows the policymaker to ignore the realities of the particular real-world context that we are facing. Moreover, this ability to distance one's analysis from context leads us to ignore the utter complexity of the latter. There is a dimensionality to real situations that ineluctably exceeds that of our self-contained systems, and this is where our book begins.

The Goals of the Book

The basic intentions of this book are simple. We would like to find ways to go beyond the mythological and to bring contextuality and complexity back into policy analysis. As a result, we should seek out ways to increase the dimensionality and authenticity of our analyses. To do this, we would like to achieve a number of things in this book, namely:

- Map the terrain of policy analysis thus far, and point out directions for extending these analytics beyond the limits of their self-contained models.
- Enable analysts to increase the dimensionality of their analyses by gaining a facility with multiple policy languages.
- Develop new directions for analysis that explicitly bring context, experience, and complexity back into the analytic.

The main goal is to propose new approaches to analysis that can speak to the ineffable complexity of policy situations. To do this, however, we need to cover some of the existing ground of analysis to peer into the limits of these situations and begin envisioning directions forward. In each case, we point out the limits of their scope and problems with how they have been used. Sooner or later, we begin to realize that each of these approaches speaks to differing aspects of a policy situation. There is another reason for purposely walking the reader through a number of different policy lenses. Sooner or later, the analyst learns that to respect the sheer complexity (or, to put it in geometric terms, dimensionality) of policy situations, we each have to learn to speak different policy languages. For this reason, the analyst should benefit from some familiarity with them. In another sense, we need to go over the present terrain of analysis as a foreshadowing of the latter part of the book, which sketches out new directions in policy analysis.

Analysis in the Twenty-First Century

The century begins with a deep skepticism in institutions — at least, the ideals that we hoped these institutions would embody. Surely, we have by now seen the degree to which we have abused notions such as freedom, development, patriotism, and statehood, but it is perhaps because these constructs, and the institutions patterned after them, did not live up to the needs and conditions of our lives to begin with. Perhaps, these notions were constructed completely apart from the immediacy and complexity of those conditions that move us in the most real ways. In the tumult that we have witnessed thus far in this new century, there arises an even greater need for some semblance of clarity of thought, of a point of view that might be likened to finding some, however fleeting, refuge in the eye of the storm.

Writing from this eternally sunlit spot on the West Coast of the United States, I cannot help but muse on the irony of the colossally simple ideal of the American Dream, which was evidently conceived with no thought about the economic, racial, and political fractures that so divide the country. And, so, the book is an attempt to ground analysis in the common and complex ground of our living.

Immediately, the reader will see some strong conceptual predispositions here — first, I do state, boldly but not flatly, that the politic of the everyday does touch us all in complex and common ways. Whatever the extent to which we dream of achieving a common vision, it is the complexity and immediacy of the everyday that brings us all together. Increasingly, people find themselves asking, amidst the backdrop of contending claims and ideologies, what do things really mean? Now, this is not a simple question, and we should not expect simple answers. This is where analysis begins.

It is sometimes supposed that policy truths are constituted by whatever stories are fashioned by those who are best at playing the policy "game." This is not the ground of policy, however. Rather, policy has to be capable of reflecting the immediacy and complexity of our everyday condition. Regardless of how we fashion and refashion our conceptual universe(s) with regard to the refugee who finds herself strewn in an empty, far-flung camp on the edge of catastrophe, we cannot deconstruct away her hunger or her grief. To the welfare worker who six months before could barely manage programs that were bursting at the seams from the sheer demand for services and now finds her position terminated by the latest budget cycle, we cannot substitute ideology. Nor can we simply treat as discourse the very workings of the institutions and practices that evolve around these real conditions. This reflects another strong conceptual stance taken herein: that is to insist that policy, and our analytic, be judged through the test of our experience. This calls for an analysis that can speak to the manifold complexity and richness of the real.

This takes us to an important point of this book, which is to say that policy, in order that we might transport it away from the realm of mythology, requires grounding. The grounding we speak of is not an act of compromise of some theoretical ideal — rather, it is the opposite. It is this grounding that will enable policy analysis to attain the dimensionality to handle, in effective and theoretical ways, the contingencies of experience. In fact, toward the latter part of the book, we begin to see how a return to context and experience leads us to new and richer bodies of theory and practice. Still, we are cognizant of the main point of policy analysis, which is to, somehow, arrive at solutions that are, as one author put it, "ongoing strategies for structuring relationships and coordinating behavior to achieve collective purposes" (Stone, 1997). The point this book makes is that finding such strategies requires grounding. Grounding, in turn, requires a return to the real, and we can start by examining a sample of real-world policy questions as they arise in context.

- You are running a nonprofit that, over the last four years, has created walk-in counseling and training centers for recent immigrants. More recently, however, federal and state support has become increasingly strained, and trends toward faith-based and private services are increasing. The needs and conditions of your clients are evolving also, as are the skills demanded by employers. How do you begin to reorient your practice and even to consider how the organization itself needs to change?
- You are a planner who finds herself in the middle of an already congested city where there has not historically been a strong tradition of planning. You are imbued with a desire to build more sense into the planning process, but where do you begin and what change can you realistically hope to pursue? The largest project in the works involves the siting of a new upscale retail complex, but what appears to be driving the decision process are deeply embedded influences within city council to engage in real estate speculation. How does one begin imagining reform in such a situation?
- You are a project coordinator in an international development agency and are presently in a unit devoted to supporting coastal resource management in developing countries. There has evolved, over the years, a healthy and broad communication among nongovernmental organizations regarding best practices, and this shows in the project proposals you receive. Increasingly, however, you cannot tell one proposal from another or begin to assess how each funded project is coming along. How does one begin to search for lessons, new insights, and needs in the middle of an increasingly homogeneous discourse?
- You are a legislative analyst for a public interest group. The state senate is proposing a bill to lower tariffs on imports of corn syrup, which hurts your constituents, many of whom are local farmers. However, the bill also has a rider that provides a new debt relief program for lower-income families, many of whom are also your constituents. What is your group's position on the proposed bill?

But the policy field may include situations and questions that one might not ordinarily include in its scope.

- You have been part of an increasingly large corps of chronically homeless in the inner city. To survive, you used to combine state relief subsidies and food stamps with nonprofit shelters to which you turn toward the end of the month when your funds ran short and you had to leave the so-called hotels in the area. With the recent change in unemployment compensation, however, you find yourself running out earlier and earlier in the month. How do you find new ways to make ends meet?
- You are the supervisor at a border patrol station where, on the one hand, there are new initiatives from the department to increase scrutiny of border crossings but, on the other, you also have to respond to a trend of increasing violence displayed by the border guards. How do you begin reforming this institution?
- You are a political analyst in a nation that is presently considering a complete overhaul of its political system. The reason that the proposal (e.g., moving from a parliamentary to a presidential system) seems to be gaining ground with members of the legislature seems not to have anything to do with the public good, however, but entirely to do with the ambitions of political entrepreneurs who intend to profit from times of transition and political uncertainty. How do you analyze such a proposal?

Moving beyond the Mythological

Why do we talk of metaphors? It is because policy analysis is driven by models, which really are extended metaphors. Metaphors and models are fictive devices. More to the point, models are hypostatizations, i.e., fictions that stand in for reality. But, and this is a central point, policy cannot reside within the self-contained terrain of the model. To take a simple example, a model plane cannot fly or, if it did, cannot be ridden. If it did, on both counts, then it would not be a model. Models can be used and manipulated, but not so the world. This problem is so much more complex when we deal with not just material, but social realities as well. We use models to supplant reality because we can control and manipulate the former. A model is a world of our own making, and, in this world, we are its queens and kings.

Now, there are other metaphors that we can speak of. For example, some talk of policy as a social construction. That is, policy is a device that is used to create an artifice (of ideas), and these artifices are freely exchanged, manipulated, but never pinned down. This is well and good, but let us make the point that to so completely give our understanding over to the notion that policy is purely a construct is to so easily justify artifice. However much policy has been constructed, it cannot simply be artifice. One of the points we make in this book is that the twenty-first century ethic should be a turn toward the real and the substantive — in other words, a turning away from the mythological. This is the main difference between policy, as it should be understood, and the policy model — policy is and should be an enacting, a setting into motion. This is one of the main points of the book, that policy is not simply a construct. We have to engage in more than hypostatization. This is a sentiment that, for lack of a better word, we will, at various points in this text, describe as "postconstructionist."

What happens when we venture outside the hypostasis of policy? We take up this theme later in the book, but for now, let us start with an innocent (but presumptuous) working definition of policy analysis.

> Policy analysis is the process by which we arrive at a course of public action that will effect beneficial change in the situation at hand.

Why is this presumptuous? Because it embeds the notion of action in the definition. By action, we mean real change in real situations — that is, molecules must move. This is a radical notion nowadays. By public, we simply mean any event affecting any social group, whether formal or informal. Some changes do not at all involve physical activity. For example, say that townsfolk set the following policy: "From now on, let us call our town Middle-Earth." But even within this example, with some circumspection, we realize that molecules do move. It is the policy analyst's task to see what real changes result. By real, we begin, though not necessarily end, with the notion of the physical. Let us begin with an eye toward changes in the material conditions by which people in society live, and then move on from there. Analysis, we claim, is a return to the here and now.

The focus on the real is crucial. Increasingly, in this Internet-enabled world, analysts finds themselves in a position of being able to access great amounts of information (census information, maps, environmental data, commerce, etc.) about a community and then to process the information into some project report, all without ever actually having set foot in the place. One of the things we question, in our postconstructionist frame of mind, is the ability of analysts to study, assess, and recommend solutions to a problem without leaving their cognitive perch. Analysis requires grounding. Yet, for policy analysts, this leaves us with the question: If we do indeed boldly venture outside our cubicle and spend time in a place, how would this possibly affect our analysis?

As we will see, much of the analytic we have built around the policy sciences are geared toward the insular mode of analysis, which really does not require grounding. If we look beyond this model, however, what insights do we arrive at when we experience a place, walk its broken pavement, sample its trendy emporiums or dingy eateries, or come to know its residents? More than this, how do we incorporate this element of experience into our analysis? That we may struggle to find good answers to these questions underscores the great distance we have to travel.

Consider one powerful methodology used in the policy sciences, that of statistical analysis. In this model, we seek after large numbers of cases — the larger the more statistically significant. But in the pursuit for large numbers, what happens to our cognitive stance? Let us say that we want to compare changes in the quality of life in large cities over the last ten years, in terms of different parameters. Now, the larger the numbers of cases (or cities, in this example), the less able we are to focus on any one place and be attentive to it. Physically, this precludes our getting to know a place beyond the mere assemblage of figures we may collect for each and every case study. In fact, we can only look at data that one can systematically measure in each and every one of the cities, which reduces our relevant observations to the statistically relevant. Census data are the easiest to obtain and most commonly utilized type of data for this kind of analysis. Using statistical power is like getting into an epistemological balloon and floating farther and farther away from the landscape until we see the broad shape of the region, its hills and valleys but not its puddles and mounds — that is, until we are far enough to take it all in without reeling from its sheer detail. But life exists not in the panorama, but down in the dirt. Notice that from the rarified air of the upper troposphere, we cannot see people. We might see cities and corridors, or we might get a sense of land uses and infrastructure, but we would not see people or understand places. The point to be made is that policy affects not society writ large, because society is itself a fictive device, but people and places. What would analysis look like when we descend back to the particulars of a context? What about the beauty of a place, its charm, its dingy streets and back alleys? What of its people? When we aspire to an analytic that operates by projecting the world onto a unitary field, we lose this kind of richness. But if we decide to return to the richness of this kind of knowledge, which we will call "experience," what kind of policy analytic could possibly incorporate this? How do we link experience to policy recommendations? How do we systematically study experience so that our analysis is both insightful and rigorous? Could we possibly proceed as policy analysts once we walk away from our laptop and standard-issue cubicle? While the statistical approach brings with it the certitude of replicability, experience speaks to a different criterion, that of authenticity.

In this book, we employ two main strategies in order to move analysis beyond the mythological:

- Policy situations exceed our models in terms of dimensionality, so there is a need to employ multiple perspectives and frameworks for understanding and describing these situations.
- We need new policy models that give a better accounting of context and experience and are more suited to dealing with the inherently complex phenomenon of policy.

The first is taken up in Parts I and II of this book, and the second is the subject of Part III, which builds upon the previous sections of the book to sketch out new directions in policy analysis. In so doing, we encounter different policy "languages" — from the utter mathematization of policy in Part I, to the staunchly anti-positivist frameworks in Part II, to models that challenge formalization, altogether, in Part III, the latter presenting new trajectories for policy thought.

Different Traditions

What do analysts do when they do analysis? To put it another way, what is the analyst's conceptual accounting stance? Analysis is, after all, figuring out the right way through the universe of infinite possibilities, and so how does one go about this? For now, let us look at two routes, represented in Figure 1 and Figure 2, that each, in their own way, depicts this search.

Consider the figures shown. They are both seated, each of them aspiring toward and somehow searching for the truth. But notice, too, how different they are. How would you describe each? How would you contrast them? Compare them physically — though both seated, they are each in quite different states. Most importantly, what do these figures symbolize?

The figure on the top is in search, as we said. How do we discern this? We see it in the furrow on his brow, in the arch of his back, in the muscles that are tensed with effort. What sort of effort is this we wonder. It is perhaps a yearning after eternal truths, possibly a reflecting on one's future, or maybe a pondering of the demise of the king of Denmark — at any rate, the figure approaches the question through the sheer dint of effort, almost agonizing in his attempt to divine the truth. The figure attains the goal by lunging after and seizing it. The figure is saying: "Thought is effort, and

Figs. 1 and 2 Two seated figures.

I have to strive to reach after the answer." The figure has, in fact, become a human question mark.

The figure on the bottom is also in search, but in a radically different movement than the first figure. Whereas the thinker on the top arches forward in a motionless yet powerful movement forward, the figure on the bottom sits back in a tranquil state of peace. The thinker arches forward as if trying to get at his prize, while the lotus-positioned figure stays back in a motion of perpetual acceptance, ready to take in and be part of the truth. The figure on the bottom has assumed the answer and has become it. He attains the answer by letting go and abiding in a cosmic symmetry. In a sense, there is in this motion some of the grounding that we speak of, except that here it is an inseparable being in a here and now that knows no limit. Whereas for the figure on the top, truth is to be arrived at through thought, for the figure on the bottom, truth is something that is simply experienced and entered into until all the preconceived formulas of knowing fade away, leaving an entirely new consciousness (that is, *satori*).

As we venture into the theoretical underpinnings of classic policy analysis in chapter 1, we will understand that much of the philosophical foundation of policy analysis is founded on the figure on the top and not on the bottom. This is a limitation that we strive, ever so incrementally, to begin to escape. The prevalent notion of rationality that pervades the policy analysis field is a Western one. We begin to undo these foundations, however, as we progress farther away from the so-called rational purposive model. Later in the book, in what is perhaps a distinct movement closer to the other, Eastern model, we seek ways to locate policy in the ground of our experience, and by entering deeply into the phenomenon of that experience, begin to understand it in new ways, as if for the first time.

The Outline of This Book

The book is organized into three parts:

Part I   The Positivist Foundations of Policy Analysis
Part II   The Postpositivist Turn
Part III   The Postconstructionist Sentiment

We begin this book by taking up the classic model of analysis, which is a rationalist one in which policies are analyzed and judged according to some all-encompassing rule. Whether known as a *summum bonum*, social welfare function, program goal, objective function, or other, the rational model seeks to collapse all of the relevant factors into one measure and then maximize this. It is a model that turns policy decisions into something like an objective exercise, where values only need to be measured for the different contributing factors and the course of action that maximizes the total value chosen. The rational model, which draws much from the positivist school of thought, is the subject of Part I. In this part, we walk through the history and theoretical underpinnings, and critically reflect on the limitations of approaches based on the rational model. We also discuss how we might begin to resolve some of these limitations.

To this classic model, there have arisen a number of important alternatives, which we might lump under the term "postpositivism" — a reaction to the classic, rational model's reliance on objective measures and standards. These alternative models, in their own way, portray policy as something other than the exercise of measurement and calculation. The term "postpositivist" implies a greater willingness to consider subjective and interpretive elements of policy decisions as valid and, in fact, necessary. A more pragmatic, pluralist model portrays policy as crafted not out of some rational ethic, but out of the sheer contest of competing proposals. In this latter model, the emphasis is not on the optimal course of society, but in explaining what dynamics create policy outcomes. Related to this is a policy model founded on critique, which understands policy outcomes and processes as political moves to create gains for power-wielding groups and which seeks to portray the injustices and inconsistencies of these policies. The so-called postpositivist turn is the theme of Part II, in which we learn about various policy analytics that belong to this movement.

In Part II, we take up a more interpretive mode of analysis, which understands the policy process as a contest over what policy means. In an interpretive world, policies are narratives that are crafted by storytellers. Groups or individuals may see different things in a situation, and policy now becomes a question of whose understanding is influential in the policy process. Another version of the interpretive is a constructivist (or constructionist) approach, which sees policy as a social construct (Berger and Luckmann, 1966). In its strongest form, this model posits policy as pure construction — text devoid of any ultimate meaning but only subject to contests over interpretation. Authorship becomes a contested issue at this point. In this rarified air, the question becomes not what the reality of policy might be, because even reality is constructed, but, rather, the issue of how a policy is constructed, who constructs it, and how effective the construct is. In some cases, analysts seek ways to reconcile conflicting constructs or narratives, e.g., by developing a suitable metanarrative. In this book, we study the divergence between rationalist and postpositivist models but also inquire into commonalities between them. In fact, both are constructionist, in the sense that policy (or truth, nature, reality) is whatever is constructed by the analyst's will. These are, after all, self-contained symbolic systems.

We learn how both movements (the classical and postpositivist) can serve to entrench the mythological nature of analysis. To take an example, consider the strong and, as we discuss later in the book, somewhat artificial dichotomy created when we set apart policy from implementation as two discrete phases in a policy process (Pressman and Wildavsky, 1979). This strong notion has so influenced policy that we have come to think of this logical sequence as a natural rule. That is, policy is formulated in some center of decision making and then implemented in the field in an arrangement that is presumed to be temporal as well as spatial. This is entirely in keeping with the rationalist model, which begins with the assumption of a center of intelligence. The postpositivist or constructionist notion of policy also helps further this dichotomy because now policy can be seen and understood as simply text. As text, policy need only be formulated, then taken from its origin and imported into each and every place, and enacted by the state and other policy actors. Whether policies are reflections of enlightened reasoning in the halls of the executive or legislative branches, or the unforeseeable and contested outcomes of a pluralist, political battle, the point is that these policies are ostensibly not of the place. Indeed, as constructs, they are not of any "place." A postconstructionist bent means going beyond the mere textuality of policy and seeking out authenticity. The fidelity of our analytic to the real situation also depends on the extent to which we can aspire toward a greater complexity in analysis. Returning to the ground of context and experience, which we describe as postconstructionist, is the theme of Part III. In a sense, it is important to walk through the existing terrain of policy (in Parts I and II) because the approaches described in Part III build on them to some extent.

By the time we reach the end of the book, we will recognize that this logical progression, from the classical to postpositivist to postconstructionist, is not a progressive displacement of worn policy models in favor of ever newer ones. On the contrary, we realize that the progression is a cumulative one and that the policy models add to each other. The goal of policy analysis is to seek out a "thick description" (a phrase attributed Geertz, 1973 and, before him, Ryle, 1971) of the policy situation. Inasmuch as each of the policy lenses taken up in this book bring out differing aspects of a policy situation, we find that, increasingly, we are motivated to employ multiple lenses in our analysis.

All throughout the book, but most centrally in Part III, we seek out avenues for redirecting policy analysis back to the field of context, experience, and complexity. The analyst is urged to open up to grounded and, perhaps necessarily, innovative ways of understanding reality. We need to approach policy situations as phenomena — that is, before one can judge, classify, and categorize the situation, we must first experience it for what it is. A return to the phenomenon of policy does not mean, however, that analysis might become objective, far from it. Phenomena make themselves known to us along different dimensions, and we may end up describing some possibly utterly personal experiences of a policy situation. Moreover, the analyst should endeavor a return to complexity because the reality being studied is fundamentally complex. Among other things, this requires a suite of methodologies that can bring dimensionality back into our analyses.

At this point, we should begin to build an understanding of what the postconstructionist mode is and is not. It can, at times, be realist in that we might sometimes posit that some elements of a situation be understood as given and even objective — but it is not necessarily so. It can be phenomenological because we oftentimes find ourselves insisting that our analysis take account of the singularity of experience of policy actors — but it is not always phenomenological. It may also, at times but not primarily, be materialist. Invariably, policy involves the interpretive, but interpretation is not quite the core of the concept either. What is central to the concept, however, is our unwavering resolve to go beyond the analytic. As such, it allows us to understand and emulate the complexity of our experience. In other words, the postconstructionist sentiment involves the capacity to reach beyond the self-contained systems of the mythological. We will not go so far as to create a dictum, but if we had to, it might well be:

In policy, there is no such thing as the *a priori* analytic.

In the end, there is no getting away from the use of our cherished models. Throughout the book, we endeavor to bring out all the different ways in which each of these models, in real ways, do speak to particular aspects of a policy issue. We also speak to the limitations that each of these models possess. The point is not to pit one model versus another, but to realize that these are all analogic representations of phenomena that beg deeper analysis. The point is to consider models reflectively and to ground their workings in the actual contexts and institutions of their application. For this reason, we need to fully appreciate the existing models, including the classic models that we consider in the next few chapters. To this end, too, we devote increasing attention to the issue of context. In Part III, we take on the theme of analytical grounding more explicitly and consider how we can bring our analysis closer to the context of a policy. We begin to think about *contextualization*, or the process by which policy actors and communities take a policy (that may have been conceived elsewhere) and make it their own. The end of this should be some degree of *institutional coherence*, i.e., a sense that the policy, in the process of remolding and evolution, becomes a better and better fit for the particular needs, motivations, and meanings relevant to a certain context. To be able to reconstruct our modes of analysis, we find ourselves having to approach policy situations as phenomena — that is, complex, multifaceted instances that continually exceed our ability to take them all in, much less describe. The problem begins when analysis comes from the other direction, which is to force a policy situation, in all its complexity, to fit our preconstrued analytical framework.

At times, we pose the policy problem in terms of the separation of text from context. This problem takes on many forms, but in its most immediate, it is seen in a policy regime that is formulated by the state or other center of knowledge and authority, and subsequently transported far afield, where it is simply imposed upon the populace. As we will see, certain epistemological assumptions embedded in various policy models allow this to occur. As we will also see, real policy cannot be so simply understood as the generation of a signal and the fidelity by which it is transmitted. Rather, policy can be individually or jointly constructed, it can be reinterpreted and adapted to local contingencies, and it can be a moving target, constantly shifting in both meaning and application. Once we establish how it is, exactly, that policy analytics achieve the separation of text and context, we move on to the question of how we might hope to bring them closer together.

To the Reader

There is no telling who might pick up a book such as this. The study of policy encompasses more fields than we dare list, including public administration, health care, environmental management, social services, urban planning, and many others. Much of this book, particularly the last four chapters, speaks to emerging research in the policy "sciences." However, this book should also be central to those students and practitioners of public policy, i.e., the study of the formulation and evaluation of public programs. Students of program evaluation will find many of these analytics to be quite apropos to their work, and so they are also encouraged to investigate the material in the book. But again, there is no telling who might pick up a book like this. To the reader who approaches the topic from a distant land, e.g., art history or particle physics, know that the only prerequisite for jumping into the study of policy is an inquisitive and open mind.

The ultimate goal of the book is to describe research on new frameworks for policy analysis, which are discussed in Part III. However, it is important to enter deeply into the existing terrain of analysis if we hope to understand what developments are needed — new frameworks build largely on this existing ground. However, the reader who feels already too well acquainted with the foundations and foibles of both rational and postpositivist frameworks can choose to leap directly to Part III (with caution). On the other hand, for those not yet well versed in this area, they can use the first two parts as something of a handbook on policy analysis.

One of the main points of the book is that we should strive to approach policy situations in their complexity and appreciate the richness of their context. It is only right, therefore, that the book makes much use of real-world case studies to illustrate each of the policy lenses taken up. Most of these case studies are relatively recent research projects in which the author is grateful to have participated. It is hoped that the case studies help in making policy analysis real to the reader, in the most immediate way possible. In a similar vein, the reader is urged to try out some of these analytics in their own professional or academic milieus. One should approach analysis as a pig might approach a mud puddle — just politely introduce one's self to it, and then proceed to splash around.

Part I
Positivist Foundations of Policy Analysis

CHAPTER 1

Background: Some Origins of the Classical Model

In this chapter, we trace the evolution of what is today's dominant policy model, that of policy situations as rational decisions involving goal-maximizing choices, whether the goal is to increase utility or some other objective function. This history is traced from the Enlightenment onward to the modern-day utilitarian theories of games and decisions. In this treatment, we do not merely (temporarily) focus on the abstract theories stemming from utilitarianism because of their theoretical merits. Rather, we dwell on them to try and show how these theories have been used in policy discourse to justify strong policy models and, sometimes, ideological positions. In all this, it is important for the student to be aware of the historical and epistemological underpinnings of these discourses to better understand and, invariably, critique them. Toward the end of the chapter, we hint at murmurs of the postpositivist and the beginnings of movements away from the rational model. Part of this turning away leads us to the discussions, and models, found in the latter parts of the book. However, this chapter, along with chapters 3 and 4, are important even for the rational model's critics because we can best move forward and reform policy practices by being thoroughly versed in the discourse and theory of classic policy analysis.

Philosophical Tradition (1700s)

Descartes is the philosopher most commonly associated with the model of the mental, that is, a radical separation of the person from nature. When he posited nature as basically something that is entirely doubtable and landed upon the conclusion that, therefore, the only thing that was indubitable was his own capacity to doubt, this signaled the strongest movement toward an intellectual tradition that associated knowledge with pure thought.

> Yesterday's Meditation has filled my mind with so many doubts that it is no longer in my power to forget them...I convince myself that nothing has ever existed of all that my deceitful memory recalls to me. I think that I have no senses; and I believe that body, shape, extension, motion, and location are merely inventions of my mind. What then could still be thought true?...have I not thereby convinced myself that I did not exist? Not at all; without doubt I existed if I was convinced for even if I thought anything. Even though there may be a deceiver of some sort...he can never make me be nothing as long as I think that I am something. I am something real and existing, but what thing am I? I have already given the answer: a thing which thinks.
>
> From Descartes' Meditations, 1641

In the most emphatic way, Descartes was paving the way for a tradition that associated truth seeking, analysis if you will, with mental life. The human person was, in his conception, definable only as *res cogitans*, the thinking being, inasmuch as everything else had to be laid open to doubt. This concept of knowledge as the mental is a striking movement away from any notion that knowledge might be embedded in experience (which involved sensory input, emotion, moral reasoning, and aesthetic sensibility). In fact, this led to scientific traditions that, for centuries onward and to this day, categorized emotion and other nonmental sensations as mere affect.

The model of thought, of course, stems from much earlier. For example, consider the following passage from a text from the Sung Dynasty.

> I sat quietly by the desk in my official room,
> With my fountain-mind undisturbed, as serene as water;
> A sudden clash of thunder, the mind-doors burst open,
> And lo, there sitteth the old man in all his homeliness.
>
> Chben, from Suzuki, 1962

It is the notion of the mental (or contemplative) life, freed from the vagaries of nature. At any rate, the model upon which learning and, as we will see, policy analysis, is founded begins with the notion of thought as, while acting upon and influenced by material reality, essentially independent of it. But, of course, the mind itself is, among other things, material reality, a notion to which we are just beginning to return. As an aside, one cannot help but note the parallel with current notions of the World Wide Web as a freely floating medium, existing independently of any place. But of course it is not since each and every bit of information on the Web necessarily must lie in at least one computer's hard drive. Ideas, like bits, have a home. These realities will have implications for our analysis, as we see later on.

At any rate, Descartes made the argument, in the deepest way, for two important notions: first, the notion of the person as essentially and ultimately individual, and second, the notion of the individual as essentially a thinking thing: *res cogitans*. Knowledge is *ratio*, truth arrived at through a mental process. But what, then, of external nature? When Descartes pondered upon a melting slag of wax, surely he could not have thought those thoughts if not for the reality of something like wax? Such was the debate that ensued between the rationalists, of which Descartes was the foremost voice, and the empiricists, who included in their number writers like John Locke and David Hume. The latter insisted that nature and material reality were the ultimate source of knowledge and that, by itself, the mind would have no knowledge whatsoever unless it came to it from outside. The empiricists likened the mind to a blank slate that knew only what was written into it through sensory experience. Descartes would say that we know that two and two equals four by reasoning, while Locke would say that we know it by observation, e.g., that I am as full after eating two two-egg omelettes as I am after eating one four-egg omelette *(ceteris paribus)*.

Kant attempted to bring both fields together by stating that nature did exist and did create in us knowledge, but not by nature's own action. Rather, all knowledge of nature was possible because the mind is able to create categories to which sensory input could be assigned (Kant, 1787). The mind is, prior to any experience, equipped with the capacity to classify and order, e.g., to assign a notion of proximity to objects seen by the human eye. Thus, the myriad points of green, yellow, and red light coming to our sense from a tree can be understood by the human mind as belonging to one object (the tree) and not just a jumble of sensory input like dots swirling on a TV screen. This was an even more radical conceptualization than Descartes' since, in Kant's concept, the mind was the organizer of the universe. The universe did exist, but only through the categorical process of the mind that gives it meaning. Perhaps we can appreciate more fully how completely radical this concept was by considering what central event marked the beginning of the European Enlightenment in the first place: the printing of the first encyclopedia, a systematic classification and ordering of knowledge. This was a radical notion, that we could essentially define truth, reality, and the universe through none other than our individual, mental capacity for classification.

But the primacy of individual reason still left important problems to solve, e.g., morality. First of all, while we certainly can believe that an individual can figure out the best course of action or the most reasonable depiction of the truth for her or himself, how could a group of individuals do this together? That is, since we exist as social beings, how does a society reason? How do we engage in moral reasoning, which is reasoning applied to social reality? How do we arrive at the *summum bonum*, or the good of all of society, not just the individual?

Kant posited that reasoning individuals, through cogitation, should be able to arrive at some basic truths and that all individuals should be able to arrive at the same conclusion. This is because some principles hold regardless of context (i.e., outside of the particularities of a person's experience). These universal rules were true universally and regardless of the particularities of a time or place or person and, as such, held independently of experience. These truths are *a priori* or prior to experience and, so, are universal. For example, consider Kant's categorical imperative:

> Act only on that maxim whereby thou canst at the same time will that it should become universal law.

> Kant, 1785

which Kant posited as the universal rule by which we derive other universal rules.

Thus, all that was required was to be sufficiently thorough in our cogitation, whether done as individuals or by many persons together, and we should arrive at these *a priori* principles, the *summum bonum*. The practical difficulty with this prescription, of course, is that it is notoriously difficult for different people to agree on the same first principles. Could a group of people who cannot even agree on a choice of pizza ever possibly find a way to come to the same conclusions about more fundamental questions like Social Security? How practical a prescription is Kant's for the formulation of public policy? In chapter 8, we take up the application of Kant's deontological and other ethical theories to the area of public policy.

At around this same time, there arose a voice from across the Channel, and his promised a prescription for public policy that seemed much more amenable to actual application. Taking his cue from the empiricists,

Jeremy Bentham sought to ground social principles on reasoning processes that did not involve more than individual thought. Starting from the individual, Bentham posited that the course of action that was best for an individual is none other than that which gave this individual the greatest pleasure or benefit. But what of society? By a process of philosophical induction, Bentham reasoned that, inasmuch as what was best for one individual was the maximization of one's greatest pleasure, what would be best for society was whatever resulted in the sum total pleasure, aggregated over all individuals in that society. The implied mathematical operation is not merely an allusion. Bentham really did propose a moral calculus: to divine the best state for society, one only needs to find out which action gave the largest sum of pleasures, added up over all the individuals in society. To do this, pleasure (or its negative, pain) had to be commensurate — and one had to have ways to actually measure it. Otherwise, one could not carry out the additive operation. This stemmed directly from Bentham's empiricism, in that, in place of the moral reasoning proposed by Kant, Bentham's was simply an exercise of measurement. Simply measure the amount of pleasure or pain for each individual, then simply add up all these measurements over all the individuals, and this gives us the implication for society as a whole. In Bentham's words, the *summum bonum* consisted in securing "the greatest good for the greatest number" (Bentham, 1789). This notion was further developed by John Stuart Mill, who took up the utilitarian tradition after Bentham.

> According to the greatest happiness principle, as above explained, the ultimate end, with reference to and for the sake of which all other things are desirable — whether we are considering our own good or that of other people — is an existence exempt as far as possible from pain, and as rich as possible in enjoyments, both in point of quantity and quality...I must again repeat what the assailants of utilitarianism seldom have the justice to acknowledge, that the happiness which forms the utilitarian standard of what is right in conduct is not the agent's own happiness but that of all concerned.
>
> Mill, 1863

This was the first principle of utility, or the basic tenet of the school of Utilitarianism, which has exerted its powerful influence over the policy sciences ever since. This was an important step for policy analysis because this prescription allowed one to bring in the notion of a societal, collective will simply by replacing it by an ersatz society, the aggregate, thus bringing to full circle the model of the reasoning individual. We begin with some principle by which an individual might arrive at some judgment. Then instead of problematizing how to extend this reasoning process over many individuals, Bentham simply substituted a different individual, the "collective," whose opinion on a matter was simply the register of the sum of individual valuations of good or bad for each person in the collective. Instead of attempting to find a common ground among a thousand people, one simply posited a collective individual whose likes and dislikes were the simple aggregation of the likes and dislikes of the thousand.

But Bentham's operational solution, to mathematize away the moral problematic, also introduced other problems, such as "How do we measure good and bad, pleasure and pain?" These were not traditional objects that one could measure with an instrument in empiricist tradition. Doubtless, if Bentham had available during his day, the type of sensors we have today to record electric impulses from our nervous system, he or one of his students would certainly have tried actual measurement. What Bentham and his student J.S. Mill essentially prescribed was to measure societal good and bad by simply having each person express the level of good or bad experienced by an individual as a result of some action. That is, instead of simply measuring inanimate objects, utilitarianism involves the measurement of subjective cognitions from animate and reasoning subjects. It is almost as if a boulder reported its own weight back to us. Utilitarianism introduced the notion of a social calculus: the treatment of moral questions involving good and bad as empirically commensurable things while not departing from the primacy of the individual, because good and bad were subjective claims made by animate subjects.

Utilitarianism also underscored another important notion: that of the individual as a self-satisfying automaton. That is, each individual need not ponder on the welfare of society as a whole or even of the person next to him. The social calculus took care of that and left to the individual the simpler operation of determining only what was good or bad for him or herself. The only input to this social calculus is the individual expressions of personal welfare. Persons only had to concern themselves with their own good or bad. This is the notion of the person as a utility maximizer. Having been freed from the Kantian obligation to think universally (i.e., to seek the good of all), each person need only worry about individualizing, which, taken to its logical end, simply meant that the dictum is for each person to simply opt for actions or states that maximized their individual good or utility.

We see then, stemming from the Enlightenment thinkers, a number of distinct schools of thought, all of which contributed, in their own ways, to a number of central notions that are influential in policy analysis to this day.

1. The basic unit of analysis is the individual, and knowledge is arrived at by the individual.
2. The basis for morality is reason, and social questions can be treated as exercises in reason.
3. Individuals tend toward seeking individual utility.
4. Society can be treated, analytically, by understanding it as a collection of individuals.
5. Scientific empiricism can be brought to bear on social questions.

This has led to modern institutional models based on the assumption of the atomistic, self-directed, personal utility-maximizing individual. We should note that even Mill's model (as suggested in the previous excerpt) did not posit this utterly individualistic notion of the person but, instead, conceived of the person as someone with an inclination toward the social good, at large. The former, versus the latter, conceptualization of the individual has come to dominate policy thought today.

Modern Decision Theory (1940s On)

While Bentham and other Enlightenment thinkers introduced the first glimmers of the mathematization to the field of policy, it was not until the twentieth century that its most formal and utterly mathematical formulation would appear. In 1944, John von Neumann and Oskar Morgenstern published an altogether monumental book: *Theory of Games and Economic Behavior* (von Neumann and Morgenstern, 1944). In this treatise, von Neumann and Morgenstern (vN–M) took some of the same concepts that grew out of the Enlightenment and proceeded to systematically build up a number of powerful theories based on them. Over the rest of the chapter, we discuss the basic conceptual movements that stemmed from this treatise and their further development as others proceeded to develop these basic models. We leave for the succeeding chapters, however, the actual theory in its detail. While the history of the classic rational model spans many, many writers, we have space enough to treat just one of the more recent branches, that of the decision sciences. It is not possible to cover the many intellectual schools that revolve around the rational model, including the empiricists, later to be followed by positivists (e.g., Comte) and logical positivists (e.g., Carnap). We do not even venture into the rich history of scholars who helped shape the course of public policy curricula, e.g., Laswell and others, which any policy student should feel obliged to become familiar with (Laswell, 1970). Instead, to focus in on the assumptions behind the rational model, stated in their purest and starkest form, we simply concentrate on the decision model that came out of the original work of vN–M.

In their book, vN–M posited two basic models for judgment: that employed by the individual and that employed by a group of individuals. The individual, in this rarified formulation, was simply a walking register of utility whose judgment and action was governed by the principle of utility maximization. That is, starting from the utilitarian prescription of self-satisfaction, vN–M built their theory upon the supposition that each person in society can be modeled as an ideal utility-maximizing machine. In the following two chapters, we concentrate on those particular policy models that derive from the fundamental work of vN–M, noting that these are simply a part (though, an important part) of the diverse approaches and frameworks that are linked to the rational model.

The theory of individual judgment is now known as decision theory. This model provided the mathematical description of individual utility maximization. To do this, vN–M modeled "judgment" as ineluctably a *choice* among competing *alternatives*. Each alternative would be judged by the individual and, ultimately, valued and assigned its level of utility. The individual would then, having evaluated every alternative and assigned them scores (utility), simply pick that alternative that gave the highest score in the individual calculus. This is the mathematical equivalent of Bentham's utilitarianism. The extension to multiple individuals is the same operation as Bentham's. Having calculated the utility to each individual from an action, we simply add up the utilities over all individuals and choose the alternative that gives the highest aggregate utility. But, again, the extension to many individuals is done by simply positing one "collective" individual whose utilities are simply the sum of all individual utilities. This assumes a centralized decision maker, capable of making these judgments, choosing the solution, and making sure that the choice is carried out. The centralized decision maker is, of course, simply the logical extension of the reasoning individual. Instead of the individual person, posit the individual state.

What if there is no centralized decision maker capable of choosing and enforcing one course of action for all members of society? What if each of a thousand individuals, instead of being given one course of action determined by the state, had enough liberty to choose a thousand different individual courses of action? That is, what if these thousand individuals engaged in private decisions, and not public decisions as posited in decision theory. With regard to a transportation example, a public decision might mean the choice of a public transport measure that, automatically, all in society would receive, whereas a private decision might mean the individual choice of a car or a choice of whether to use the car, bus, or feet to get to work each day. The second theoretical frontier created by vN–M formalized the modeling of this second type of judgment, where each individual is free to choose his or her own solution. How would we model the kinds of consequences that might result given that each individual is autonomous? This body of theory is known as game theory. Again, vN–M model the individual as a simple utility-maximizing machine.

Figure 1.1 depicts the development of theory that stemmed from vN–M onward, mentioning some authors whose work is discussed in the succeeding chapters. Of course, we should always keep in mind that the decision sciences represented in the figure are simply one "branch" of a much larger set of traditions revolving around the norm of rationality that emerged from Enlightenment thought.

The social calculus, decision theory, has developed into two related, yet sometimes distinct, sets of methods known as multiattribute utility (MAU) on the one hand and cost-benefit analysis (CBA) on the other. The main differences are the attempt to simulate, within CBA, actual markets, which entails the measurement of all values in terms of currency. This brings to the fore questions about the influence of income and ability to pay on valuations of costs and benefits. Difficulties with CBA involve the fact that the real significance of a dollar to a given person varies with that person's utility and the payoff received. That is, utility is nonlinear with currency. On the other hand, CBA may be intuitively close to human cognition owing to our everyday experience with actual markets. MAU does not bring everything to the level of currency and uses units of utility that may be nonlinear with currency. Moreover, there is more attention paid in MAU to the functional form of the social aggregation equation. For example, utilities might not be simply added across the range of things being

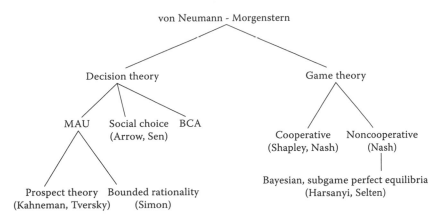

Fig. 1.1 The "family tree" of decision sciences.

valued or across the range of individuals being considered, but might be aggregated using other functional forms (e.g., multiplicative). At any rate, this branch of the hierarchy encompassing both MAU and CBA basically involves the expression of individual utility in terms of numbers, or cardinal utility. This allows us to simply add (or use some other mathematical operation) the utilities to get at the collective answer.

There is another branch, social choice theory, that stems from the individual person model and, yet, does not involve cardinal utilities. This theory is based on expressions of personal preferences not in the form of numerical valuations but simply as rank orderings. That is, given a set of alternatives, the decision maker does not assign cardinal values to each alternative but, instead, merely orders them in terms of most to least preferred. In other words, in social choice theory, preferences are expressed in ordinal, not cardinal, terms. Ordinal data are simpler and less information rich than cardinal information and, so, are easier for people to determine. Note that cardinal data automatically lets one rank order alternatives — this is what we mean by cardinal data being richer in information. How does one aggregate preferences across individuals then? Not by addition but by some other social choice rule. The easiest example is that of voting, which involves people registering ordinal information. A social choice rule used to aggregate a group of individuals' preferences for, say, a president might be a majority of the votes or some other rule. The ease with which these calculations are carried out can come at a price. In particular, later theorists like Arrow and Sen have provided examples by which counterintuitive results would result and, in fact, have provided proofs that there is no social choice rule that would never produce counterintuitive results (Arrow, 1951; Sen, 1970).

There are yet other variations that we could not fit into the hierarchy. For example, one school posited that frail, imperfect humans could not possibly live up to the ideal of a perfect, utility-calculating machine. Thus, this school, including people like Hebert Simon, posited the notion of bounded rationality and the prescriptive principle of satisficing rather than maximization (Simon, 1957). We should also note the contribution of Savage who posited that humans, not having access to perfect information, could still proceed by the expected utility mode of reasoning by employing subjective probabilities in situations of uncertainty, which is a distinct modification of what had been, to that point, a frequent notion of uncertainty (Savage, 1954).

As depicted in Figure 1.1, an important development in utility theory came to be known as prospect theory (Kahneman and Tversky, 1979). Prospect theory developed out of observations, mostly by cognitive psychologists, of systematic departures from the expected utility hypothesis. For example, when put in hypothetical situations wherein subjects had to weigh an expected loss of some amount versus the foregone gain of the same amount, subjects routinely chose one over the other. These heuristics and biases, these researchers concluded, were systematic and built into the very cognitive framework of the individual. The important thing to note, at this point, is that, though it is a significant movement from expected utility theory, prospect theory still can be thought of as firmly entrenched in the basic class of models that stemmed from vN–M.

On the right side of the hierarchy, game theory branches out into several different fields. Starting from the basic premise of vN–M of trying to model outcomes from multiple utility-maximizing decision makers, each making independent decisions on their own, vN–M posited two types of games. The first, cooperative game theory, assumes that the individuals can coordinate their individual actions by agreeing on mutually binding contracts, and that this group can enforce any such contract. Such a contract would specify the payoffs that each player would get from the contract. At any rate, cooperative game theory studies the different "contracts" that might result from a given situation and the properties of each type.

On the other hand, suppose that these individuals, even if they could specify an agreement, had no way of enforcing such a contract? The reasons may be numerous: There is no authority for enforcing the contract, there is no feasible way to monitor each player to ensure that each does follow the contract, etc. When this is the case, we are left with a game in which each player acts purely as an individual. An individual may adjust his or her actions depending on how others act or are poised to act, but there is no coordination between individuals. When this happens, what we have is a set of individuals each pursuing his or her own utility-maximizing strategy without any thought of the consequences for the other individuals. This field is known as noncooperative game theory. Von Neumann and Morgenstern showed how you could predict solutions, i.e., equilibria, for zero-sum games involving two players. Zero-sum simply means if one player gains an extra dollar, then the other player loses an extra dollar. Equilibrium simply means that rational players can figure out what their optimal strategies are and, moreover, can figure out their opponent's optimal strategy, having no reason not to play this strategy. That is, given that both players are rational, we can expect them to land in the same equilibrium each time, playing the predicted actions and obtaining the predicted payoffs.

Later pioneers in game theory have extended the vN–M models in different ways. In noncooperative game theory, Nash proved the existence of equilibria for more general games that are non–zero-sum and that involve even more than two players. While he proved the existence of these so-called Nash equilibria, these are not necessarily unique (Nash, 1950, 1951). Later theorists, i.e., Selten and Harsanyi, extended this model to include the effect of uncertainty, resulting in the concept of Bayesian Nash equilibria.

On the side of cooperative game theory, theorists such as Shapley produced a number of noteworthy solution concepts (or ideal formulas for "contracts"). Gillies and Shapley introduced the notion of a core, which is the set of possible contracts that are satisfactory enough for any player or subgroup of players such that none of them could do better by not joining in on the contract (Gillies, 1953; Shapley, 1952). Later on, Shapley proved the properties of the most well-known cooperative solution concepts, later on named the Shapley value, and showed how such a formula possesses some desirable properties or axioms (Shapley, 1953). We include Nash on this side of the field, also, since he formulated an axiomatic approach to characterizing a solution concept for two players (Nash, 1950). We see more of these theories in detail beginning with chapter 2. For now, suffice it to note that all these currents of thought sprang from the original work of vN–M. For now, you might use Table 1.1 to keep track of this rich ground.

The important thing is to keep in mind the manner in which concepts from the 1700s and earlier have been formalized and embedded in these more modern models. Most important is the fundamental adoption of the model of choice by vN–M. That is, social judgment is modeled as the choice of the best alternative from a field of possible alternatives. These alternatives already exist and are known — hence, the natural use of the

Table 1.1 Models produced by the theory of games and decisions

Decision Theory			Game Theory	
Multiattribute Utility	Cost-Benefit Analysis	Social Choice	Cooperative	Noncooperative
Individual preferences are expressed as cardinal utilities	Individual preferences are expressed with cardinal monetary values	Individual preferences are expressed with ordinal rankings	Groups can make and enforce contracts	Individuals cannot have binding contracts and only act individually

word "analysis" to describe this concept. Judgment is modeled as the search for the one optimal path, solution, or concept from a field of alternatives. Within this field, one only needs to deduce which one member is "best." This involves a process of evaluating each alternative and choosing one. Moreover, analysis, in this model, ends with the final choice.

There are typically many factors that are involved in weighing the merits of any alternative. For example, in choosing a home, one has to consider not just one factor (e.g., price), but others like safety, aesthetics, peace and quiet, proximity to the park, etc. The models that vN–M developed assume that one can bring all these diverse factors onto the same plane of comparison. That is, all of these elements (price, safety, etc.) can be expressed in the same units of utility (or, as in the case of CBA, in dollars). Another important feature of these modern models, then, is the assumption of commensurability. That is, any factor can be measured along a scale of utility or value. This strong empiricism has consequences for the way policy analysis is carried out, as we see further on. Since everything can be measured and expressed as value, then we can compare everything. For example, we can compare a house that is cheap but with no view to another house that is expensive but that has a great view of Mt. Fuji. This notion of comparability goes hand in hand with that of commensurability. (Actually, in chapter 2, we discuss how, so long as everything can be compared, we can often derive cardinal measures of worth.) At any rate, realize that without the ability to compare, the model of social judgment as choices between alternatives would not be possible. That is, in vN–M's universe, anything can be compared with anything else, and, moreover, these comparisons can be made by comparing cardinal values attached to each alternative. If you believe that comparisons cannot be made or that measures cannot be formulated, e.g., resetting the speed limit requires being able to compare lives lost with dollars saved, then you cannot use these models.

Even more fundamentally, analysis is essentially a mental or cognitive exercise. One can perform these calculations removed from a situation. In fact, in some circles, the common wisdom is that analysis should be performed by neutral observers who are not too familiar with or too personally involved in the situation. Decisions are best made, in this formulation, by the analyst as *res cogitans*, the thinking thing removed from nature but able to ponder it from an epistemological distance.

The Postpositivist Turn

In chapter 4, we begin to talk of a turning away from the strongly positivist nature of classic policy thought, beginning with the hermeneutic tradition and leading to the more recent school of poststructuralism. For now, we simply note that all the while that both the rationalist and empiricist schools were developing systematic systems of philosophy leading to the present bodies of classic theory we find today, there were numerous voices that reacted to the reductionisms of the classic models. One will readily recognize in the Kantian, Humean, and Benthamite systems the strong notion of a separation of the internal from external (or, similarly, of mind from nature). In Part II of this book, we take up systems of thought that do not so irreconcilably posit two independent spheres of reality. We also should recognize the strong notion of the *summum bonum,* (whether couched as philosophy or social policy) as an objective principle if not fact. When one is willing not only to set aside the grandness of the *summum bonum,* but, moreover, accept its permanent absence, what system of thought might we be led to? While some of these alternative accounts have, by now, become standard fare in the realm of theory, they still have to work their way firmly into the policy disciplines. In Part II of this book, particularly from chapter 4 onward, we attempt to chart these movements. We then peruse some of the frayed edges of both the rational and postpositivist movements, and attempt to propose new directions in Part III.

CHAPTER 2

Decisions

Introduction

The very first model that we take up is probably the one that has been most influential in policy analysis: policy formulation as decision making. In this chapter, we enter, in some depth, into the fundamental theory of decisions. Later on, we examine how it is applied to policy situations. Our goal is, first, to point out in great detail what assumptions, operations, and conceptual positions are taken in the decision model, and second, to begin charting directions forward. This entails both evaluating the extent to which the model of decisions furthers the mythological and considering directions for reforming this practice, which we take up toward the end of the chapter. To be able to evaluate, critique, and reform this policy model, we first need to understand the concepts and workings of the model in some depth, which we proceed to do next.

Theory: From Comparability to Commensurability

Remember that, as we discussed earlier, decisions are taken to mean the choice of one optimal alternative from a set of competing alternatives. More explicitly, the focus of our analysis is the unitary decision maker who, like all of us, faces several, perhaps many, or even an infinite number, of alternative actions to take. For example, should we zone this wilderness area for recreation or development? Or, what is the best insurance plan to get from the set of a surprisingly large number of health plans? The task, then, is for the decision maker to be able to study the alternatives and select the best one. Again, this involves analysis — the unearthing of an answer from within a field of inquiry. The answer is already in the set of alternatives somewhere inside this set, and all the decision maker needs to do is figure out which one it is and choose it. The process by which the universe of alternatives is recognized or constructed remains inscrutable.

To be able to divine the best among a set of alternatives, we need to be able to compare one alternative with any other one, and, making this comparison, judge whether the first is better than the other, the other better than the first, or they are equally good. When we can make comparisons like this, then our preference structure is said to be complete. By "complete," we essentially mean that there are no gaps in our ability to compare. All alternatives can be compared with everything else.

Let us see how far we can get just through sheer comparisons between pairs of alternatives. Consider three possible homes (that are up for sale in the market) to choose from. You proceed to compare them two at a time and arrive at these results.

Home A versus Home B → Choose B
Home B versus Home C → Choose B
Home A versus Home C → Choose C

This then allows us to construct our rank ordered preferences among the three alternatives.

Rank 1 most preferred   Home B
Rank 2 second most preferred   Home C
Rank 3 least preferred   Home A

Of course, if you have a lot of alternatives, then you may have too many pairwise comparisons to make. For example, with a list of just 4 alternatives, you would need to make 6 pairwise comparisons in order to establish the relative rank orderings; with 5 alternatives, you would need 10 pairwise comparisons, etc. A more efficient way of doing this is to simply assign a value (or utility) to each alternative independently, as follows:

Alternative	Utility
A	0.0
B	1.0
C	0.7

and simply use the values to give us the same rank ordering (B-C-A). Most important, it is easy to then figure out our solution, B, which is the alternative that gives the highest utility to the decision maker. This is the simple definition of efficiency in the case of one decision maker, and alternative B is said to be the efficient solution. There arose the question, however, of whether it is always possible to produce cardinal valuations for alternatives. Some theorists have shown that provided one can make comparisons between mixtures or combinations of alternatives, then one can always derive a cardinal utility scale (e.g., see Herstein and Milnor, 1953). Probably the easiest thing to do is to think of a "mixture" in terms of a probability. For example, suppose that we can conceive of an alternative being a 50% probability of getting alternative A and a 50% probability of alternative B. We might then compare this against the sure, 100%, probability of getting alternative C and choose the better one. This essentially amounts to a mental experiment involving the choice of one of two boxes. In one box, there is one ping-pong ball marked "C," and, in the other box, there are two ping-pong balls, one marked "A" and the other marked "B". You would then choose a box, reach into it, and pull out a ping-pong ball. The mental model of the box with the two ping-pong balls is also sometimes called a "lottery," wherein choosing this alternative means some chance that it actually results in alternative A and some chance that it results in alternative B.

Compare 0.5A, 0.5B versus C → choose C.

We might proceed to vary the mixtures of A and B

Compare 0.55A, 0.45B versus C → choose C

incrementally, until we get a tie.

Compare 0.64A, 0.36B versus C → tie.

At this point, we simply assign arbitrary values of 1.0 to A, the most preferred, and 0 to B, the least preferred, and derive the value for C.

$$U(C) = 0.64U(A) + 0.36U(B) = 0.64(1.0) + 0.36(0) = 0.64.$$

This is an important step. One of the arguments often made against the utilitarian model is that there are things or situations to which we cannot assign numerical values. Take the example of the worth of a human life, for which many, perhaps most, will say that a life has an immeasurable (or incommensurable) value. It is impossible to assign any numerical value to such. Now, the counterargument to this is closely tied to the example above, and it states that we can assign numerical values and implicitly do so whenever we make any choice that is more risky to humans but less expensive. Another way of saying this is that dollars and life are comparable in actual practice. Take the example of speed limits. Whenever the Department of Transportation (DOT) raises the speed limit, some analysts interpret this to mean that society (for which DOT ostensibly stands in) is making a trade-off between lives and dollars, inasmuch as raising the speed limit saves us travel costs while increasing the number of highway accidents per year. If you would agree with the argument that we do indeed make implicit trade-offs between income and life, then it is a short, short step from this point to making this trade-off explicit and actually assigning a dollar value to life. For example, say that the increase in the speed limit saves a state $1 billion (B) a year because less time is spent by the public on the road, commodities are delivered faster, less gasoline is used, etc. At the same time, insurance actuaries estimate that an additional 250 deaths per year will result from the increased speeds. Let us also assume that the savings in time are just enough to convince legislators to change the speed limit despite objections by prosafety advocates. Analysts who believe in the comparability of life and income could then proceed to calculate a value of human life as:

$$\$1 \text{ B}/250 = \$4 \text{ million (M) per statistical life.}$$

where analysts use the term "statistical life" to ease society's conscience about the loss of life (i.e., the new policy isn't killing anyone in particular, but in general) and assign a statistical and faceless entity to what might otherwise have been posited as an actual living, breathing human being.

That is, believing in the comparability of things like life and dollars leads immediately to the notion of commensurability — if we can trade off money and life, then we can express the value of life in terms of money (or other, perhaps more general, measures of utility). But this is the same argument shown mathematically above. The point is that the mathematics of it, which can be at times elegant, leads us to strong assumptions that we may or may not agree with, philosophically. What is needed is an ability to discern what these hidden assumptions are and to analyze them explicitly. A good exercise for the policy student is to try and put together, in the space of a few paragraphs, arguments for and against the commensurability assumption. These arguments, more than the calculation or legal hairsplitting, are exactly what policy analysis is all about.

Let us make a bit of a minor point. One school of decision theory, that of cost-benefit analysis (CBA), expresses everything in terms of dollars (or other currency). Other analysts, espousing different methods but lumped in Figure 1.1 under the title "multiattribute utility" (MAU), object to this, however, saying that a dollar is worth more, in real terms, to a pauper than a prince. If you are a billionaire, a couple of dollars here and there means almost nothing to you, but to a homeless person, it may be worth enough for him to spend a day perusing the city for recyclable cans. That is, we could just as easily have expressed our values in terms of utility, where utility is not necessarily linear with money (i.e., as you get more money, the utility of the next dollar diminishes).

Utility

Our first practical model, then, for professional policy analytic work stems from rationalist and utilitarian notions of analysis, calculation, and optimization. For the unitary decision maker, the model entails simply listing all the alternatives or directions of action open to you, calculating the utilities of each, and choosing the alternative with the highest utility as the solution. This mode of understanding is referred to as "consequentialist," in that to calculate utilities, one has to figure out the consequences or outcomes of an action and then assign utilities to these consequences. The issue is that there are different kinds of outcomes from an action, and the exercise of coming up with a value for the alternative translates to coming up with values for each outcome associated with the alternative.

Let us suppose that one alternative being considered by the DOT is as follows:

Action (or alternative) A:	Raise speed limit to 70 mph (112 kph).
Consequences (or outcomes):	Total annual savings to society of $2.4 B a year.
	One hundred and twenty additional deaths a year due to the new speed limit.
	Additional expenditures of $420 M a year due to automobile wear and tear.
	Increased noise of, on average, 20 decibels to residents along the highway.

Each of these kinds of consequences is sometimes referred to as "criteria" or "attributes" in the MAU school, and "goods" in the CBA school.

How are we to determine these consequences (i.e., consequences relative to what)? The rule is to compare the state of the world with the alternative versus without the alternative. It is not necessarily comparing things before and after an action was taken because the mere passage of time between the "before" and "after" can produce changes. This is a mental exercise, pure and simple, but then we already admitted that much of analysis assumed the primacy of the mental. Even given that it is a mental black box exercise, we still need to assume some kind of baseline or default situation that would occur in the absence of our proposed action. In the case of the DOT problem, it seems simple enough to assume this "without-alternative" scenario to be continuing to use the existing speed limit. That is, all the consequences specified above are relative to the baseline no-alternative scenario of the existing policy, and a savings of $2.4 B a year means that if we stuck with the present policy, we would be spending $2.4 B a year more than with the new speed limit. Evaluation then entails assigning values or utilities to each of these effects and, then, simply adding them up to get the total value or utility of the action (alternative A). We can do this in units of dollars or more general units of utility. The exercise looks something like that shown in Table 2.1.

We could have done the same exercise in units of dollars instead of utility and produced something like that shown in Table 2.2, where we do not have to recalculate the value of things like dollar savings since they are already expressed in terms of our ultimate measure of value, which is money.

Table 2.1 Calculation of total utility of measure A

Outcome	Unit Value	Utility
$2.4 B savings	100 per $B	+240
120 statistical lives	1 per statistical life	−120
$0.42 B cost	100 per $B	−42
20 decibels	0.5 per decibel	−10
	Total	+68

Table 2.2 Calculation of total net benefit of measure A

Outcome	Unit Value (in $)	Utility
$2.4 B savings	Same	+$2.4 B
120 statistical lives	$8.33 M per statistical life	−$1.0 B
$0.42 B cost	Same	−$0.42 B
20 decibels	$4 M per decibel	−$0.8 B
	Total Utility	+$0.9 B

The final "worth" of alternative A should be pretty much the same, regardless of whether you use MAU or CBA, although assuming nonlinearity of utility with income in MAU may tend to vary the final value to some extent. The unit values in the previous examples are essentially weights that translate the different criteria into the same units of utility. For example, we may tally up the characteristics of a used car that we are thinking of purchasing in terms of the following:

Price = $15,000
Mileage = 40,000 miles
Fuel efficiency = 24 mpg

Clearly, it would not be right to simply add up these numbers (15,000 + 42,000 + 24), especially if fuel efficiency was very important to the decision maker.

The more important point is that the exercise of evaluation is essentially the same and can be summarized in the following flow diagram.

Criteria: List the criteria (e.g., life, money, noise, aesthetics, etc.).
                              ↓
Alternatives: Determine the set of alternatives.
                              ↓
Outcomes: Measure or estimate how each alternative performs vis-à-vis each criterion.
                              ↓
Evaluation: Evaluate (i.e., attach values) to each alternative's outcomes.
                              ↓
Choice: Select the alternative that gives the highest total value or utility.

Whether we use MAU or CBA, the question is how do we derive the values? Basically, the same way we mathematically derived cardinal utility from ordinal rankings — by making comparisons. We might do this using hypothetical trade-off exercises (which in CBA is known as "contingent valuation"). We might, alternatively, do this by looking for actual situations wherein people made this implicit trade-off. For example, you might want to see how much, on average, people paid for a piece of land with a view (e.g., of Mt. Kilimanjaro) versus land without a view. From this, the analyst might derive the dollar value of a view (for a CBA analysis) or the simple exchange rate between dollars and a view (in an MAU analysis). If, for example, we find that, on average, lots with a view are about $140,000 more expensive than similarly sized lots (and, in fact, keeping everything else but the view similar, i.e., *ceteris paribus*), then we could use a value of $140,000 for the utility of a view of Mt. Kilimanjaro.

At this point, we should point out something the student may not have noticed in all the discussion about utility categories — the easy, almost sleight-of-hand transition from the one-person case to the societal analysis, which the previous discussion represents. Here, instead of registering values or utilities to one person, we simply enter the total value added up over everyone in the affected community. Again, this is the power of the utilitarian model, in that we begin with a decision problem for one person and simply replace this unitary decision maker with a collective, unitary entity whose utilities are simply the raw sum of utilities over each individual. This stirs up unrest in some quarters over the model's neglect of the distribution of benefits — something that game theory explicitly treats (we see this in chapter 3). This neglect of distribution is undeniable, and in the positing of a collective entity, the model does wash away difference, disenfranchisement, and the minority's voice. There are no losers or winners in this model, merely a unitary collective. Something even more fundamental has occurred, though, and this is the hypostatization of the concept of the public weal. We have reified the otherwise fictive concept of aggregate welfare and proceeded to treat this as a seamless whole — in fact, a surrogate for society. This operation, besides the very real leveling of difference and distribution, allows us to proceed with analysis. The reason this type of analysis is so dominant is that policy making in the public sphere, which inevitably calls for a public process, can be reduced to a positing of a self-contained conceptual model, entirely outside the public realm, and to find within this same model the sought after result. Analysis, as traditionally carried out from Descartes and Kant, is an inwardly directed operation, taking the rational mind away from nature and into introspection.

Expected Utility

There is a complicating factor to all this utilitarian reasoning, and that is uncertainty. We used the term "consequentialism" to underscore that utilitarian models require that we look at the consequences of an action. This is because we arrive at conclusions through valuation, and we need to be able to measure something to value it. Something has to result in some change because we are only able to measure change. Recall the roots of modern analysis in empiricism. Change that is measurable tends to be mostly physical change, and so there is a strong empirical bias toward the consequentialist practice of looking for or predicting physical changes and basing our evaluations on their measured degrees of change.

The assumption of a consequentialist mode of analysis is not an innocent one. It assumes away purely ethical considerations, for one. For example, consider that in an empirical, utilitarian mode of analysis, throwing a rock at a pedestrian and missing said pedestrian (who never even noticed a rock sailing past his head) really registers hardly a blip in the utility scale (except for some positive value assigned to the satisfaction of the rock thrower, but this is a minor thing). But what about the rightness or wrongness of an action? Surely a morally wrong action should be assigned a much lower value in our analysis than a morally right action? In this case, we should assign some negative value to rock throwing purely out of moral considerations. But this is not the case in this type of consequentialist analysis. Perhaps an everyday example of this argument is found in the supermarket check-out line. Suppose you are standing in the middle of a long, long line of people and that, out of nowhere, someone furtively sidles into the line in front of you. Consider the small real impact on you of this sneaking in. Physically, at least, all it really costs you is perhaps half a minute's delay. But, then, consider the unadulterated rage that comes over the people waiting behind this cad. The consequentialist would not mind much, really. In physical terms, it really is of small consequence. But in real terms, it can be a very consequential thing, which suggests that what is physical does not encompass the real, and consequences do not encompass significance.

Even if we wave away the nonconsequentialist arguments, there still persists the problem of uncertainty. Here, uncertainty is used as a concept to include all types of contingencies in all their manifold manifestations in our lives: the tenuousness of one's employ in recessionary times, the lack of tenure or security of residents in informal housing along a river, the lack of health insurance, our mortality, etc. All of this is collapsed, in this model, into a problem of predicting consequences. That is, consider the path from the here and now to the future and some uncertainty where exactly this path leads. To take a simple example, if I buy this lottery ticket that the grocer is waving in my face, what consequence would result? There are two obvious possible consequences, of course, and uncertainty lies in our not knowing which one would result. The model we are talking about treats this kind of uncertainty as simple probability. That is, in the lottery ticket example, we treat uncertainty as some probability that you would win the lottery and some probability that you would not.

But recall that the decision model posits that we calculate a utility associated with the alternative (which, in the example, is buying the lottery ticket). What is the utility of this action? In this model, it is simply the sum of the probability of winning times the payoff (or utility of winning) and the probability of losing times its payoff (which is zero). This is the model of expected utility, and it requires that we estimate these probabilities. That is, assume that you estimate the probability of winning the lottery to be 0.001% and the jackpot to be $2 M, then the calculation would be as follows:

$$\text{Expected utility (buying a ticket)} = 0.00001(\$2 \text{ M})$$
$$+ (1 - 0.00001)(\$0) = \$20,$$

which means that, if the grocer were charging you $2 (or anything less than $20) for the ticket, then most reasonable people who have the money to spend should go ahead and buy the ticket — that is, if they actually reasoned in this manner.

There are some variations to this procedure, of course. Von Neumann and Morgenstern's (vN–M) original work allowed for departures from simple expected utility. For example, risk-prone decision makers would be people who would buy the ticket even if it cost a little above $20 (since they just love the gamble). In this case, we would adjust the expected utility of buying a little upward. Risk aversion, on the other hand, pertains to those who would only buy the ticket if it were significantly less than $20, in which case, we would adjust the calculated utility of buying a ticket downward. Risk neutrality simply means vacillation between buying and not buying a $20 ticket, i.e., you feel just as well off either way.

The main point that we are making, however, is that the decision-analytic model treats contingency, uncertainty, trepidation, anxiety, etc., using the simple construct of probability. More explicitly put, uncertainty is interpreted to mean a probability distribution over a range of possible future outcomes. But, as with most of the central assumptions of these models, this one comes with a large epistemological price. Perhaps one meaningful way of introducing this question is to look at one specific type of probabilistic uncertainty analysis: risk assessment. Risk assessment is a set of methods that have grown into a full-fledged discipline developed to conduct analysis on topics like human health impact assessment, safety failure analysis, and others. Consider a town that has been picked as a site for a nuclear plant. Consider, also, that the expert analysis of the possibility that the plant might actually leak radiation suggests that there is a one in a million chance (or probability) that this might happen over the life of the plant. These same experts sometimes then evince some surprise that the amount of public outrage seems off the scale considering the small, almost miniscule risk of failure of the plant. But part of the problem stems from the use of probability as a stand-in for a lot of elements that attend to the phenomenon of uncertainty. The phenomenon is one that carries with it a host of experiences: a feeling of betrayal, a suspicion of motives, a loss of esteem, an existentialist fear, a moral outrage. And yet, to this spectrum of experiences, we have assigned as a surrogate the concept of probability. Probability is a frequentist notion that represents the frequency that something would result were a situation to be repeated over and over. In this concept, we implicitly carry these notions of the innocuousness of repetition and experimentation, really, and the positing of conditions that one might call "average," and assign a normative dimension to them. However, not everyone, or perhaps no one, would find it acceptable to be the guinea pig in a social experiment, no matter how infrequent an adverse result would occur on average. In the phenomenology of the victim's experience, there is no such thing as an average, and the entire matter rests on just one case: this one. There is no repetition of the present situation — this is, in fact, it. The same reservation exists for unique or catastrophic situations. In these cases, there is no frequency to speak of because the one event cannot simply be considered as a single case in a set.

Optimization and Satisficing

The most explicit notion, in this whole construct, is that of optimization, which is an operation enabled by the hypothetical construct of utility. We have discussed the use of aggregation as a cognitive device to allow analysis to proceed. The hypostatization of utility, along with the operation of equating the good of the public with aggregate utility, allows us to treat policy as an optimization problem. The logic is simple: If you can identify what is good for society, then the more of it, the better, and at the limit, whatever maximizes this good is the best course for society, the *summum bonum*. But, one eventually is moved to ask, what is this good or utility? Enough analysts have pointed out that utility cannot be simply income because utility changes with income. Perhaps, this concept of the good, which is to be maximized, is some combination of income, health, joy, ambition, sentiment, etc. But how would we find and define what constitutes utility? We might watch what choices people make and try to guess what it is that increases with each rational choice (the idea of revealed preference). But this is a circular argument. Not able to define what it is that really makes up utility, we resort to the argument that "utility is whatever it is we maximize." But we needed a prior definition of utility to figure out what to maximize to begin with. This "entropic" definition of utility is what one inevitably ends up with:

> Policy is determined by maximizing utility.
> Utility is whatever we maximize when we set policy, which is convenient for analysts since this is a no-lose proposition.

At this point, we introduce a geometric representation of the decision problem to better explain the theory of optimization. Suppose that we are trying to decide on a home to buy and that we have a range of homes that vary over two criteria: design and view, ranging from 0 to 200 on an "architectural" scale and a 0 to 100 rating on a "scenic qualities" scale, respectively. To simplify things, we just assume that no other criterion is important or variant enough to warrant consideration — all the houses could cost the same, for example. Then, suppose that we have a lot of alternatives and, in fact, an infinite number of alternatives. The set of alternatives can be represented by the shaded area shown in Figure 2.1.

The question is: Which home (which is just one of all the infinite points contained in the shaded area) should we buy? If we wanted to maximize architectural qualities, we would pick point A. If we wanted to maximize the scenic view, we would pick point B. But, what if we valued both? Then, we would need to determine how much we valued one criterion relative to the other. But this is the same operation we had seen before, where we simply do pairwise comparisons and determine the rate of exchange between architectural quality and view. Let us suppose that we trade off architecture to view on a 3:2 ratio. Our utility is calculated as follows:

Utility (alternative C) = 3 * architectural value (C) + 2 * scenic value (C)

for some alternative C. The task is then to calculate the utility for all the points in the feasible set and see which point gives the highest utility. We cannot process an infinite number of calculations, of course, so we look to the geometry of the problem to suggest an easier solution procedure. Notice that the utility function is actually the equation of a line:

$$U = 3 * x + 2 * y$$

where the line can shift toward or away from the origin depending on the alternative being measured. We sometimes call this equation the "social welfare function." Thus, if we want to get the utility of alternative C, we simply draw the line through C and see what value of U we obtain. For alternative C with x and y coordinates of (100, 0), we calculate a utility of 300. For alternative D with x and y coordinates of (75, 75), we calculate a utility of 375. Obviously, the farther away from the origin the line is, the higher the utility. This is illustrated in Figure 2.1. To find the alternative that gives the highest utility, we simply look for the point that brings the movable line farthest away from the origin. It is easy to see that this is the point E, which is right on the outer boundary of the feasible set. In fact, E is the point at which the line and the feasible set are tangent.

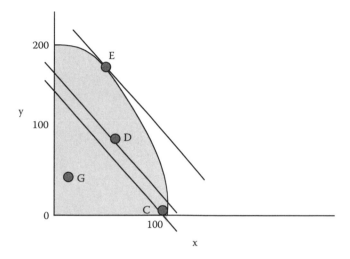

Fig. 2.1 Feasible set of alternatives.

If we have a different exchange rate, say, 4:1, then this simply gives us a different sloping line, as shown in Figure 2.2. The solution for this case, with the new rate of exchange between style and view, is simply the point of tangency between the feasible set and the movable line, or point F. Notice that, regardless of what the exchange rate is, this optimal point will always lie on the outer boundary of the feasible set. This outer boundary is called the "Pareto frontier." The Pareto frontier is the set of nondominated (or "Pareto optimal") points, which are all the points that are not dominated by any other point. Domination, in turn, means that a point is bested by another point on all criteria. This is the case between alternatives E and C, where E dominates C since E is better than C on all counts (style as well as view). The Pareto frontier for this example is shown as the boldly drawn curve. If you think about it, to solve this problem we could pretty much ignore all the points interior to the curve and just concentrate on the Pareto frontier.

The exercise of narrowing our scope so that we need only look at a subset of alternatives is called "screening." Various ad hoc techniques are used by policy analysts (and others) to screen away clearly unacceptable alternatives. The theoretical justification for screening operations stems from a subfield that grew out of decision theory and that came to be known as "bounded rationality." As proponents of this field, such as Herbert Simon, argued, humans are fallible and cannot attempt to come close to the ideal model of the utility-maximizing person. Specifically, among our other limitations, real humans cannot figure out all the possible alternatives to

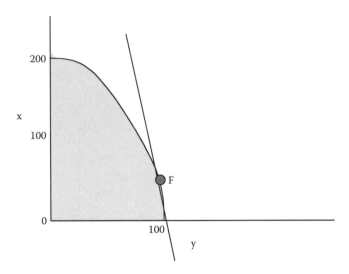

Fig. 2.2 Feasible set of alternatives (new utility function).

an action, cannot perform the utility calculations required, and cannot even approximate the requirements of optimality (Simon, 1957). They argued that a more common mode of decision making is that of "satisficing." That is, rather than assign a utility to each and every alternative and rank order them from best to worst, humans often simply "score" alternatives on a simpler, dichotomous scale: acceptable or not acceptable. Their model of the human is that of a limited analyst seeking out alternatives until he or she comes upon some one alternative that is good enough. This is still rational behavior but in a bounded, limited sense.

Satisficing is something we obviously practice much of the time (but proponents might say, all of the time). It also provides us with ad hoc rules for screening. That is, we simply look for rules by which we distinguish acceptable from not acceptable and apply these rules to the set of alternatives. This allows us to screen away alternatives that clearly would not make the grade, no matter how we calculated utility.

This also introduces an important variant of utility and that is the notion of a threshold. In its ideal sense, a threshold is something that, below which, no alternative would possibly be acceptable, no matter what. This suggests that in the human cognitive universe, utility is not simply a smoothly varying measure but instead can be characterized by sudden jumps (as the scale passes from the zone of acceptability to nonacceptability). Sometimes, these rules are induced by moral principles, which we return to in a later chapter. Suffice it to say that thresholdlike structures and processes do seem to exist in our cognition — whether these are absolute thresholds is a debatable matter. Utilitarians would say that there are no absolute thresholds — everything has a price or a rate of exchange with any other good. To deny comparability means that one espouses notions of value that depart from that of utility. Later on, we discuss some of these nonutilitarian notions. At any rate, a threshold may look something like the following rule:

Never accept candy from strangers.

or something more ad hoc like the following:

Given my cash flow situation, I will not consider cars priced higher than $16,000.

Whether driven by nonutilitarian, moral, or practical reasons, satisficing gives us some ways of effectively screening our list of alternatives. This might be employed in graduate school admissions deliberations (or not), and one might find a department employing some such set of screening rules like:

If: GPA less than 2.5
or GRE less than 750 (verbal + quantitative)
or time to degree greater than 10 years,
Then: Deny admission.

We have discussed two kinds of screening rules, as summarized below.

Rule 1: Discard all dominated alternatives.
Rule 2: Discard all alternatives that register values for any criterion below the threshold of acceptability for that criterion.

Geometrically, these two operations are depicted in Figure 2.3 where we see that the feasible set is first reduced by throwing away the lighter regions that fall outside the respective thresholds for the two criteria: style and view. Then, the remaining subset is further delimited by removing all its dominated alternatives, which essentially means considering only the bold outer perimeter contained in the subset (i.e., the portion of the Pareto frontier that remains after the thresholds are applied).

Prospect Theory

In the 1970s, there arose a number of studies beginning with Kahneman and Tversky (1979) that involved testing the expected utility hypothesis

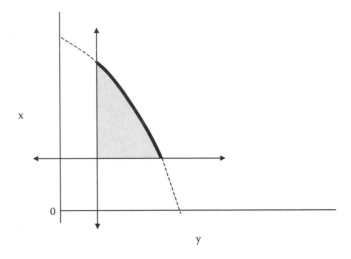

Fig. 2.3 Screening using acceptability thresholds.

in simulated decision situations in the laboratory. Their studies found consistent deviations of the subjects' behavior from that normally predicted by expected utility. For example, when asked to choose between the following situations:

Situation A: Sure gain of $1000
Situation B: 50% chance of gaining $2000, 50% chance of gaining nothing

most people would choose Situation A, though the expected utilities of both situations are equal. On the other hand, when given the choice between the following situations:

Situation A: Sure loss of $100
Situation B: 50% chance of losing $200, 50% chance of losing nothing

most people chose Situation B. The patterns they found were consistent enough that it seemed to beg modifications to the expected utility hypothesis. Based on these patterns, one might say that many people are averse to risk when it comes to winning money, i.e., they would rather be paid a guaranteed amount rather than risk it all for double that amount. On the other hand, when it comes to paying a debt, people are more likely to be prone to risk, i.e., they would rather get a chance not to have to pay a debt even though this exposes them to some probability that they would have to pay double. That is, if we plot dollars against utility and plot

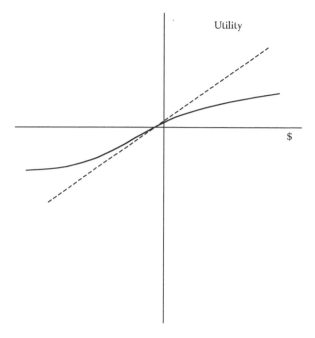

Fig. 2.4 Departures from the expected utility hypothesis.

winnings on the positive scale and losses on the negative scale, we find a utility curve that looks like that shown in Figure 2.4. By way of contrast, someone whose preferences completely matched that predicted by expected utility would show a utility curve like the dashed line in the figure. The point to be made, however, is that while prospect theory does show departures from the expected utility hypothesis, in that people do seem to consistently reveal asymmetries in how they value gains versus losses, the theory is still very much within the basic framework of the vN–M model. The main difference is, as Kahneman and Tversky suggest, people use biases and heuristics to maneuver their way around decisions. This is not to say that people are less than rational, but perhaps it is a way of saying that rationality, as found in real individuals, is not perfectly modeled by the vN–M model.

Policy Considerations

The decision-theoretic model of human judgment is meant to be a universal one, and so it is applicable to any situation involving individual or social decision making. It is, first of all, meant to be a comprehensive model of how humans reason. From a policy standpoint, however, its power lies in its ready application, in concept, to practically any policy situation — in concept, because while policy situations are easily described in terms of the model, getting the data for the model is quite another matter.

First, while not all the details of decision analysis are always followed, one most commonly finds that the basic essence of rational model appears in different policy situations. It is important to be able to detect this rational model embedded in different policy processes. Consider the following decision procedure used in conducting environmental impact analysis for new projects:

Scoping: Construct list of decision criteria in public hearing.
               ↓

Alternatives: Come up with a reasonable range of alternatives for the proposed project.
               ↓

Screening: Test the alternatives against any thresholds of acceptability (referred to as significance thresholds, where significance refers to degree of environmental impact).
               ↓

Choice: Select the environmentally superior alternative.

The rational model, and the more specific model of utilitarianism, is ever present even when not explicitly evoked. For example, consider the argument often used to justify maintaining the NASA (National Aeronautics and Space Administration) space exploration program. As the argument goes, the cost of running the NASA program is more than offset by the future benefits stemming from it, the latter consisting of spin-offs in terms of new products and commodities from the market, using technology developed for the space program. Environmentalists have used a variant of this to try and convince politicians to agree to cuts on emissions of greenhouse gases. By learning how to design and run industries to be cleaner, we will be forced to create a new generation of industrial technologies that can then be sold to other countries for a profit. However, the problem with these types of arguments is that they drown out the nonutilitarian aspects of the issue — for example, it is possible that, for many, the most important arguments in favor of space exploration or of reducing greenhouse gases are those that are not about monetary costs and benefits at all.

Utilitarian arguments also lie at the heart of one important mode of policy analysis: the so-called rational choice model. This model is used as a tool for explaining why policy actors behave as they do. Rational choice arguments are used to analyze almost any and every social situation, ranging from group membership (e.g., see Olson, 1965), fertility (e.g., see Cain,

1977), and religion (Young, 1997). For example, using whatever variables might be actually measurable, an analyst might try to explain high fertility rates in the developing world as a rational calculation by the decision maker (parent) in which the latter balances the gain from additional children (in terms of utility to the family from future income or agricultural productivity) versus the cost of additional children (for rearing the infant, food, education, etc.). Obviously, untrammeled use of rational choice can violate other (as in moral) sensibilities in how or with what constructs we can or should understand different social realities. The unhampered use of rational choice can also lead to perhaps dubious conclusions. As an example, one recent analysis (Tsebelis, 1990) concluded that, through utilitarian calculations, a potential criminal should, ironically, not base his or her decision to commit a crime on the degree of punishment involved. However, in pointing out the severe limitations of the rational choice framework, the analyst should not fail to see situations in which this type of analysis would yield highly valuable insight. For example, although there are many different ways of studying and understanding corruption in bureaucracies, certainly one relevant mode of analysis is a rational choice perspective wherein the potential "corruptee" is motivated by strong motivations toward utility maximization (e.g., Rose-Ackerman, 1999).

The Mythology of Decisions

The critique of the model often begins with the implausibility of the calculating "machine" that persons are assumed to be — to some extent, theories such as that of bounded rationality address this. There are other, even more fundamental critiques. The decision model, in its utilitarian formulation, implicitly brings in an assumption that borders on the mythological — the hypostatization of the state. The extension of the individual decision maker to all of society posits the existence of a unitary state that is able to act as the locus of decisions. This furthers the notion of the state as unitary, monolithic, representative, authoritarian, and omniscient. The problem is that this flies in the face of the state as we know it, which is a complex polity that is beleaguered by a multitude of contending voices, forces, and motivations. Furthermore, positing the state as a locus of knowledge is problematic, given the removal of state actors from the everyday circumstances of community life, commerce, and individual pursuits. The critique of the state was most ebulliently voiced by Hayek who reacted by going to the liberal extreme of positing the notion of catallaxy, i.e., the ultimate location of efficiency and knowledge in the dispersed actions and motivations of countless atomistic individuals (Hayek, 1948).

However, the most fundamental construct that underpins this model lies in the conceptualization of utility. The mythology of utility entails the construction of some hypothetical entity that captures the manifold motivations of individuals and, by extension, the whole of society. As we can see in chapter 3, this can lead to a strong assumption of behaviorism, which does dominate classical policy analysis. It is problematic because there really is not any such identifiable entity, and utility serves as a place-holder for the *summum bonum*. For example, it is easily shown that money is an inadequate measure of utility. The deepest issue, however, is the circularity of the reasoning behind the construction of the concept. The premise is that we can model individuals and society as all seeking the maximization of utility. However, the construction of utility as a positive measure has, so far, been impossible. Is it a complex function of wealth, fame, affection, friendship, butter, ships, art, and others? But what possible function might this be? Given the sheer intractability of defining utility, we are essentially left to positing that utility is whatever people maximize when they do any action — that is, utility is something like entropy, which is increased whatever happens in this universe. However, the circularity of this reasoning is only too self-evident. The fact that we cannot measure utility is an outcome of this more fundamental problem.

In short, the model of decisions achieves a drastic simplification of human motivation to that of utility and of polity to that of the unitary state. The act of decision making is also largely an objective one, in which, given the same universe of choices and utilities, the same decision should hold in any context. Missing in this account is the role of history, culture, morality, doubt, indecision, love, and a host of other notions that essentially define human existence.

The most fundamental impact of the vN–M–Bentham model on policy analysis remains that of positing policy as an act of choice. Choice, we remind ourselves, is modeled after the individual decision maker applying a personal utility function to a set of alternatives and seeking that alternative that maximizes her or his calculated utility. This precedes and enables the mathematization of policy questions, which is needed to transform the question to one of analysis. At this point, we merely note the rarified simplicity of such a model. Consider the impossibility of constructing discrete, analyzable alternatives in a policy debate surrounding educational reform. In this case, to simply construct a set of competing alternatives neglects the more important dimensions of institutional capacity, cultures for organizational performance, professional learning, bureaucratic trans-parency, and a host of other issues that necessarily have to enter into an effective policy discussion. Positing policy discussion as a decision-theoretic choice reduces the entire question to a unidimensional analytic. In this example, this unitary dimension onto which all policy questions collapse is understood, in a performative sense, as choice and, in the cognitive sense, as utility. Other policy approaches, some of which we discuss later, also involve similarly radically reductive operations, Consider the more recent focus on participation, which can be reduced to the championing of the formal nature of participation and not the substantive.

Portraying the policy question as a choice between competing alternatives and, importantly, alternatives as competing states of the world has cast its pall on policy analysis. This reduction of policy action as a simple act of choice among readily consumable states of the world is a real limitation on our ability to conceive of policy action in other terms (such as institution building or policy evolution). First, notice how, epistemologically, this description allows the model of *res cogitans* to be translated into real practice. As a neutral, distant maker of choice, the decision maker need only gaze upon the alternative states of the world and pick one. This waves away the real and significant position of the decision maker as embedded in the very world that is being reengineered and the necessary aspect of policy as an enabling of a course of action to transform social reality. Positing policy as mere choice leaves out the necessity to encounter community, to mobilize and organize, to seek common understanding, to train policy actors on the ground to assume new roles, to study the past in order to gain a sense of what is potentially achievable, and myriad other dimensions to policy action.

To take one of these examples, consider the way in which history is simplified in the vN–M–Bentham model. In the model, the past is categorized as, simply, sunk cost. Whether one should or should not keep waiting for a bus is determined solely by the probability that the bus will arrive in the next so many minutes and the utility (or, more correctly, disutility) to the waiting person. The amount of time already "invested" in waiting should have nothing to do with the decision to keep waiting or to go. That is, to make a decision, one need only take into account all the consequences that are laid out in the future and their attendant utilities. The analyst need only look down one path, to the future. However, consider a policy situation wherein formerly warring factions (whether tribal or social) are to be brought together in a collaborative regime for regional development. In this situation, one could not proceed with policy without entering into the past. Why is this? Quite simply, it is because history is not buried in the distant past, but, in real terms, exists as a component of present-day social reality. To enact (not merely choose) policy, one must design and engage in processes that allow people to work across and in the midst of ever-present structures of division. That community building is often absent from the definition of the policy process is a serious failing of policy analysis.

Positing alternatives as ready-made states of the world can have more serious consequences for policy work than one might first realize. Consider the predilection of planning and policy agencies for long-term planning reports that spell out utopian visions for their planning areas. Consider, at the same time, the frequency with which these policy and planning reports are relegated to irrelevance. The envisioning of states of the world is only one component of policy. It is, moreover, an element that encourages ever more distant policy horizons over which to envision the alternatives. The reason for this is that choices and alternatives can become more distinct or comparable with time and distance. One could not sufficiently construct alternative states in a day, and in real terms, one needs a 25-year time horizon to be able to spell out distinctly competing alternatives for public transportation (e.g., elevated rail or subway). For example, in 1989, the City of Los Angeles put out the Advanced Planning Report (City of Los Angeles, 1989). This pioneering plan was a blueprint for facilities over a 100-year time horizon. Why did the planners choose such a distant horizon? According to one city manager, part of the rationale was that one needed to get far enough in time that the report became apolitical. This echoes our point about the epistemological distance that policy analysts try to assume. There are other dangers to this distancing, however. One is that, as a social process, policy formulation is necessarily political (i.e., engaging the polity in debate, consensus, and paralogy). The other is simply practicality — vision occurs on the horizon, but action happens in the here and now. The day the Advanced Planning Report came out, it was already "wrong," beginning with the requisite population projection.

The most important policy question is often not what we can envision in the distant future, but the relevant question: Where do we go from here? This second model of policy is too incremental, too embedded in present-day and messy goings-on to be incorporated well into the choice-theoretic model. As important, this alternative model is also too close to home for the policy analyst who is, after all, embedded in present-day politics, economic realities, and job constraints. Distance is needed for the policy analyst to be able to clamber onto the epistemological perch and, from these heights, divine society's highest good. The enlightenment model of rationality does not take the point of view of a fish swimming in the ocean, so to speak, but something more like Hamlet perched atop the castle looking down upon the sea. It is this epistemological distance that is sought after to achieve analytic clarity.

When we give up this artificial clarity, however, what kind of analytic is possible? We will proceed to enter into these questions from chapter 5 onward. In the end, the greatest influence of the utilitarian model is in the area of legitimation of policy arguments. Rational choice models for explaining social phenomena would not be possible were the analyst not able to reduce dimensions of society onto the unitary, featureless plane of utility and so allow for social phenomena to be described simply as movements along this plane. The very ethic of globalization and its vision of a global market owes its fundamental logic to utilitarianism, in that in the positing of the social calculus and the mathematization of policy, one can find the reduction of all social phenomena to the logic of market transactions (which are, after all, modeled as mere exchanges of utility).

Reforming the Practice of Decision Analysis

How do we reform the concept and practice of decisions? As we will see in the rest of this book, the first thing we need to do is be open to a richer notion of policy making. In this alternative formulation, policy results from a manifold of parallel, sometimes competing, logics and processes, of which the decision model is but one. The consideration of utility and choice remains an important facet of policy, but it exists side by side with other considerations. Later in this book, particularly in Part III, we illustrate how to combine the logic of decisions with other modes of analysis.

If we are open to the possibility that the model of decisions only partially captures the horizon of analysis, then we should also be open to the idea that utility is, at best, a proxy measure that is applicable to a subset of policy considerations. Not everything can be captured by the notion of utility. This leads to reflection on the analyst's part about what elements, things, or considerations are treated by individuals and society as if they were utility. In other words, what sort of things do we maximize? Related to this is the question of what sorts of things are commensurable and can be quantified into elements that can enter into a decision analysis. This leads us to creating an explicit category within our analysis for elements of a policy situation that are utility commensurable. In many practical applications, this may amount to a separate categorization of those elements that are expressly captured in the market and for which valuations can be arrived at. Furthermore, an analysis should well consider the impact of any policy on changes in these utilitarian measures but acknowledge that these are just one of various sets of analytic considerations that need to be taken into account in policy design.

Later in this book, we see how we can juxtapose and integrate decision theory with other logics — for example, less teleological, more normative models for policy design. Still, the biggest problem with the utilitarian model remains the utter loss of dimensionality when we collapse features and meanings of a policy situation into a single dimension of utility. In this manner, we also collapse the meaning of what it means to be a person to a planar concept — a person is a utility bearer and, moreover, someone who behaves so as to maximize that utility. When we have reduced everything onto the plane of utility, then we can easily work out problems and solutions to problems. In the planar universe of utility, there are optimum strategies. The problem is that we then take these prescriptions out of their artificial context and impose them upon the real, multiplex, and multidimensional realm of experience. It is this seemingly circular, but irreversibly reductionist, operation that constitutes the mythology of the decision model.

At any rate, the paucity of dimensionality of the vN–M–Bentham model, and its utter and elegant simplicity, may be a large part of the reason that, first of all, this model so dominates policy analysis and thought; and second, most policy analyses serve mostly as tools for justifying policies formulated through some other logic or as ornamental shelf liners that can transform a drab office into something like the congressional library.

While many policy questions, some of which we discuss later, involve complex phenomena and manifold processes that cannot be described as decision-theoretic choices, some policy problems are readily describable in terms of this model. For example, siting and purchasing decisions by public agencies are inherently matters of choice among competing alternatives and so are ripe for this type of analysis.

A related note is that, though the decision-theoretic model is most easily applied to policy situations, it is generally used not so much to drive a decision, but to justify it *ex post*. Often, a cost-benefit analysis is used to explain why it was that a decision already previously made was wise. Or, such an analysis is often done midway through a project to check whether it is, in fact, working as planned or needs correction (e.g., see Portney, 1990 or Palmer and Portney, 1995 for some analyses of the efficiency of the environmental regulation). In other words, decision theory is used often as a tool to respond to criticism. Its most common use is not for judgment but for legitimization.

If the last point is true, what, then, drives policy formulation? The most common answer is: the political process. This process is most often described as a process by which multiple policy players vie for a policy outcome, competing with each other, sometimes cooperating or forming temporary coalitions, and through this pluralistic melee, some policy results. However, oftentimes, society does not coalesce like the unitary collective assumed by the utilitarians. Also, there may not be a political force strong or influential enough to enforce a unitary-driven decision. In these cases, it may be too overbearing for an analyst to assume that one can simply proceed with analysis by washing away differences in position and, instead, assuming the unitary collective fashioned after the rational individual. This political arena, with multiple players who ineluctably refuse to be lumped into a collective, is the subject matter of chapter 3.

Games

Noncooperative *n*-Person Games

Introduction

In this chapter, we explore the other side of the influential von Neumann and Morgenstern (vN-M) treatment of social judgment by considering the theory (or rather, theories) of games. As in the last chapter, we have several objectives for the chapter, the first being the capacity to thoroughly understand the theory, power, and limitations of games for modeling policy situations. Here, we inquire into questions such as: Why is it that games have been such an influential model for policy phenomena? What assumptions are embedded in the notion of a game, and how do we begin to reflect more deeply on them? How might we begin to move the theory of games beyond its present reductionisms and onto richer, more contextual, and more meaningful planes of analysis? Most immediately, this chapter speaks directly to the consequences stemming from the mathematization of analysis and how this took analysis along a direction that excludes many other analytical possibilities. To do this, we need to retrace some of these steps, at least to some extent.

The theory of games is perhaps the most extreme form of the rational model, and it is particularly fitting to study it in some depth to bring out its limitations and the potential for extending its use in more grounded, complex descriptions of policy situations. An analytical look at game theory is also instructive if only to see, most clearly, the problem of what we might call the "*a priori* analytic." Moreover, we would like to discover why it is that games (and concepts like the equilibrium) have been so influential in policy discourse despite its extreme reductionism, and how we might find in it useful insights to inform our analysis. We wonder whether a grounding in the real institutions and contexts of policy situations can inform our employment of games and make them informative in ways beyond their present use. Lastly, having reflected on the limitations of the game as a policy model, we begin to chart ways to deepen our analysis and bring back the dimensionality that was lost when we projected the policy situation onto the plane of the rational-purposive. To be able to chart directions beyond the austere formulation of game theory, we first need to understand it in some depth.

For the most part, game theory has been used in the discourse of policy as a way to justify certain policy prescriptions in an abstract sense, more than in the actual modeling of real situations. Toward the end of the chapter, we insist that these concepts move from the abstract-theoretical to the immediately real. We study these models primarily with the intent of introducing a reflective element to this study. The point is that these models need not remain in their abstraction but, instead, be increasingly used in routine analysis of real programs and projects. Other than having the model drive reality and refashion institutions, we can use real-world institutions and policy considerations to drive the exact form of the game that we should analyze or to assess whether the game is a proper model to begin with. Before launching into the directions in which game theory departed from the decision theoretic model discussed in chapter 2, it is helpful to remind ourselves of the concepts and assumptions that game theory inherits from decision theory. These are as follows:

- Social policy situations are best described as decisions involving choice of one among multiple alternatives.
- Decision makers are individual utility-maximizing people.
- The goodness or badness of situations may be described by assigning values (called "utilities") to consequences that characterize these situations. Decision makers employ the notion of expected utility under conditions of outcome uncertainty.

In fact, most of the assumptions carry over into game theory intact. The one departure is that game theory, unlike decision theory, assumes away the possibility that:

- A social decision may be made by considering a collective unit standing in for all the individuals in society, and, therefore,

- One cannot simply impose upon society the alternative that results in the highest total aggregate utility.

Game theory assumes that one cannot impose these preceding operations, and so has to fall back to the original problem of how to characterize decision making of a multiple number of individuals. The key, here, is that the individuals still act and decide like individuals. To better understand how game theory works, let us start with a hypothetical policy problem.

Case Study I Consider a large lake on the edges of which are found two towns, A and B. Each town is presently enjoying a substantial income from two sources of revenue:

- The fishing industry located in each town
- A generating station (i.e., power plant) that each town owns and operates and that allows them to produce electricity and sell the same to other towns farther away from the lake.

Now, each town is contemplating whether to add one additional generating station to be able to increase its annual revenue from the sale of power to other towns. However, the problem is that generating stations use lake water to cool their turbines; the used water is then discharged back to the lake. The result is a slightly warmer lake water temperature, which is bad for freshwater fish. Thus with each additional generating station, the lake water gets warmer and warmer, resulting in increasing losses of fish catch. Let us describe the consequences of each potential set of actions, below. Note that each scenario involves two actions, one by town A and another by town B.

Scenario 1:	Neither A nor B add generating stations.
Consequences of Scenario 1:	No change in annual revenues to either town.
Scenario 2:	A adds one generating station, and B adds none.
Consequences of Scenario 2:	A gets an additional $20 M/yr. in revenue and a loss of fish catch of $7.5 M/yr. (leaving a net additional revenue of $12.5 M/yr.). B only gets the $7.5 M/yr. loss.
Scenario 3:	B adds one generating station, and A adds none.

Consequences of Scenario 3:	B gets an additional $20 M/yr. in revenue and a loss of fish catch of $7.5 M (leaving a net additional revenue of $12.5 M/yr.). A only gets the $7.5 M/yr. loss.
Scenario 4:	Both A and B add one generating station each.
Consequences of Scenario 4:	Both get an additional $20 M/yr. revenue. But both also suffer fish catch losses amounting to $25 M/yr. each. The reason the drop in catch is so high is that the combined effect of warmer discharge water from towns A and B is precipitous to lake water quality.

This "game" is summarized in Table 3.1.

Note the terminology. We call each individual decision maker a "player" and each alternative action a "strategy." In Table 3.1, strategy S1 is a town's decision not to add an extra generating station, and S2 is the decision to add an extra generating station. Each player in this example has to decide on one of two competing alternatives, S1 and S2. So far, it sounds like the decision problem in the previous chapter where all we had to do was select a best alternative for all of society. In this model, each player gets to make an individual decision and choose a best alternative for that player. In the previous chapter, there was one decision to be made. In this model, there are n decisions in a situation involving n players (in this example, $n = 2$).

Table 3.1 summarizes the consequences of the game. Again, note the consequentialist nature of this model, which posits that we need not pay attention to how the situation unravels but, instead, just focus on the end result (the consequences). Each cell in Table 3.1 represents the outcomes in terms of payoffs, of one possible set of actions taken by the players. For example, if both players choose S1, then there is no change in the present situation and the change in payoffs to either player is zero. If, on the other hand, player A chooses S1 but player B chooses S2, then we find ourselves

Table 3.1 Payoff matrix for two-person game (Case I)

		Player B	
		Strategy S1	Strategy S2
Player A	Strategy S1	(0, 0)	(–7.5, 12.5)
	Strategy S2	(12.5, –7.5)	(–5, –5)

in the upper-right cell of the table, which tells us that player A receives a negative payoff of –$7.5 M and B receives $12.5 M. If both players choose S2, then both receive a loss of –$5 M each, relative to their incomes today.

What would each player do? To answer this, we go through a mental exercise. First, suppose you were player A (without forgetting that player A is actually an entire town, perhaps its municipal government). For sure, the best outcome for you would be if you played S2, and player B played S1, which Table 3.1 results in a payoff of $12.5 M to you and a negative payoff (loss) of –$7.5 M to player B.

However, how can player A be sure that player B does indeed play S1? If player B played S2 instead, they both end up receiving –$5 M. The way the mental exercise goes is to consider your payoffs under each possible strategy that player B might take. The reasoning goes like this:

If player B plays S1, then player A gets zero by playing S1 and $12.5 M by playing S2.
Conclusion: If player B plays S1, then player A should play S2.

If player B plays S2, then player A gets –$7.5 M by playing S1 and –$5 M by playing S2.
Conclusion: If player B plays S2, then player A should play S2.

But look at the above conclusions and comment on the insight you derive from them. The key insight is this: Whatever strategy B does play, it makes the most sense for player A to play S2. And, since we assume A is rational, we can conclude that A would, indeed, play S2.

Now consider the same mental exercise for player B. What conclusions do you arrive at? This is the second key insight of this game: Because the game is symmetrical anyway, player B ends up making the exact same decision that A does, which is to play S2. We can figure out that B thinks the exact same way as A because we assume them to be identical (that is, utility-maximizing individuals).

The bottom line is that you can, just by doing these mental exercises, figure out how the game will be played. That is, the resulting set of strategies should be (S2, S2), and the resulting payoffs should be (–5, –5). Now, take a step back and ponder on the entire game and, then, consider the final result we obtained. Comment on this result and whether it makes sense to you. We return to the logic of this game later on.

For now, consider what we have accomplished so far. We have modeled a situation wherein each decision maker is able to make a decision independently of the other people in this society. Moreover, we have shown that we can predict the result of this game, which essentially means that we can predict how each person will decide. How do we know that we can solve these games? Let us go into the theory of it a little bit.

Analysis: Two-Person Zero-Sum Games

Von Neumann and Morgenstern introduced this basic model of social judgment as a game played by individual utility maximizers. Moreover, in their book, they also gave von Neumann's theorem that showed how you can actually predict these results for one specific type of game: that involving two players and zero-sum payoffs. By zero-sum, he simply meant that type of game wherein whatever you receive comes from the other player. For example, if the result of the game is that you receive a payoff of 24, then the other player must receive a negative payoff (or loss) of −24. Table 3.2 gives an example of such a game.

For this type of game, von Neumann proved that you can predict the result to be the so-called max–min solution for the game. However, von Neumann did not give a proof of the existence of more general games (e.g., non–zero-sum or for three or more players). Consider the original game in Table 3.1, which is a two-player game but not a zero-sum game. In this two-player, non–zero-sum game, we found a predictable result just by going through a set of mental exercises. However, consider a different two-player, non–zero-sum game as found inTable 3.3.

Notice that if you went through the same mental exercises, you would find that you do not arrive at a definitive result. Resolution of this type of game awaited a later proof, as is discussed next.

Table 3.2 Payoff matrix for two-person zero-sum game

		Player B	
		Strategy S1	Strategy S2
Player A	Strategy S1	(0, 0)	(−7.5, 7.5)
	Strategy S2	(7.5, −7.5)	(−5, −5)

Table 3.3 Payoff matrix for two-person zero-sum game

		Player B	
		Strategy S1	Strategy S2
Player A	Strategy S1	(0, 0)	(5, 2)
	Strategy S2	(−2, 5)	(7, 0)

Analysis: Non–zero-Sum, n-Person Games

A more general model for games would involve the possibility of not just having two players but three and more and payoffs that are non–zero-sum. John Nash proved that these more general types of games always had solutions. To understand what "solution" means, let us consider the game shown in Table 3.1. Why is the strategy pair, (S2, S2), considered to be a solution? More than anything else, it is a solution because we can predict that both players will play this way. There is another way of stating this same thing, which is useful for our discussion: (S2, S2) is a solution to this game because no player has any incentive to play any other strategies than the ones assumed. That is, given that player A assumes that B will play S2, then there is no incentive for A to play anything other than S2. Similarly, given that B assumes A will play S2, then there is no incentive for B to play anything other than S2. Thus, each player plays the strategy that the other player assumed for him or her (and that we assumed).

Consider the strategy pair (S2, S2). If player A assumes B to play S2, then for A to play S1 would result in a payoff to A of –7.5, while playing S2 would result in a payoff to A of –5 — so, player A plays S2. On the other hand, if B assumes A to play S2, then B's best response is to play S2. Thus, each player's best response to the other player's assumed strategy is identical to the strategy that the other assumed they would play in the first place. Their final decisions reinforce the initial assumptions about what each would play.

Initially, the proposal was to call such a solution a "stable point." However, others (specifically Lloyd Shapley, Nash's colleague at Princeton) thought that this might not be the best thing to call such a solution concept (communication between Shapley and the author). For example, take the following analogy of a ball resting on a porcelain vessel (Figure 3.1).

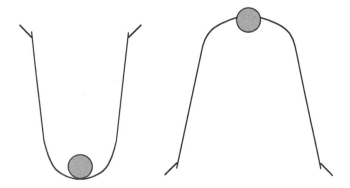

Fig. 3.1 Stable versus unstable equilibriums.

We see that, while in both cases, the balls are motionless, the ball in the figure on the left is clearly much more "stable" than that on the right. For this reason, the name for the solution concept was changed to "equilibrium" since the latter term merely points to all forces being in balance (as in either of these situations — otherwise, the ball would not be still). An equilibrium can be a relatively unshakeable one (e.g., picture someone literally shaking the table on which the ball and porcelain laid) or relatively tenuous, while nonetheless being in a state of equilibrium. The very idea of an equilibrium has irrevocably influenced policy analysis ever since. In some cases, the concept suggests we might envision some sort of policy "utopia" where policy goals, stakeholders, and strategies might be static, stable, and objective.

The notion of an equilibrium did not start with these game theorists, of course. It is a notion that goes back to ideas about natural homeostasis in nature and other physical phenomena. It is a fairly important concept that has influenced policy analysis (and institutional practice) in fundamental ways. Perhaps, the most important aspect of the notion of equilibrium has to do with its natural origins (as in homeostasis or chemical equilibriums). Employment of this notion of natural equilibriums allows one to import the idea of states of things coming to rest even in the very human and social dynamics of policy. A policy that is contentious can be idealized as the very arena of combat, with pitch battle being fought between very active combatants. On the other hand, policy resolution might be idealized as that state wherein policy players are at peace, content with their spoils and, well, sitting in the shade in motionless bliss. What this allows policy is to posit equilibriums as not just a normative idea that one should aspire to. In this model, it is also posited as a positive concept that actually describes how the world would look if one were to implement the solution. A policy is thought to be resolved (in this rarified model) when no one makes a move to contest, change, or revise it. In this state, the positing of society as a collective actually might be realizable, allowing the policy analyst (or other authority) to step in and work her or his wisdom. Through this idealized model, we can legitimize policy analysis. The relevance of this idea to real policy situations is discussed later in this chapter.

At any rate, there is an easy, graphical way to solve for the equilibrium of such a game. First, consider player A's choices given some assumed strategy for B. That means, first consider what strategy A would play if we assumed B to play S1 (the latter meaning that we only need to concern ourselves with the first column). We see that A would play S2. To remember this, underline the payoff to A under (S2, S1). Then do the same thing

Table 3.4 Payoff matrix illustrating solution procedure

		Player B	
		Strategy S1	Strategy S2
Player A	Strategy S1	(0, 0)	(−7.5, 12.5)
	Strategy S2	(12.5, −7.5)	(−5, −5)

assuming B plays S2. Then consider B's choices and do the same thing except, now, we proceed row by row. Assuming that A will play S1 means we only need to consider the first row. We underline the payoff to B corresponding to B's best response if A plays S1. We then do the same assuming A plays S2 (which means concentrating on the second row). The resulting figure should look like Table 3.4.

The way to identify the solution is to simply look for cells wherein all the payoffs are underlined. As seen above, the cell (S2, S2) does have all the payoffs in it underlined and so is a solution to the game. Solutions to these games are known as "Nash equilibriums."

Now, try this underline method on the game shown in Table 3.3. We do not find a solution to the game. Moreover, if we try to test whether any cell is an equilibrium by asking whether any player has incentive to play another strategy, we find that we cannot stop at any cell and that this mental exercise has us moving from cell to cell to cell. For example, say that in Table 3.3 we try to assume the cell (S1, S1) as an equilibrium and proceed to go through the mental exercise. If player A assumes B will play S1 (i.e., assumes that this cell is the solution), then A figures out that S1 is best for him or her. On the other hand, if player B assumes A will play S1, then B figures that S2 is better for him or her. Thus, we move to a different cell (S1, S2). But, if we assume that (S1, S2) is the equilibrium and proceed with the mental exercise of determining each player's best response, then we end up moving again to the lower adjoining cell. And, so, we find ourselves moving from cell to cell without ever stopping, as shown in Table 3.5. This reinforces the model of equilibrium as a state where policy debate, and moves from stakeholders, comes to rest.

This notion of policy solution as a state of inactivity is a strong one that has influenced the way we think about and proceed with policy formulation. With regard to games such as the one shown in Table 3.5, we find that we cannot identify any solution that allows us to stop the policy cycle once and for all. Let us call one of these cells a "point" in "policy space" (where any other possible solutions or cells are other points in this policy space). Then, if we start with (S2, S2) as a point in this policy space, we find that applying the mental exercise, which we will call a "response function" because each player determines his or her best strategy assuming the

Table 3.5 Payoff matrix illustrating absence of pure strategy equilibrium

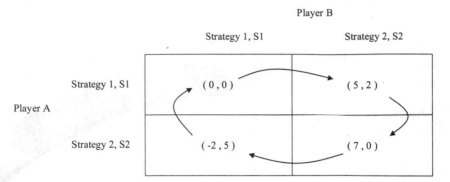

other players play as assumed, shifts us to another point in this policy space. And, if we start with this second point and apply the response function, we shift to yet a third point, and on and on. This is illustrated in Figure 3.2 where each point is a cell in the original table. Now, Nash proved that we find solutions (i.e., Nash equilibriums) provided that we are able to conceive of mixed strategies, which are best interpreted as probability mixtures of different "pure strategies," the latter being defined in the game shown in Table 3.5 as simple solutions (e.g., S1 or S2). The student will recognize the exact same notion applied in chapter 2, where we called these "lotteries." At any rate, a mixed strategy for player A would involve a probability mixture of A's two pure strategies:

$$(0.25)(S1) + (0.75)(S2)$$

which can be understood as a 25% chance that player A actually plays S1 and a 75% chance that A plays S2. Suppose that a player could actually decide to play such a strategy (how?). How would this change Figure 3.2? First of all, realize that this strategy greatly increases the options to either player. The set of possible pairs of strategies is now represented by the entire gray region in Figure 3.3. Now, player A need not have to choose only between S1 and S2, but from an infinite number of combinations of S1 and S2. The figure then becomes as shown in Figure 3.3.

If we simply pay attention to the pure strategies, we find the same cycling as discussed earlier, which is depicted by the endless path shown in Figure 3.3. However, Nash proved that in this expanded (the mathematical term is "convexified") policy space, we can always find at least one point that, if we were to start there and apply the response function, we would arrive at the same exact point (Nash, 1951). This is called a "fixed point," which is a convenient allusion to our idea of an equilibrium as a point

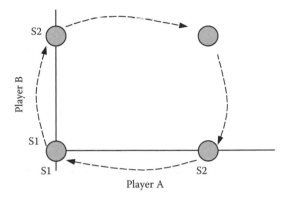

Fig. 3.2 Shifting strategies in a policy space of pure strategies.

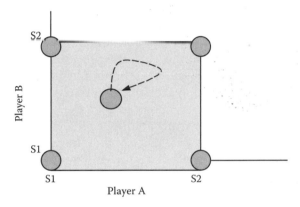

Fig. 3.3 Illustration of an equilibrium policy space with mixed strategies.

where movement ends. At this fixed point, each player can go through the mental exercise and still end up concluding that he or she was where it was best to be, after all. Another way of saying this is that we can always find a fixed point that always maps back onto itself. This seemed to be the proof that was needed to reassure theorists that the game-theoretic models could be counted on to have solutions.

However, though Nash did prove the existence of equilibria under various conditions, he could not show uniqueness. That is, there can be more than one, and perhaps an infinite number of, equilibria in a given game. This is seen in the game in Table 3.6.

In Table 3.6, we see two Nash equilibria (actually, the game has three, including one mixed-strategy Nash equilibrium). This poses a problem in that we do not know which one of these we should predict for the outcome of the game. The other way of talking about this is to wonder which of the

Table 3.6 Payoff matrix in game with multiple equilibria

		Player B	
		Strategy S1	Strategy S2
Player A	Strategy S1	(5, 5)	(–6, 2)
	Strategy S2	(2, 2)	(7, 4)

equilibria would the players prefer? Player B would prefer (S1, S1), while Player A would prefer (S2, S2). So, we are torn over which of the equilibria to recommend.

Later on, two other game theorists, Selten and Harsanyi, introduced several concepts that might help in deciding which of multiple possible equilibriums a set of players might actually choose (Harsanyi and Selten, 1988). The first insight is that in many situations it might best be modeled as requiring a series of decisions from players and not just a one-shot decision from each. In such a game, a final outcome can be a Nash equilibrium even though each single decision might not in itself be optimizing. Selten introduced the notion of subgame perfect Nash equilibria wherein each decision made along the route is a Nash equilibrium in itself (Selten, 1975). Here, a subgame is simply the game that results when you take that particular decision as the starting point of a smaller game (leading up to the final outcome). Selten's concept allows an analyst to narrow the choices for Nash equilibria in these kinds of multistage games.

Harsanyi introduced the related notion of Bayesian Nash equilibria, which posits that a player can assume some subjective probability distribution for the other players' moves. In the games we have talked about so far, each player's moves or decisions are perfectly transparent to the other players.

Policy Applications of Noncooperative Games

As in decision theory, the theory of games has had its biggest influence in the area of policy discourse: justifying certain models or directions for policy. One particularly influential example concerns the modern-day microeconomic proof of the invisible hand, which has been used as a policy discursive tool to justify institutions ranging from globalized trade to school cash vouchers. The original idea stems from Adam Smith, of course, and merely states the tenet that individuals should be free (through a free market) to make individually utility-maximizing choices (Smith, 1776). Through these choices, however, individuals move the entire society to a state that is Pareto optimal. The mathematical restatement and proof of this principle, however, needed to wait till the 1950s.

Arrow and Debreu published a paper that essentially gave a veritable restatement of Nash's paper on the (Nash) equilibrium (Arrow and Debreu, 1954). The original notion in Arrow and Debreu's paper was to describe markets in the terms of Nash's game-theoretic constructs wherein buyers and sellers were the players, and choices of quantities of goods bought and sold represented the feasible set of alternatives open to each player. In addition, they posited one additional player, that of the "market" (or "nature"), whose choices were the actual level at which prices of goods were set. Other than this, the entire paper was a basic allusion to and restatement of Nash's proposals. As in Nash, Arrow and Debreu proceeded to argue how in such a game one could rely on the existence of equilibria in the form of fixed points. In this equilibrium, buyers and sellers find themselves at positions (of quantities of goods bought and sold) from which no one had any incentive to deviate. In other words, at this equilibrium, the market found itself to be in a state of Pareto optimality. At this state, markets cleared (purchases equaled sales) and prices were stable. In this manner, Nash's notion of a state of equilibrium was essentially imported into an economic formulation and used to describe the end result of a smoothly functioning market. This end result, known as a "Walrasian equilibrium," is the embodiment and manifestation of the invisible hand that drives the market through the individual rationality of multiple players, unerringly to the final, stable outcome. It is the same logic through which a group of players arrive at, and play, a Nash equilibrium in an n-person game.

The point is that were it not for the game-theoretic foundations set by von Neumann and Morgenstern and later developed by Nash and others, there would not have been a microeconomic proof of the invisible hand. The mathematization of the market, and its model of equilibrium, is an important element in the present-day neoclassical school of economics.

Of course, this economic restatement of the noncooperative n-person game also inherits the latter's more problematic features. As in the general theory of games, though we can prove the existence of Nash (or Walrasian) equilibriums, we do not prove their uniqueness. Thus, in an ideal market, there can be multiple (even an infinite number of) Walrasian equilibria. The starting point of the transaction, which is the state of affairs or endowments of money and other goods that individuals have before the market works, can radically change the equilibriums that result. Therefore, as a policy prescription, positing the model of the invisible hand says nothing to society about distributing endowments. An even more basic reservation stems from the three-pronged hand waving that has to occur for the analyst to forget that:

- The idealized market does not correspond to the idealized n-person noncooperative game.
- Real markets do not correspond to the idealized model of the market.
- Real individuals do not actually behave like atomic utility maximizers.

For example, we realize the first point when we understand that even idealized markets deal with monetary exchange and not that of utility, as posited by the noncooperative game. Moreover, even an idealized market deals with purchases and sales of discrete amounts of goods. On the other hand, situations involving a handful of players can be modeled as a noncooperative game while the idealized market requires the hybrid assumption of a finite yet uncountable number of players (and a more sophisticated model as found in Aumann and Shapley, 1974). The analyst should reflect on the departures of real markets from the idealized. Most real consumers have only a limited number of choices between discrete alternatives. Indeed, marginally subsisting consumers are sometimes thought to have essentially no choice.

Tragedy of the Commons

One famous application of the theory of noncooperative games (specifically, the $n = 2$ case) concerns the so-called prisoners' dilemma, later reinterpreted by Hardin in his article on the tragedy of the commons (Hardin, 1969). In this model, Hardin posits a common pasture, owned by none and open to all (hence, the term, commons) on which two farmers are herding their cows. Each rancher currently owns one cow that presently grazes on a certain pasture. Rancher A is contemplating whether to add another cow (making it two in all). The other rancher, B, who shares the pasture with A, is contemplating the same decision (i.e., to keep only one cow or to add a second). The thing is that, when there are too many cows on the pasture, they interfere with each other, compete for grass, disturb each other psychologically, etc., such that the resulting weight of each cow is reduced as more cows use the pasture. In fact, the expected weight of each cow is as shown in Table 3.7. How many cows does Rancher A send out, and why? What does Rancher B do? Note that, for various reasons,

Table 3.7 Payoffs for tragedy of the commons game

Total Number of Cows in Field	Tons per Cow
2	3
3	2
4	1.25

Table 3.8 Payoff matrix for two-person tragedy of the commons game

		Rancher 2	
		1 cow	2 cows
Rancher 1	1 cows	(6000, 6000)	(4000, 8000)
	2 cows	(8000, 4000)	(5000, 5000)

you cannot communicate with the other rancher at all. The payoffs are shown in Tables 3.7 and 3.8.

The student can easily solve this game and see that it, indeed, has a Nash equilibrium in pure strategies. The model then suggests that we take this analogy and apply it to a host of policy situations that might be modeled as a tragedy of the commons games. Note that the analogy extends to greater numbers of players and has been generalized by its advocates to capture the essentials of many social situations wherein each individual player has an incentive to defect from the cooperative strategy even though society as a whole benefits from cooperation. In the case of the ranchers, both ranchers know fully well that they would both benefit more if both were to maintain only one cow each. However, both decide that they have no choice but to renege on this and to send out an extra cow, thus hurting both ranchers. The power of this analogy is its applicability, discursively, to any number of policy situations (e.g., instead of cows on a pasture, imagine cars on a highway, litterers on a street, contributors to a public fund, nations emitting carbon dioxide, and countless other situations). Indeed, the model has been used to justify two strongly contrasting solutions to problems of the commons — either strong coercive action by the state (forcing each rancher to stay put with one cow) or privatization (such that each rancher puts a fence around his or her half of the field and has no incentive to add an extra cow).

Cooperative *n*-Person Games

Introduction

In the previous section, we learned about noncooperative games wherein individual players behaved only like individual players. That is, individuals could not form groups. The assumption used to construct the noncooperative game is that of the nonenforceability of contracts. Perhaps, it would be best to restate a definition from Harsanyi (1966):

> A game is cooperative if commitments — agreements, promises, threats — are fully binding and enforceable. It is non-cooperative if commitments are not enforceable.

Case Study II   The cooperative model posits, as before, n players. However, the model allows the formation of a concerted group effort involving these n players. For example, let us consider the following example (depicted in Figure 3.4) wherein players are taken to be three private water supply entrepreneurs, one in each of the three towns in a region, all in the vicinity of a large river, their common source of drinking water.

In this example, suppose that each of these three private vendors is contemplating building a water treatment plant in their own town to take water from the river, treat it, and use for drinking water (and other purposes). Each private entrepreneur would get some profit from the sale of the water to townsfolk (where profit is revenue minus cost). Here is the genius of the formulation and, in real terms, real actors that decide to act collectively — it would cost less, due to economies of scale, to build one large treatment plant to serve all three communities than the total cost to build three separate, smaller treatment plants for each community to use. If the three players decided to pool their resources and build one central treatment plant, they would spend significantly less, meaning the total profit could be appreciably greater.

The problem in the cooperative model is not so much what strategy does each player pick, but rather, assuming that all n players decide on a common, cooperative strategy, how should the costs and benefits of the cooperative venture be allocated among the n players? In the noncooperative game, one needs to solve for each player's best strategy since we assumed away cooperation in that model. In the cooperative model, we assume the formation of a cooperative venture that, almost by definition, is the best collective strategy. We say that this is "almost by definition" since a cooperative venture can also mean each player acting individually (the noncooperative outcome). As in the noncooperative

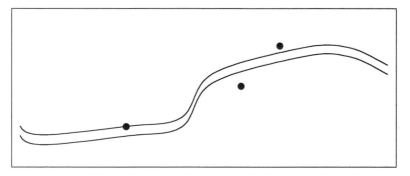

Fig. 3.4 Water treatment example.

model, here we also want to solve for the final payoffs that each player gets from the game.

The question is then a normative one. For example, should each player pay equally toward the joint treatment plant? How would you argue against an equal-split solution? Should only one player pay (this specious proposition almost needs no argument but is often the case in real life)? Doubtless, you will have raised some important concerns that we should consider in starting to formulate solutions to this allocation problem.

- A player will cooperate only if he or she cannot do better acting alone.
- We have to start talking about what each player deserves to get out of the game.
- There is also the possibility that players collude in not cooperating with the others.
- A strong cooperative bond can only form if the final allocation seems good or fair to all.

Players actually have more options in this model than in the noncooperative case. Here, a player can cooperate (or collude, depending on how conspiracy minded you are) with one or more other players. The likelihood of cooperation increases with the benefit each player gets from cooperation and the perceived fairness of the arrangement. To formally analyze this model, we need to introduce some new terminology.

Terminology and Symbols

Players are called "players," as before, and we use small integer-convention letters (i, j, k) or numbers (1, 2, 3) to refer to individual players. Each set of players, e.g., (i, j), is called a coalition, and the set of all players, n, is known as the grand coalition.

Whereas in the noncooperative model, where we posited multiple alternatives for each player, in the cooperative model, we cut to the chase and assume only one course of action for each player. This course of action is assumed to be whatever action gives that player the greatest utility. The player is already assumed to have figured out what that best action is and what the payoff to him or her would be. We use the following symbol to refer to the payoff that each player gets from his or her optimal individual strategy.

$v(i)$ = the payoff (in terms of utility) to player i from i's best course of action, acting alone.

We need to consider the possibility of a player joining one or more players in a joint action. The model assumes that the group of players has already figured out what action results in the greatest utility. Note, however, that we finessed the question of "greatest utility for whom?" Like true utilitarians, theorists merely look at the aggregate utility and assume that the group will choose that course of action that maximizes their total, aggregate utility. We use similar symbols to refer to the payoff to coalitions.

$v(ij)$ = the total aggregate payoff to coalition $\{ij\}$ from their best joint course of action, acting together.

$v(n)$ = the total aggregate payoff to the grand coalition, n, from their best joint course of action, acting together.

For example, if the grand coalition were composed of the players i, j, and k, we could write either $v(n)$ or $v(ijk)$ to refer to the same thing. Lastly, we note that the payoff to the entire coalition, $v(n)$, is a lumped amount that does not spell out how this aggregate amount is distributed among the n players. Some kind of allocation rule is needed to determine how much of $v(n)$ goes to player 1, how much to player 2, etc. This allocation rule is what we will call a "solution concept." We use the following notation to represent the individual allocations, as well as corresponding notation for each subgroup's actual aggregate allocation.

$x(i)$ = the actual payoff received by player i; this is some portion of $v(n)$.

$x(S)$ = the aggregated actual payoffs received by all the individual players making up the coalition, S.

For example, if the coalition S is made up of players 1, 2, and 4, then

$$x(124) = x(1) + x(2) + x(4).$$

Analysis: Cooperative Games

For Case II, let us use some hypothetical numbers to illustrate the analytic. Suppose that the entrepreneur (call this player 1) in town 1 were it to build a treatment plant, estimated that it would incur a cost of $4 M/yr. and earn $6 M/yr. in sales (i.e., earn $2 M/yr. in profit). Suppose that player 2's situation is identical, and that player 3 is looking to build a slightly larger plant for $7 M/yr. and earn $12 M/yr. in sales. Now, we realize that, were each of the players to build their own plant, the total amount they would spend would be $16 M/yr. to build and operate the plants. On the other hand, were they to cooperate and build one centralized, joint treatment plant, the total cost would be only $12 M because of economies of scale. The total sales of $24 M/yr. would be the same, so the total profit under the joint arrangement would be $12 M/yr. If they agreed to the joint venture, how much would each player pay toward the joint treatment plant? This is the same thing as asking, how much net profit should each player get out of the arrangement?

Let us introduce one additional complication. A subgroup of two players, e.g., 1 and 2, could cooperate just by themselves and build a joint treatment plant just for the two towns, leaving the third player to fend for itself. Let us suppose that the cost of a joint treatment plant for towns 1 and 2 was $5 M/yr. We assume similar costs for other possible subgroups, e.g., players 2 and 3, and formalize the problem as follows:

Solve for each $x(i)$, assuming:

$$x(1) \geq 2$$

$$x(2) \geq 2$$

$$x(3) \geq 5$$

$$x(12) \geq 3$$

$$x(13) \geq 7$$

$$x(23) \geq 7$$

$$x(123) = x(N) = 12.$$

These relations are known as "rationality constraints." The last constraint, $x(123) = 12$, simply states that the aggregate payoff received by the grand coalition, N, from the joint venture is to be completely divided up among the participating players, no more and no less. To explain, take the first constraint, $x(1) \geq 2$, which simply means that, whatever payoff is allocated to player 1, it must be at least equal to (and, ideally, greater than) what player 1 would have received if it acted alone. That is, there must be some incentive for each player, and subgroup of players, to join the joint project. There may be more than one possible solution to the above problem. The set of all the possible solutions that meet all these constraints are known as the "core," a concept jointly developed by Gillies and Shapley (Gillies, 1953; Shapley, 1953). The core is the set of potential solutions that are said to be defection proof. The core is the first major solution concept that we will study. We can depict the solution space and the core graphically in the following diagrams (Figures 3.5a, b, and c).

A good analogy is that of a person biting away at an apple until one is left with the core of it, hence the name of the solution concept. The core is an important concept that has myriad potential applications to situations beyond the classic allocation game. In fact, we can use the concept to represent all potential agreements that might induce different stakeholders to opt for a cooperative solution.

Any point within the core is a potential point of agreement. However, we can go further and inquire, given that all the points in the core meet some standard for acceptability, can we pinpoint a single point in the core that is best? To do this, we need to employ other criteria for judging which solutions are better than others, given that they all meet the requirement of lying in the core. For example, take one of the simplest solution concepts, the even-split or Kalai-Smorodinski solution (Kalai and Smorodinski, 1975). This involves simply dividing up $v(N)$ equally among all n players. For the game described in Case II, we find the following even-split solution:

$$x(1) = x(2) = x(3) = 4.$$

How do these solutions compare against the rationality constraints given above? Immediately, one sees $x(3)$ falls below player 3's reservation payoff and so would not be acceptable to player 3. That is, player 3 has incentive to defect. Another way of saying this is that though the even-split solution satisfies some criterion of egalitarianism, it fails to satisfy the rationality requirements represented by the core, i.e., the even-split solution falls outside the core.

Probably the most intellectually intriguing and well-known cooperative solution concept is the so-called Shapley value. This solution concept posits a number of desirable properties that one would like to find in a solution, namely:

1. Symmetry: if $v(S \cup i) = v(S \cup j)$ for all S, then $x(i) = x(j)$.
2. Dummy property: if $v(S \cup i) = v(S)$ for all S, then $x(i) = 0$.
3. Additivity: if $v'(S \cup i) = v(S \cup i) + \epsilon$ for all S, then $x'(i) = x(i) + \epsilon$

For example, the symmetry property states that if two players are identical with regard to the values of all the coalitions they join, such that one could interchange one player for the other in any coalition and get the same value, then their final allocations should be identical.

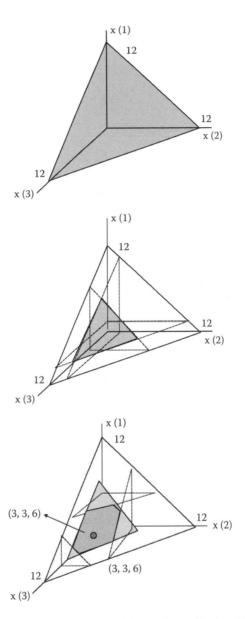

Fig. 3.5 (a) Feasible set of alternatives; (b) feasible set after application of individual rationality constraints; (c) core, or feasible set after applying all constraints.

Shapley showed that there is one unique solution that meets all these ideal properties, which was subsequently named the "Shapley value" (Shapley, 1953). The formula for the Shapley value is as follows:

$$\varphi_i(z) = \sum_{\substack{T \subset N \\ i \in T}} \frac{(|T|-1)!(n-|T|)!}{n!} \ [v(T) - v(T/i)]$$

solved for all proper subsets T of N, and within each subset T for each individual player, i, of T. Using this formula on the game in Case II, we solve for the allocations in this manner:

$$x(1) = 3.67 \qquad x(2) = 3.67 \qquad x(3) = 4.66$$

i.e., players 1, 2, and 3 receive payoffs of 3.67, 3.67, and 4.66, respectively.

Policy Applications of Cooperative Games

The theory of cooperative n-person games has not been as widely utilized in the field of economics, but this is partly due to the desire on the part of economists to found their discipline on a positive theory that does not purport to say anything about what is ethically or socially good (which would be a normative theory) but only describe how people behave. The theory of noncooperative games is an attempt to base the discipline on a model that does not introduce normative considerations but simply describes and predicts what outcomes might result from different situations. As an aside, we note two questionable things about this last statement: first, that the decision not to explicitly introduce the normative is itself a normative statement and, moreover, the construction of the noncooperative game itself, along with the atomistic, utility-maximizing actors who play it, is itself completely saturated with many, oftentimes hidden, normative assumptions. For example, the assumption that an individual's sole norm for behavior is personal utility is a strong normative position.

Cooperative theory, on the other hand, deals explicitly with ethical issues. The Shapley value, for example, recommends itself on the strength of a number of desirable normative principles that characterize it (e.g., symmetry, additivity, and the dummy player property). The Kalai-Smorodinsky solution has its basis in a strong ethic of egalitarianism. More than anything else, cooperative theory gives us a formal construct for testing the fairness of different institutional arrangements.

Cooperative theory has been widely employed in situations that naturally involve allocation problems. Water resource allocation has been a traditional area of application (e.g., see Young, Okada, and Hashimoto 1982; Dinar, Ratner, and Yaron, 1992; Lejano and Davos, 1995). However, the potential for more extensive application should be considerable. The notion of the core is an important one that can be interpreted in any social situation involving stakeholders who have the option of cooperating with other players or going it alone. We might use the concept of the core to study the fairness of different alternative arrangements.

The theory is potentially useful for analyzing a wide class of policy problems. The mathematics of it, along with the complex nature of solution concepts, hinders its application. If we are, in our postconstructionist bent, to move analysis away from the artificial and onto the pragmatic, how do we adapt a theory to the real world? One way is to reduce the mathematical complexity of the concept. We see this in negotiation literature wherein one rule for assessing potential deals is that no agreement should result in a payoff for any player that is worse than the best payoff this same player would get by acting alone — also called a BATNA, the best alternative to a negotiated agreement (see Fisher, Ury, and Patton, 1991; Susskind, Thomas-Larner, and McKearnan, 1999). This concept is, the student will recognize, the same as the core, except that, in negotiation theory, one does not consider coalitions in determining the BATNA. The second pragmatic step that real stakeholders can take is to appreciate the normative principles embodied in the different solution concepts without having to enter into the mathematics of them.

As it is, however, cooperative theory has not been used to as great an extent as it should, in this author's opinion. The concept of the core can be a potentially valuable tool with which to understand and explain deals and no-deals, and coalitions that form in real-world situations, and to structure favorable allocation rules.

Postscript: Grounding the Model in the World

Games have been used, both in their noncooperative and cooperative forms, to model real policy situations. However, their greatest use in policy has been, by far, in conceptualizing policy situations and justifying certain ideal forms of solutions. The two most influential game-theoretic policy models are probably the general equilibrium model of the economy and the tragedy of the commons model of public goods (or bads). In the first case, economists were able to construct a rigorous proof, based on Nash's concept of the equilibrium, of Adam Smith's invisible hand. In the second instance, a simple two-person game was used to justify institutional solutions to a host of real-world problems.

In general, games have been used less for modeling and solving actual situations than for positing hypotheticals and testing institutional designs in concept. However, they are used to legitimize strong policy positions. For example, recent calls for less stringent zoning and more regionally open zoning and land use practices draw their justification from utilitarian reasons. We refer to policy arguments such as the so-called Tiebout hypothesis, which posits that local land use planning agencies need not be so active in determining land use in the city (Tiebout, 1956). Rather, local agencies should allow for a more unregulated, *laissez-faire* housing and land market to exist in the region. Tiebout's argument is that so long as a market is created in which individuals can express their preferences for the best mix of land use, amenities, housing, and price that is available to them, all things considered, then the state need not step in and dictate who lives where, what amenities each city should have, and other decisions that can be made by individuals through the market. To the argument that public goods (parks, cleanliness, etc.) are not allocated through the market, Tiebout argued that an ersatz market exists, wherein individuals "vote with their feet" and register their preferences and willingness to pay for public goods by moving to their preferred neighborhood. The Tiebout argument draws from the same logic of the simple two person prisoners' dilemma and other games. So, then, we see that, while games may not be so commonly used to actually model people's preferences, actual utilities, and actual decision parameters, these games are used to legitimize institutions and policy regimes.

How do we then bring these abstruse models closer to the here and now of actual experience and practice? In one sense, we cannot so long as real people and institutions function in ways other than the atomistic utility-maximizing players posited by the theory. In another sense, we can use these models to study how much social actors depart from the norm of utility maximization and the vN-M sense of rationality. Regardless of whether we do engage in utility-seeking behavior or not, there is in us and in our institutions at least some inclination to consider how we might maximize utility. The models may be too lacking in dimensionality on which to found institutional designs, but surely these lend us some insight into the limits of a society wherein this kind of reasoning does hold. The utility of these models may lie not in their use for modeling actual social situations but in merely pointing out, when actual behavior comports with these simple games, situations when utility-seeking action may indeed be present.

We may, when it provides insight, use games to analyze real policy situations but at no point do we insist that when we find discrepancies, reality be assumed to follow the model. This would be like insisting, as in a market, that the grocer bring out real peaches that were mottled and pastel like Cezanne's. Rather, we use these models to explain whatever little in a policy situation might be explained by them. We might even try to understand a cultural phenomenon like a Javanese cockfight as, in some respects, resembling an *n*-person game, but that is in *some* respects (Geertz, 1983). Let us state what this means exactly — for policy to be policy, we cannot have the analytic consist of just the model by itself, i.e., if we want to escape the mythological. If we attempt to use a model like that of rational choice, we do so by tempering or calibrating our analysis according to experience. Personal and social inclinations can then not simply be posited as one form of rationality (e.g., utility maximization, zweckrationalitat, efficiency). As we will more emphatically state later in the book, a model of a policy situation as a game cannot speak to policy unless it is seen from the perspective of other concepts. Unless we are willing to introduce a reflective component, then the model falls from the weight of its own sheer ethereality.

How can we attempt to utilize the model of games as part of a more grounded theory for analysis? Real-world situations involve fundamental uncertainty, incommensurability, social considerations, moral principles, historicity, and other elements that are not prone to modeling.

In general, games are not that useful for actually solving real-world policy situations. Yet, games can be useful in yielding insights about factors that one should look for in analyzing real situations. A good example of this kind of work is found in Ostrom's analysis of real-world institutions for resource management as games over common property resources (Ostrom, 1994). Starting with the one-shot tragedy of the commons game, Ostrom reasoned that real situations are more like repeated games, for which a larger set of equilibriums can be achieved. In these real situations, which include everything from fish catch allocation quotas in Nova Scotia to irrigation traditional Panchayat forest management systems in India, there are elements that one would imagine allowed transformation of the situation into a repeated game of sorts and, presumably, allowed these longstanding systems to endure over time. Consideration of these repeated games led these researchers to look for design elements in the real institutions that take care of variables important in the model — elements like the ability to monitor each player's behavior, clear rules about membership in the group, fair allocation rules, and boundaries. What arose was a new research agenda to search for these local practices that are needed to not have the situation degenerate into a commons game.

Most of all, the theory of games provides us with a useful heuristic tool for analyzing aspects of many situations. The most important point, however, is to remember that these games can shed light on patterns of behavior of real-world actors but not stand in for real social behavior. Real policy actors are neither atomistic nor optimific. Real situations do not present themselves as choices among well-defined alternatives. However, there is a place for this type of analysis. To say that the rational model is a failed simulation of social reality is not to say that the model does not provide us with a useful glimpse into some dimensions of social behavior or motivation. While real policy actors are not utility maximizers, it would be wrong to say that real individuals never engage in trying to increase personal gain. But we need to increase the dimensionality and contextuality of these analyses. In the following, some brief prescriptions are provided in an attempt to increase the relevance of the rational model.

1. We need to consider ways to reduce the absolute and stringent requirements on data. This means that we should begin to consider that preferences between situations are not necessarily something we can equate with utility — other motivations, such as culture, normative considerations, and institutional context drives how people make decisions. For this reason, if we are to employ game-theoretic reasoning, we should be able to attempt analyses in which preferences are not expressed as cardinal utility (perhaps using ordinal comparisons, for example).

2. We need to find ways to modify or adjust the design of the game to better match the realities of real social situations, not the other way around. For example, bargaining games in which players negotiate over some distribution of payoffs, often modeled as repeated games, are notoriously sensitive to the particular assumptions made in positing the rules of the game. Real bargaining situations, however, are characterized by flexible and fuzzy rules, sloppy bargaining, no requirements regarding turn taking, etc. To better understand real bargaining situations, some of which may well bring out the classic patterns of utility-maximizing behavior, we need to create games that are not so precise and that do not lead to exact solutions. In some cases, mathematical descriptions of the game and their outcomes may give way to more descriptive, even narrative treatments. For example, in some bargaining models, the first mover has a decided advantage, while in others, it is the last mover — it is all in the assumptions one uses to construct the game. However, real bargaining situations do not resemble any of these in the least bit, and the real task is to begin to assess how the workings of real bargaining contexts operate. These real-world rules and heuristics should inform how we "model" the game. For example, we can ask, in what instances would the first mover have any advantage at all, and when do we see these conditions in real situations?

3. We need to find better ways to modify our models to allow them some capacity for portraying individuals and groups that are driven by multiple motivations — moral as well as utilitarian, economic as well as cultural. In many cases, this will lead to "models" that are not positivist but are, instead, thick descriptions of individual and group behavior. In other cases, we may be able to develop mathematical models that help us simulate some of these patterns. However, the inescapable notion that underpins all of this is that we use the models to suggest patterns to look for in real life — not to predict real outcomes or, worse, rework real institutions to match the recondite assumptions of these abstract games.

4. Lastly, we have to be critical in searching for all the aspects of policy situations that prevent their explicit modeling through games. Foremost among these aspects concerns the misfit between real-world contingencies and the model of social action as choice, the reductionistic model of choice as contests between players for a homogenous and allocable good called "utility," and our basic inability to model the richness of real-world institutions into our conceptual games.

Could there possibly be a "postconstructionist" theory of games? Grounding, if it is possible, would need to occur in at least two ways. The first is to more and more leave the absolute conditions of the toy games used in the literature and instead find insights into real-world "games" that we might analyze, using frameworks from the theories of games to discover decision rules and procedures that apply in real life. The other direction is to be able to build richer models that allow for multiply motivated players and more complex notions of what it means to be rational. We might mention, at this point, some earlier attempts to relax the conditions of rationality that game theory imposes and to create a notion of bounded rationality (Simon, 1957). This book leans the other way, in that real decision makers are not so much simpler than the theory requires but actually more complex.

Lastly, we need to be more reflective about how these simple models have been used to construct policy discourse. Consider the notion of the equilibrium, which from Adam Smith onward has given the analyst a mathematical equivalent of the social utopia. Consider further how the idea of it is used to justify an entire regime of institutional designs (e.g., the neoliberalist penchant for turning every social situation into some form of market transaction) even though reality could hardly be farther removed from equilibrium. The model of the game, and the related notion of the equilibrium, allows us to, misguidedly, conceive of solutions to policy situations without dealing with the conflicted polity. In fact, when these notions are used as a model for Smith's concept of the invisible hand, it does not even require the presence of the state (except, of course, as a way of enforcing the rights of the individual and ensuring the functioning of the market).

Up to this point, we have been well entrenched within vN–M's framework, wherein we posit policy as an act of choice among alternatives, and the divining rod for this choice being that of utility. From the next chapter onward, we take a radical turn and begin to ponder on policy situations that we may not feel are amenable to interpretation in the spirit of vN-M. The analyst should begin to think about real policy situations and consider when and how they might not be well described as decisions. How should we then begin to conceptualize these, if not as decisions subject to considerations of utility? From the next chapter onward, we consider a number of alternative frameworks for constructing policy, and how we might use them to add depth to our insight. We should also appreciate the fact that, in many cases, proponents of these alternative models were directly commenting on and challenging the strong, recondite, and hegemonic assumptions embedded in the rational model. Since the latter is most often associated with the privileging of the scientific (or positivist) route to knowledge and reason, we collect these alternative frameworks under the label "postpositivist."

Part II
The Postpositivist Turn

CHAPTER 4

Background: Voices of Postpositivism

Although critiques of the classical model of rationality began well before, it was in the twentieth century that the most decisive steps away from the rational model were taken. The lineages of these diverse strands of thought are numerous, and we only take up some of the most immediately relevant in this book. The origins of the critique, moreover, are numerous and not at all mutually consistent. For example, one set of contrary systems of thought arose in philosophy, most profoundly so in the writings of Wittgenstein (1922) who challenged the notion of logic and, in fact, the most basic concept of literal meaning itself. By arguing that all knowledge was a form of language game, he and others opened the doors to other constructs that lay apart from the positivist-rationalist system of the classical model. After all, if everything were a language game, then all alternative constructs were equally valid. This presented a direct challenge to the core concepts of the Enlightenment, namely the primacy of the ratio (the cognitive subject) and sense (the empiricist route to knowledge). Later writers, among them Kuhn, Latour, and others would construct a similar challenge to the dominant intellectual discipline arising from the Enlightenment, which was the model of science. In particular, they would argue how science itself was a social construct, subject to tradition, consensus, and prejudice.

The most sustained attack on the rational model came from a group of sociologists associated with the Frankfurt School of Critical Theory. In a series of works that, while not all systematic and quite broad in coverage, challenged different dimensions of the classical model, the Frankfurt

School furthered an intellectual task that stemmed from earlier work by Marx (1887) and Weber (1864). The Frankfurt School developed Marx's thesis of the alienation of persons through the commodification of labor and proceeded to work out how alienation was carried out completely, not just through the systems of production but that of art, advertising, popular culture, and other aspects of society. Perhaps even more comprehensive a critique came from Weber, who postulated the irreversible tendency of society toward rationalization, or the transformation of institutions and social processes according to the dictates of instrumental value. The concept of rationalization was further developed by the Frankfurt School and traced to the human drive to master nature. While Horkheimer and Adorno (1972) wrote about the narrowly technocratic notion of reason that characterized social institutions, Marcuse (1964) decried the stifling effect this had on the individual.

While unclear in charting the alternative to the rational-purposive model, these thinkers, particularly Adorno (1975), did succeed in describing a negative dialectic, which took the founding assumptions of the classic model and revealed inherent inconsistencies. As the century drew on, however, it was unclear exactly whether their critiques were solely a negative exercise or whether any utopian vision could still be attached to it, e.g., the liberation of the working class from alienation or the freedom of human philosophy from utilitarian thought (or, in Adorno's words, "identity-thinking"). At any rate, by the time their project began to draw to a close, the Frankfurt School had succeeded in crafting a multipronged assault on the instrumentalist, utilitarian mode of positivism associated with the rational model. Habermas, one of the later sociologists to be associated with the Frankfurt School, probably came closest to resurrecting a noninstrumental notion of rationality, putting forth the idea that reason might be found in intersubjective communication (Habermas, 1987) instead of a privileged subject (whether the enlightened individual or the emancipated proletariat).

These thinkers drew from another philosopher, Nietzsche, who considered social institutions to be fundamentally founded on a fundamental human will to power — thus, domination is the rule rather than the aberration (Nietzsche, 1901). This fundamental notion would be furthered by later writers. For example, Foucault's histories of institutions such as the clinic or school suggested that domination is to be found embedded in an infinitude of social spaces and not merely in the structures of class or hierarchy (Foucault, 1977). A related critique would also be developed by a line of feminist writers who rejected the gendered nature of the historical-philosophical subject (e.g., see Gilligan, 1982). For example, if we revisit the figure of the seated thinker in the Introduction, one could not fail to see how rationality has traditionally been equated with the masculine. Very related critiques would also come from postcolonial writers who began to reject the assumed primacy of the Western (or Occidental) over the Eastern (or Oriental) in modern-day thought (e.g., see Said, 1993). There is a general notion behind these critiques and that is to reveal that modern-day institutions are so structured for the furtherance of the status quo, which is the dominance of the already powerful.

Another influential line of thought came from the field of pedagogy and, later on, development studies. By challenging the common notion of Western-style education, Freire provided a deep critique of that model in which knowledge was transmitted in linear fashion, from expert to recipient, according to classic modes of legitimization (Freire, 1973). This classic model of pedagogy stemmed, of course, from the technical-rational model that drew its most basic epistemology from the scientific, positivist framework. As positivist in philosophy, knowledge need only be measured or determined by the expert and transmitted, unaltered, to the student. Freire countered by developing curricula in which the students, primarily drawn from rural Brazilian communities, discovered knowledge on their own terms and became their own experts. These methods were later applied, most broadly, by rural development practitioners (e.g., Chambers, 1983) seeking to undo the subservience of rural populations in the developing world. These developments are seen today in the growing use of participative modes of deliberation or governance. This line of thinking had some parallel with that of Dewey (1925) who posited that learning came out of practical engagement of the person with the environment and other pragmatists who rejected strictly idealist or empiricist epistemologies in favor of learning-in-action (a phrase from Argyris and Schön, 1996). This, in turn, had some parallel with work of the phenomenologists who grounded truth not in received knowledge or rational calculation, but in experience (e.g., Husserl, 1913; Heidegger, 1927). However, by experience, they did not simply mean empirical sense perception but the subjective understanding of an event or condition. In each their own way, these writers challenged the classic dichotomy of the subject and object in which knowledge was either purely subjective (as the rationalists maintained) or, even if objective, was to be understood as a reality that needed only to be measured (as the positivists maintained).

There were other notable intellectual developments in the twentieth century that furthered the critique of the classic model, such as Freud's psychoanalytic theory that legitimized the irrational (Freud, 1899) or that of Piaget, which underscored the active part that the individual and society play in constructing knowledge as opposed to a notion of meaning as simply existing outside the person (Piaget, 1929). Each of these theories decentered the subject away from the ratio. More recent decentering impulses came from various other disciplines, including feminist and postcolonialist theories that challenged the assumption of the Western, male ego as the archetype of reason (e.g., recall the sculpture of the Thinker from the Introduction). Central to these movements were other bodies of thought, such as symbolic interactionism, which developed a theory of society and meaning as negotiated and interpreted entities (e.g., Mead, 1934; Goffman, 1958; Blumer, 1969). In this book, we touch on those directions of inquiry that directly led to the policy models that we discuss from chapter 5 onward. To help guide the reader through the rest of the book, we diagram some of these diverse lines of reasoning in Figure 4.1.

All these lines of inquiry led to a growing willingness to question the very idea of *logocentricity*, i.e., the idea that the meaning of a text (or reality) is fixed and that its meaning ultimately lies in the author. For example, the truth about a natural phenomenon such as light is something that can be verified with scientific measurement (e.g., like reading a text) and that this truth need only be revealed by the author (e.g., the scientist). If thinkers from Wittgenstein onward were right, then truth is something to be contested, and there is no authoritative source of meaning on which to base the right version of the truth. This allows one to construe meaning as something subject to interpretation. In its most radical form, where people

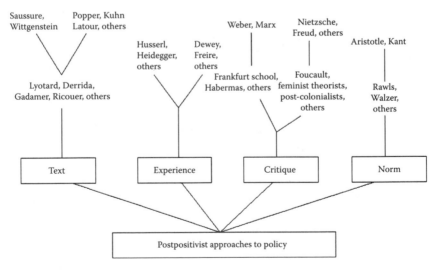

Fig. 2.1 Major constructs of postpositivism.

previously thought there was truth, there is only text, subject to interpretation. This takes on its boldest statement in the work of Lyotard who, in providing the first statement of postmodernism, trumpeted the death of all grand narratives (Lyotard, 1979) and, in more sociological terms, in the work of Berger and Luckmann who argued that social institutions were like text also, i.e., mere constructs of people or groups in society (Berger and Luckmann, 1966). The idea of the "constructedness" extends even to the discipline(s) of science, to which the work of Latour (1987) is a good example. Some point to a middle ground between the rational and postmodern, wherein rationality is seen to lie not in the individual ratio, but in the communicative process that transpires between subjects (Habermas, 1984). The postpositivist turn succeeded in bringing to the fore various representations of knowledge as interpreted, socially constructed, and power laden.

The interpretive, postpositivist treatment of policy has given rise to various approaches that take policy as text and subject it to interpretation. Later in this book, we encounter interpretive models such as found in the area of hermeneutics (Gadamer, 1960; Ricoeur, 1971). We see a marked postpositivist turn in more recent books in the public policy field (e.g., Schön and Rein, 1995; Stone, 1988; Roe, 1994; Yanow, 2001; Schneider and Ingram, 1997; Fischer, 2003; and others) that understand policy to be the outcome of discursive practices and contests. In these treatments, policy is a game in which the winner is able to insert their particular interpretation, narrative, or text into the public discourse. Alternatively, policy can be a conversation in which meaning is something worked out intersubjectively through a communicative process. Parallel to this evolution in theory, there have been developments in crafting institutions and practices built around communicative rationality (e.g., see Susskind et al., 1999; Healey, 1996; Fischer and Forester, 1993). The willingness or need to consider policy as a social construct, which these more recent policy works manifest, is reflected in the use of the term "constructivist" or "constructionist" to describe these approaches.

Many of these constructs reject the epistemology of the *ratio* along with the empiricist route to knowledge. These alternative theories differ in how each portrays knowledge and the knower. For Nietzsche and Foucault, knowledge was an instance for power and mechanism for domination. For the linguistic philosophers, knowledge is a construct that requires certain competencies of the knowledge holder. Moreover, knowing has a primarily social aspect. For Weber, rationality had become equivalent to *zweckrationalitat*, residing completely in the technical-instrumental dimension of knowing to the exclusion of other dimensions. For Habermas, knowledge is attained through agonistic and intersubjective processes. Nevertheless, they each rejected the underpinnings of the classical framework of knowledge as objectively measured and of the individual subject as the font of knowledge. Each challenged the classical model's strong logocentricity, where policy language (and policy) exists as referents to fixed realities. From this point onward, meaning would be contested terrain.

As we will see, this has deep implications for analysis and, as importantly, for our understanding of the analyst. No longer simply the seat of knowledge and authority, she becomes, in turn, a mediator, advocate, a node in power relations, or part of a discursive community. In the first chapter of our incursion into the postpositivist realm, we begin by questioning the notion of logocentricity, and even authorship.

CHAPTER 5

Text

Introduction

The search for a *summum bonum*, or unifying concept, on which to ground our policy analysis, underpinned the classical model. As Lyotard put it, it is the search for a grand narrative. But, in creating such an overarching, universal construct, we end up excluding possibly crucial elements in our reality that do not fit the universal concept well. Grand narratives can be hegemonic. In what would be a preamble to a still-flourishing era of postmodern thought, Lyotard boldly pronounced the death of all grand narratives (Lyotard, 1979).

This is, perhaps, a useful place to begin the chapter. We might ask ourselves: If we give up on any overarching concepts (and these grand narratives include liberalism, socialism, democracy, family, etc.), what are we left with? How could we begin to engage in public discourse, much less resolve policy questions? How could we chart our way forward, vis-à-vis important issues regarding growth, employment, education, environment, when we cannot even agree on some basic concepts that we could use to further our analysis? Most specifically, if we relinquish the strong notion of rationality (and the classic model of policy along with it), how can we begin to make sense of policy and recommend directions for public action?

In such an epistemological situation, we can begin to question the meaning of our most cherished institutions, ideals, and programs. It is for this reason that we describe this as the treatment of policy as text. When meaning is in question, then reality is like text that is subject to analysis and interpretation. If no one can have a rightful claim to be the author, or if the very notion of authorship is questioned, then policy is subject to possibly endless rounds of interpretation. It is for this reason, also, that methods that originated in literary analysis have come to the fore in analyzing public policy. Policy, like a piece of poetry, is to be read, interpreted, reinterpreted — but its exact meaning never to be fixed.

Foundations

As it turns out, a large part of the epistemological "turn" came from the field of linguistics. Saussure created a structural model of language by introducing the notion of the sign, in which meaning grew out of linking signifier (the letters c-o-w) to the signified (bovine grass feeder). However, Saussure made the point that there is no inherent meaning to the signifier, per se, and that the nature of the latter was arbitrary. There is no inherent reason why we should use the letters "t," "r," "e," "e" to stand for that thing we sit under in the park and not the letters "l," "o," "g" — it's all just a matter of social convention. More subtly, Saussure was making the point that there is nothing communicated by the word "tree" in and of itself and that it only acquires significance by difference from other groups of letters (e.g., "log") — language is a system of differences with no positive elements, only negative. He went on to point out that the concept or signified, itself, was not fixed. Dusk and twilight are two different words that stand for two related but differing concepts, but if we took the word "dusk" out of the dictionary, even the meaning of the word "twilight" would change since the meaning of any sign comes about only vis-à-vis its relative position in a system of signs. The implication was that not only is the signifier (the combination of letters) arbitrary or at least unfixed, but so is the signified (or concept) itself. Without the combination of signifier and signified, within a system of differences from other combinations of signifiers and signifieds, even our thoughts would be a shapeless, unstructured mass.

Where Saussure left off in his careful analysis, other, later authors were quick to take off, perhaps less carefully, in bold, new directions. The implication of Saussure's work, these authors claimed, was that even thought occurs only through language. And, so if language is nothing but a social construct, then so is thought and, ultimately, meaning. This decentering of meaning led inevitably to the decentering (or questioning) of the privileged position of the author. The implication of this for literary analysis was predictable: Because the meaning of a text was not fixed, then the notion of authorship is in question and text can only be interpreted. If there is no ultimate meaning, then everything is subject to (possibly endless) interpretation.

A parallel development came out of the field of philosophy early in the twentieth century when Ludwig Wittgenstein sought to question the logism that was then current, most identified with Russell and Frege (Wittgenstein, 1922). He examined how complex propositions could be built out of elemental ones. For example,

If A then B   (or A → B)
A is true   (A)
then B is true. (B)

where propositions are simple statements about objects in the world, e.g., A can mean "it rains tonight" and B can mean "our picnic tomorrow is cancelled." By combining such propositions in ways allowed by the formal rules of logic, the logical atomists posited that all the truth of the world could be communicated. However, Wittgenstein attempted to show that such complex propositions amounted to nothing but a tautological claim because the relation, A → B, is already implicit in the very construction of A and B. In this case, it may have to do with the very construction of what a "picnic" means, e.g., as a get together in the park on a typically warm, sunny day. Because we assumed or created the propositions A and B, Wittgenstein was essentially saying that the ultimate source of truth, elementary propositions like A and B, find their basis not in verifiable sources but simply in the arbitrary ways we define or construct these propositions. He was saying that, ultimately, there was no way of establishing ultimate truths about the world. In his words, communication, knowledge, and logic were all merely language games. Perhaps another way to clarify what Wittgenstein was getting at is to bring up an example from Saussure himself. Take the notion of a game, Saussure said, and imagine the innumerable situations that come under the label of a "game" — chess, soccer, gambling, business, fox hunts, courtship, warfare, etc. — and try to imagine what possible thing all of these have in common. Nothing, Saussure said, except maybe the word "game" itself. Outside the word, there is no meaning.

This poststructuralist unraveling of meaning and authorship grew out from the literary interpretation of text and onto all other fields of analysis. As Gadamer wrote, even action can be considered to be text that is subject to interpretation (Gadamer, 1960). In the following sections, we give a glimpse of how forms of interpretive analysis can be applied to diverse instances — from literary text to policy action to other types of research artifacts. Essentially, all of these things are vehicles of meaning, from our manner of dress to social relationships to moral norms.

The task then became to understand and study what different meanings are communicated and how do meanings get constructed, contested, and possibly resolved? Berger and Luckmann introduced sociological and political dimensions to these questions of meaning and suggested that meaning was a contest in sociopolitical power (Berger and Luckmann, 1966). Moreover, institutions themselves are social constructs that the powerful in society are able to maintain and enact. This has led to a constructivist (or constructionist) school of policy studies, wherein the analytical task is to understand how meanings are constructed, which meanings vie for salience in the public realm, and how constructed meanings lead to institutional change. Essentially, policy is the outcome of a contest over the construction of meaning. According to some, these contests are resolved through an agonistic process, wherein the better and more compelling narrative wins the policy debate (e.g., see Roe, 1994; Stone, 1988). According to others, contests over meaning might be resolved by constructing metanarratives that are able to include previously opposed parties (e.g., Schön and Rein, 1995). The latter notion of collaborative modes of resolution draws from a notion of rationality as embedded not in the subject but in the intersubjectivity of a community of subjects, all cooperating in the search for the true and right (Habermas, 1984). In Habermas's formulation, truth may be arrived at, but through the testing of truth claims within an open, public, and undistorted communicative process. It is as if the notion of authorship could be located within a community.

The treatment of policy as text covers a range of models: from the pluralist-political that depicts policy as an outcome of a social contest, to the interpretive that looks for deeper meaning in policy artifacts, to the poststructural, which challenges the idea of meaning, per se, and maintains that all there is, in the end, is text and socially constructed meanings. Probably the most nonconciliatory stance is associated with Lyotard who espoused a model of paralogy, which is the sheer collision of opposed ideas in the public realm, without any hope or need for resolution (Lyotard, 1979).

Analytics

Literary Analysis

It is not surprising that when we encounter models that posit policy as text, methods from literary analysis prove to be quite useful. These approaches can vary in scale and emphasis. By scale, we simply mean the unit of analysis, where one can focus on the totality of the policy narrative that one finds in the text (e.g., identifying elements of plot, characters, etc.), look for specific themes within the narrative, or focus closely on the very language used in the text.

From the most macroscopic point of analysis, one can study the text for overall narratives that seem to encapsulate the whole of the policy argument. In this, we are guided by the concepts developed in the area of literary interpretation (e.g., Ricoeur, 1991) and even the dramaturgical (Goffman, 1959). In most cases, the interpretation consists of summarizing the policy situation in one or more coherent narratives, and furthermore, finding traditional or archetypal storylines that seem to typify the particular narrative. For example, in his narrative analysis of the medfly controversy, Roe likened one of the policy arguments to the Biblical story of invaders putting salt on the land (Roe, 1994). Such a literary device need not involve only age-old, classic texts. For example, when then U.S. president Ronald Reagan likened Russia to the "evil empire," he was deliberately bringing in a familiar epic battle from *Star Wars* (and, in fact, people eventually named his grandiose and prematurely conceived missile defense system after the same movie). Whereas, in the fable, the federation was guided by the Force, Reagan's America would be guided by the ideology of small government and untrammeled markets — all going by the name of democracy.

Furthermore, the analysis might try to identify what narrative type the story belongs to. If one were to treat the policy story in dramaturgical terms, this might involve identifying the story's basic dramatic type (as in the basic types, and their corresponding definitions, below).

Tragedy: protagonists attempt to challenge fate but fail.
Romance: protagonists attempt to challenge fate and win.
Comedy: protagonists reconcile themselves with their inevitable fate.
Satire: protagonists defy fate through denial.

For example, the author and colleagues began talking with residents of the community of Vale Verde, California, which is located next to a large municipal landfill. In analyzing the narratives offered by the residents, we encountered testimonies such as the following (Lejano et al., 2005):

...In the mornings like I mentioned, well I wake up early, before we used to work at four and five in the morning. When I worked you could smell the stench but since I went in my car I would cover my nose so I wouldn't smell that filth, I would pass through there because I had to...I would say, some days, let's leave like around five in the morning, I knew what was good, the same as here but some people don't care. I would put vapor rub on my nose and when I would arrive over there I would blow my nose I would clean myself so I wouldn't smell the stench right, and I breath all that...what can I do, the air enters and you can feel the ammonia.

In the above passage, we encounter a basic tragic form where the main protagonist, a resident of this community, strives to counter the workings of fate, here represented by the inescapable air that brings ruin regardless of the hero's vigilance.

Our analysis of the text can work at different scales. For example, we can move closer to the text and seek smaller narratives embedded in the larger overall policy tale. Or, we can search for literary devices used within the overall narrative. These literary devices often include the use of basic literary tropes that authors use to bring meanings into the text. For example, some literary devices include the use of metaphor, metonymy, hyperbole, and paradox. Identifying and studying these types of literary devices help us to find new or embedded meanings in the text. Thus, when Hobbes metaphorically described the state as a Leviathan, he purposely drew in an image of government as rapacious, powerful, and monstrous (Hobbes, 1651). For example, from interviews with the same community in the previous passage came the following statement:

Well like I said now we no longer smell those strong odors. Although sometimes it still does come at night like waves sometimes. Because the wind is like that.

In this case, the agent is that of the wind, which is metaphorically likened to the surging, inexorable ocean. This is true to the tragic form, and in this case, the wind is a symbol for fate that, like the ocean, engulfs the speaker and her community. The speaker's (and community's) use of this narrative fulfills multiple functions. First and foremost, it is a convenient literary device to be able to begin expressing the loss of agency, which is one of the main attributes of the situation.

We find this narrative reflected, too, in basic grammatical structures, beginning with sentence construction. The most common form that we find in the transcripts might be called the "agent–receptor" structure that involves, first, identification of an agent and a specific action. The dynamic nature of agency often results in the specification or naming of a specific agent and association with specific, human actions. The flip side of this is the evocation of a passive, often unnamed recipient. Its lack of agency is sometimes seen in the amorphous lack of identity but, often, in specific statements that directly speak to the speaker's sense of powerlessness. The agent–receptor form might be depicted as follows:

| | [personified agent] | ... action | ... [passive receptor] |
| example: | wind | ... attacks | ... a person |

Take the following examples from the Val Verde transcripts:

Some days, the winds move in the afternoon and in the mornings and you get a cough.

...There are gases. And the wind is the same...the wind is what attacks a person.

The story is that our community is always being shaped.

Sometimes the air blows it this way and sometimes the other way, the wind is what dominates everything.

And, even more directly, we find statements that talk exactly about powerlessness:

But ever since the landfill came, all this started but, like I said, what can we do?

Well, for my part I feel bad, because there are many children (who have gotten sick) and we don't have the means to cure them.

...And what can we do in that case? If they are like that, like I said, they have the power...one feels incapable of not being able to do that.

In other words, we use methods from literary analysis to read meaning into the text. In the above example, we find that residents spoke not just about their concern over the landfill, but also about their loss of agency and the feeling of powerlessness in the face of an insurmountable obstacle.

One can go further in the analysis. Often, it can be a useful exercise to construct a narrative that is being told by the text. This entails sketching out a storyline or plot that one finds hidden in the text. This does not even entail identifying any particular literary or dramatic form, but simply answering the questions:

What story or stories are being told? Can we give a basic structure of the plot?

Who are the main protagonists, and how does the narrative depict them and their actions?

What is the main point, theme, or moral of the story?

Moreover, note that we can combine more positivist methods with the qualitative. For example, in the above case study, the researchers transcribed the text of interviews conducted with the residents and proceeded to perform content analysis on the text. For this exercise, a number of categories were constructed, which represented basic types of statements that people would use. For example, a statement or passage coded as "valuative" would be an instance where the interviewee judged a situation in value terms — i.e., using some notion of weight or measurement, and proceeding to assess the situation or judge it against others in terms of this sense of value. Figure 5.1 shows the average frequencies of the different types of statements found in the residents' texts.

The graph can then be interpreted accordingly. For example, Figure 5.1 suggests that much of the residents' talk consists of rule-like or deontological statements, and less those of pure expressions of emotion or valuation. Deontological statements are those in which the speaker expresses moral or other principles in the form of rules. For example, "No child should ever grow up next to a landfill, no one" is a statement of principle. This belies notions that residents are often exclusively emotional in the way

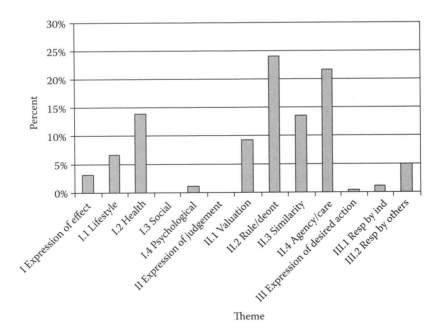

Fig. 5.1 Frequencies of statement types in resident interviews. (From: Lejano et al., New Methodologies for Describing the Phenomenology of Environmental Environmental Risk. Working Paper, 2005. Sponsored by the University of California Toxic Substances Research and Teaching Program, Davis, California.)

they judge a situation and not logical enough. In fact, deontological statements are classic statements of logic.

Hermeneutics

Text, as treated by the proponents of hermeneutics, is a system of symbols, the latter being those structures of signification in which a direct, literal meaning designates, while there exists another meaning that is indirect and figurative (Ricoeur, 1981). When trying to understand a new text, the reader attempts to "guess" possible meanings in what is being read. Such a guess is, of course, not possible from a completely neutral, unbiased point of view because we inevitably are influenced by our personal predilections, training, histories, and beliefs. Gadamer, in fact, goes further to say that such bias is necessary to be able to interpret at all, so long as it is not a fatal closing out of possibly unfamiliar interpretations and new meanings (Gadamer, 1960).

But how are we to know whether our interpretations are valid? Are all interpretations equally acceptable, or are some better than others? How do we gauge? To the initial interpretations the reader makes of the text, we introduce the grounding of context. That is, we test or assess our initial interpretations of the text for consistency with elements of the context of the situation. That is, if we consider the particular piece of text as part of the whole situation, context allows us to connect this piece to the whole. This action can occur in several (or many) stages. For example, one might go from text to context and use the latter to validate or invalidate some alternative interpretations. One can then go in the opposite direction, from context back to the text to seek a renewed, deeper interpretation. This process is known as the hermeneutic circle, as illustrated in Figure 5.2.

As an example, consider a ballot measure that was put up for a vote (and subsequently passed) in California in the late 1990s. This was Proposition 227, a move to prohibit second-language instruction in public schools. This is text that can be subject to an interpretive analysis. Of course, we start with the most ostensible meaning of the text, which is simply the cessation of instruction in any other language except English. But, we ask, what other meanings, motivations, agendas, and implications does this have? In other words, what other meanings does this text have?

To gain further insight, we can study other text. In white papers, Web sites, newspaper editorials, TV ads, and others, we encounter text written on both sides of the issue. For example, the proponents of the measure cite the need for English language proficiency in California. As the logic goes, the presumption is that second-language instruction is a culprit behind the inability of many students to gain fluency in English. It is

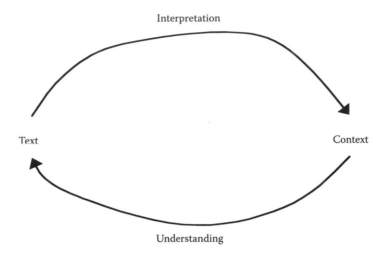

Fig. 5.2 Depiction of the hermeneutic circle.

not hard to figure out who these students are and, in fact, the same text goes on to make clear that this is a motion to bring children of recent immigrants to English language proficiency by having them use no other language in school. So far, the need to interpret beyond the ostensible meaning of the text is not so extensive.

However, we can attempt to go beyond this and inquire into other meanings of this motion. For example, we can begin by looking for symbol and implicit meanings. In this case, the very first thing we look at is the primary focus of the proposition: language. What does language signify (other than, of course, communication)? For one thing, we realize that language is also culture. The language we each speak "at home" is a good indication of some element of our cultural heritage (a fact that the decennial census is designed to track). Language is the instrument by which we join into community with others (literally joining in a conversation) or maintain a separation (picture two people switching to a language foreign to a third person standing in front of them). In fact, language is a central part of our identity, one of the ways we define ourselves.

Now, we reflect that the proposition is not talking about language writ large, but one specific language. How might we interpret this? For one, it implies a sense of competition between different languages. This proposition is about just one language, and its passage can be seen as a crowding out of the different languages competing for the public sphere. The proposition, in this sense, is an affirmation of both the identity of the larger public, and the supremacy of the one language and a signal of the primacy of the particular identity associated with it. You can see the various directions that the literary interpretation can go. Rest assured, however, that one can always gain insight by reading into the ballot measure (or other public policy) a contest over the public sphere. In other words, the measure is also about control over society.

Now, we add another dimension to it, and this is the element of context. Having interpreted the text on its own, we then see whether considering elements of place, history, social events, and other contextual things can deepen our interpretation, confirm it, modify it, or in other words, lead to deeper understanding. This is the other arc of the hermeneutic circle coming back to the text.

In the case of Proposition 227, this would require leaving the text for a moment and pondering on what was going on in the larger pale of society (i.e., California) at that time. It was a California that had just begun to recover from the social and psychological upheaval of the Los Angeles riots in the earlier part of the decade. It was also a California that was entering into its most serious depression since the oil crisis of the 1970s, exacerbated by a lax energy policy coming home to roost in the form of power cutbacks and rate increases. It was a contentious time. Why, then, would people focus on public school education and specifically secondary language instruction? In hermeneutic fashion, we ask whether the nature of the larger context supports any interpretation of the text of the proposition. In large part, it is not hard to make the connection. In the state of California at that time, the language measure was a contest, where dwindling resources and budgets posed a real fiscal contest over which public programs received the largest share of this dwindling pie. The measure can be seen as a way to secure scarce resources for an agenda shared by its proponents (e.g., it might be growth, employment, etc.) and away from the enormous expense of public school education.

But it is not just this, of course. In the light of race-torn California, the measure was also about language as a proxy for race. What the measure was saying, of course, was not just "use English" in schools but "use only English" which, we realize, also means "cease the use of Spanish." Again, we bring in context, and realize that this is also a time when the 1990 census revealed that large parts of California (e.g., the city of Los Angeles) had become, seemingly all of a sudden, "minority-majority" meaning that most of the residents in these cities were now from racial and ethnic groups that the census would categorize as "nonwhite." Moreover, projections showed that cities like Los Angeles would, by the year 2010 or earlier, become "majority-Latino," and in fact, a movement for a Latino mayor of Los Angeles was then gaining momentum. Possible meanings of the proposition become more evident in light of this hermeneutic. It might be surmised that the measure was a battle over language, but more than that, over identity and, more than that, over which group can lay claim to primacy over the public sphere. It can be interpreted as an affirmation (or perhaps false hope) by the former majority that they can still say that California is theirs, that their culture is still what California is about, and that the course of society is not to be determined by groups who talked, looked, and voted differently from them. This battle is economic, cultural, political, and psychological. It might also be interpreted as a game of laying "blame" for the state of society at that time, to wit: "It's those people who can't speak a word of English who bring the state down, use up resources in the form of social services, etc." The interpretation might be one of a battle between the races, but this is just one possible interpretation. (To be fair, there are some scholars who see the Los Angeles riots as not being about race but about class — but then again, what major social phenomenon does not involve, somehow, both?)

Of course, all this remains an interpretation, not a statement of fact. We could not prove that the measure meant this or anything beyond the exact text people voted for. But this is the difference between analysis as a positivist exercise, with its penchant for verifiability and replicability, and analysis as interpretation, where one looks for meaning that runs deeper than the positivist. But Gadamer had something to say about this — that whatever the text meant for its author, the latter was no longer the sole font of meaning. Even more important, the text means whatever it means to the reader. Whatever the authors of the measure meant by it, if you, the reader, read the word "language" and interpret that to also mean "race," then this is what the text means to you. You can affirm that this is what the measure meant "to you" and this, as Gadamer will remind us, is valid. Notice, also, the departure from the positivist ideal of the analyst as a neutral observer. In interpretive analysis, the analyst cannot help but bring her or his history, frames of understanding, and subjective predispositions to the task of analysis. The task, however, also requires that the analyst be open to new meanings, fresh assumptions, and surprise.

Figure 5.2 is also instructive in that it suggests how an interpretive approach need not regress into pure relativism. A pure theory of text can be thoroughly relativistic — in this framework, meaning can, from start to finish, be a simple construct. This strong postmodernist notion is a tempting one, especially given the radical reconceptualizations following Wittgenstein, Derrida, and later poststructuralists. However, Figure 5.2 offers us a way back. As the figure reminds us, interpretation is not the only operation that is needed. The other is that of understanding, and for this, we need to verify interpretation by checking it against the larger context. We interpret the text of Proposition 227, for example, not just on its own (e.g., as a literary piece), but in the larger context of political bargaining, race relations, and immigration policies in turn-of-the-century California, (or wherever the context may be). In Part III of this book, we emphasize this turn to contextuality and elaborate further on the necessary grounding that is needed to both understand and guide policymaking.

Analysis of Artifacts as Text

Case Study: An International Fast Food Chain   As Gadamer and Ricoeur had pointed out, the analysis of text carries over onto the social and political realm since action itself can be treated as text (Gadamer, 1960, also Ricoeur, 1971). Thus, the interpretive approach to policy analysis can be applied to an entire array of different research artifacts (i.e., meaning-carrying objects). This has motivated policy researchers to begin sifting through material that they had not previously utilized — brochures, Web sites, e-mail messages, logos, uniforms, office space, conversations, rituals, and others (e.g., see Yanow, 2001). In this chapter, we briefly take up the instance of an international fast food chain (that need not be named) and illustrate how different elements of a policy situation might be analyzed interpretively.

As this chapter is being conceived, the author is perusing the rather cheery Web site of this fast food company. The Web page displays a drawing of the planet Earth and a large magnifying glass focused on North America. Magnified through it is the company's logo, which is a large curvy letter designed to resemble a stylized set of arches, and a caption says that "it's winning time." The company's mascot, a colorful, gangly circus clown, appears on one side of the page. Later, I click onto another Web page from this same company, which talks about the company's vision for global governance. It shows a number of company employees, each of a different ethnic and racial background, and states that the company's goal is to be the "best employer in every community around the world." I then turn to yet another Web page, one wherein the chairman of the board has written a letter to the company's shareholders. This page features a gray, colorless picture of the three top managers in the company, superimposed across a bright, colorful close-up of some of the company's fast food.

Interpreting this bit of "text" is not hard. After all, it is a corporation and the slogan about "winning" is, of course, about the company winning over the competition and looking forward to a robust and profitable year ahead. There is nothing surprising in this. But how these Web pages say this is most interesting. Looking over page after page, beginning with the company logo superimposed upon the Earth and leading onto its vision for global governance, one sees a very stylized and effective restatement of the globalization ethic. This company is about making a home in communities, but not just this or that community, rather, in effect, "every community around the world." This awesome vision of global dominance becomes even more meaningful when, adding context in the manner of the hermeneutic circle, one ponders its very real domination of the worldwide fast food marketplace. When one considers the company logo, a set of golden arches, in this light, what meanings arise? One would be the immediate evocation of the arch as a symbol of triumph — to wit: Roman arches or the Arc d'Triomphe. The scene of this triumph is nothing less than the planet. Imagine conquering the world — not with spears or cannons, but with a bag of fries and a milkshake and, on top of this empire, sits its emperor with his yellow clown suit and knee-high stockings. This is a vision of imperialism in the age of globalization.

So then, we find deeper, richer meaning when we enter into these artifacts. On the one hand, we learn nothing new since companies are, after all, all about success in the global marketplace. On the other hand, we get a glimpse into the way the company (perhaps) or its shareholders (perhaps) or certainly this analyst sees its mission: empire building. This is an empire that dwarfs even the great Roman Empire in its scale and global domination. It is ironic that its mascot is a clown who evokes the richness of the circus and its vision of endless play. Clowns, however, are also symbols of irony, depth, grief, and other sentiments that run beneath the circus veneer. In fact, the shareholders' page speaks to this — despite the circus atmosphere and its image of play, the company is totally serious, even gray, in its pursuit of growth and profit. This last page is, after all, a message to its shareholders who, presumably, care less for circus fun and more about the bottom line of profit. In this last regard, the company management is not about fun and games. Sustained growth (which translates to profit margin) is, organizationally speaking, life and death.

One could then go deeper into these images, looking at other artifacts and, probably, the actual text used in these Web pages. We could employ more literary analytics to study the use of figures of speech (metaphor, metonymy, etc.) or a narrative analysis to map the structure of its storyline. We could use the methods of critical theory to test the underpinning assumptions of the narrative or discourse analysis (e.g., a Foucauldian one) to examine its goal of conquest through "ubiquity," or a cultural treatment of its effects on communities and practices (e.g., homogenization). One could analyze the Web site for how effectively it delivers its messages. The point is that meaning is not a given. It is to be read into the text, by its authors for sure, but also its readers. In another time and place, a different set of meanings might be seen in these same artifacts. The other point is that policy does work in different planes of communication — including the symbolic and interpretive, and those who are most adept at using these media have an upper hand in the policy game. The policy expert can add to the analysis by including these dimensions of symbol, interpretation, and image.

Reflecting on Text The notion of policy as text is a powerful counterpoint to the earlier models of the rational decision maker. In this chapter, we began conceiving of policy meaning as constructed by different meaning makers. This is a radically different mode of reasoning from the way meaning is portrayed in the rational model, which employs an objectivist approach to reduce meaning to that which is measurable. In contrast to the positivist mode of analysis, which reduces meaning to observable universal values, the textual treatment of policy assumes that meaning is constructed, subjective, and contested. The textual mode of policy analysis pays closest attention to the processes by which meaning and policy are created. Understanding policy as social construction entails new modes of analysis that might reveal the workings of so-called discursive practices. This can involve analyses that range from a focus on the literary qualities of a policy to a political analysis of the play of power that occurs during the process of meaning construction. This has very practical consequences for the researcher. Whereas the rational model would require the quantification of value, a textual analysis begins with the understanding that there are aspects of policy that can only be grasped by accessing them through the lenses of the stakeholder herself. As Lyotard has pointed out, this requires that we give the same primacy to more "native," narrative modes of knowing as that given to the classic, positivist "facts" within the scientific model (Lyotard, 1979).

While students of policy are quick to accept the textuality of policy, this is, in fact, much harder for the policy practitioner, who has to work with multiple publics, agencies, and communities — some of whom harbor deep suspicions of the subjective. To many, the job of the researcher is to separate fact from value and so provide some objective bases for deliberation. "Nothing but the facts," people will insist, and the policy practitioner is in no position to wave away their concerns. But, from a social constructionist frame of mind, there are no facts (certainly not in the social world and, as Latour has suggested, not even in the scientific one), only constructed meanings. The experienced policy practitioner can attest that, true enough, unassailable facts are hard to come by.

As an example, the author is reminded of an occasion where a group of academics engaged in a yearlong exercise revolving around the question, "how clean is clean?" This was meant to be a forum wherein a diverse group of researchers could talk about things like cleanup standards for environmentally contaminated sites. The forum began with some philosophical musings on what, exactly, did the word "clean" possibly mean. Did it mean that people who, later on, used a restored site would experience no risk of health (or other) effects? Well, no, people saw that the absolute absence of risk could really not be guaranteed. So, what did "clean" really mean? Well, the author observed that the same conversations were going on, at the end of month nine, that were going on in day one. Now, more than a decade later, the group probably still has no clue as to what "clean" definitively means.

Let us make the example a little more concrete. We can focus the "how clean is clean" debate to a related, but more focused, question, which is: What standards for acceptable risk do federal agencies use in determining how clean our environment should be? Such a question can be answered by looking at what standards the federal government actually does apply. This information is found in Table 5.1, which focuses on risks of cancer to people from environmental sources (e.g., contaminated air or water). In this table, risks are expressed, in true positivist fashion, in terms of the

Table 5.1 Risk thresholds under various U.S. federal regulatory regimes

Regulatory Program	Risk Threshold	Type of Regulation
Hazardous waste management		
RCRA (toxics use)	10^{-4} to 10^{-6}	Land disposal restrictions
CERCLA (abandoned sites)	10^{-4} to 10^{-7}	Clean-up requirements
Occupational Health and Safety	10^{-3}	Permissible exposures (PELs)
Clean Air Act	10^{-6}	NESHAPs
Safe Drinking Water Act	10^{-6}	Drinking water quality
Pesticides (FIFRA)	10^{-4} to 10^{-6}	Tolerances for pesticide use
Food and Drug Regulation (FDA)	10^{-6}	Tolerances for unavoidable contaminants

probability of an exposed individual developing cancer over a lifetime of exposure.

In Table 5.1, an acceptable risk of 10^{-6} (which is the same as one in a million) is understood to mean that the environment should be clean enough that a person living in that environment should have no more than a one in a million probability of developing cancer over his or her lifetime. An acceptable risk of 10^{-3}, on the other hand, means that this threshold is set at a much less stringent level of one in a thousand.

What Table 5.1 shows is that, as far as how clean the environment should be, federal agencies are nowhere near in agreement over what that the standard should be. In fact, the numbers in the table vary over four orders of magnitude. The reader should understand that these numbers represent the best science at the regulator's disposal and the closest thing to a scientific "fact." The range of numbers in the table attests to the absence of factuality. What does it mean to take an interpretive approach to this situation? First, we recognize that knowledge, fact, and value are not objects to be measured but meanings to be constructed. In this vein, we might see the numbers in Table 5.1 as socially constructed discourses. Once we take this step, however, we immediately wonder about the discursive processes within which these positions evolve. We wonder why it is that such different outcomes would result in different regulatory regimes.

Employing an interpretive approach enables us to imagine the type of discursive practices that are involved in the construction of such meanings. It helps us understand why different meanings emerge out of different regulatory regimes. First, seeing these meanings as constructed, we can surmise that different processes hold sway in each regulatory situation. There are different stakeholders, with differing degrees of political power, who contend for their particular meanings to be accepted. It should be no surprise that different meanings emerge — each situation is a different type of discursive contest with different players. It is not hard to reason why standards for factory workers or pesticide applicators are so much more lenient than that for the general public — workers in some industries and farmworkers are among those with the least political power in society (increasingly, including those who have no voting rights). On the other side of the coin, leaders of both the industrial and agricultural sectors are among the most powerful.

Table 5.1 gives us another lesson in meaning construction. The wide latitude over which the numbers range can be understood to be the sociopolitical field in which meanings are fought over. The larger the range, the higher the potential stake and, we imagine, the more vociferous the contest over meaning. There is, in fact, no such thing as fact in this situation — only outcomes of a discursive contest. What is at stake in this game is great — on one side, a slightly stricter standard can bode millions of dollars more in environmental management costs to industry or government, and on the other side, a slightly more lenient standard can translate to a host of trage-dies that can befall vulnerable individuals and their families.

At any rate, a textual approach asks much different questions than those found in the rational model. Rather than inquire into what the objectively superior policy is, the discursive approach inquires into the process by which contests over meaning are waged and how they are won. It inquires into the universe of meanings that contend in the public sphere, some of them explicit, and other meanings hidden buried in the textual landscape.

As with all the other models taken up herein, this model of policy analysis also offers us lessons on how policies might be better formulated. There needs to be closer attention paid to the processes of meaning construction, and how power differentials affect these processes. This can lead to ideas for reforming institutions for public deliberation. It gives us avenues for opening up these processes to all, making implicit meanings and processes more transparent and assisting the necessary process of meaning making. Moreover, as theorists of the consensus-building field might suggest, a better-designed deliberative process might actually help the group of stakeholders come to some common understanding of the situation (Susskind et al., 1999). In the ideal world, this may even lead to a consensus or a solution. In this model, the role of the policy analyst is transformed away from that of the scientist, measuring objective values and able to make universalist conclusions as to the best course of action for society, and closer to that of a mediator, making processes and forums available to stakeholders, listening to them as they make sense of their own situation, and facilitating the joint construction of meaning. In some situations, the analyst is only an interpreter, bringing previously hidden meanings to light.

The analyst's role can go beyond simply interpreting the situation, as understood by different stakeholders, to trying to understand how is it, exactly, that communicative processes might work to resolve policy ques-tions. Do participants, as the negotiation literature suggests, trade off different elements of the situation and so reach some generally acceptable middle ground or compromise (see, for example, Fisher et al., 1991)? Or, as others contend, it is possible for participants to coconstruct a metanar-rative around which all can coalesce (Schön and Rein, 1995)? Thus, we move from a rationalist preoccupation on finding what the best policy is to a communicative preoccupation with fostering processes by which a group might come to an understanding over a suitable course of action. When good policy is understood as created, not merely observed (or unearthed from within the known universe of possibilities), then process becomes all important, especially with an eye to fostering creativity, transparency, and the democratic exchange of ideas.

CHAPTER **6**

Critique

Introduction

As a response to the strong, overweening assumptions of the rational model, there arose important critiques from a number of different camps: sociology, political science, anthropology, philosophy, etc. In some of these instances, the critical program was developed so thoroughly that we can recognize this as its own mode of analysis. True, the critical endeavor is largely a negative one, i.e., the uncovering of inconsistencies and deficiencies in the object of criticism rather than the positing of alternative conceptualizations of policy (or utopia). Nevertheless, critique is a legitimate and often powerful mode of policy analysis with roots dating back to the earliest philosophers (e.g., the skeptical frame of analysis of Socrates and later Descartes).

As an introduction to the notions that we develop in this chapter, it never hurts to begin with the theories of two important sociologists: Karl Marx and Max Weber. Marx wrote about the material and intellectual transformations wrought by capitalism, most significantly the alienation of labor (Marx, 1887). In his concept of fetishism, Marx described how human labor, which prior to capitalism was an expression of human creativity, was transformed into an abstract entity, the value of labor, which heretofore needed only to be described through the use of a price. That is, the abstract notion of value is reified (or hypostatized) to stand in for the real entity, human work. The commodification of labor enabled the capitalist class to transform human work simply into one of the various factors of production (along with land and various forms of capital). This enabled the systematic transformation of society (beginning with modes of production) around the single pursuit of maximization of the surplus of production (i.e., profit margins). In this critique, we should realize that Marx is questioning, though not in these same terms, the same foundations of the classical mode of analysis — especially its inherent positivist utilitarianism. For example, the commodification of labor can be understood in terms of the reduction of a complex, even incommensurable entity (human worth) to a unidimensional measure (monetary value).

It was in Weber's theory of rationalization that this critique is found in its most sweeping form. Through a number of profound, though scattered, writings, Weber attributed phenomena such as the dehumanization of labor, bureaucratization of government, and the triumph of scientific over other modes of reasoning to a process called "rationalization" (Weber, 1864). In Weber's depiction, the Enlightenment was a significant turning point in human thought inasmuch as it signaled a turning away from the idea of knowledge as something received in the form of tradition, lore, or official teaching. From this point onward, the individual was free to form his or her own truths. However, Weber continues, this process of "disenchantment" also meant the splitting apart of what was once a coherent body of knowledge (i.e., tradition) into different logics or value spheres. This was a consequence of the liberation of the individual to pursue various directions of thought (Weber, 1904). For example, at this point we see the splitting off of art into its own industry, such that art was no longer integrated into the rest of society or an individual's everyday life, but occupied a dedicated place in the museum or gallery. Ethical thought grew into its own special field, also, as embodied in the legal profession. However, of the different value spheres, one came to be dominant — this was the dimension of technical–instrumental logic. This expertise, embodied in the natural sciences (and professions such as engineering and economics), involved a specific logic that entailed the optimization of the human mastery of nature. The material advantages that this narrow mode of rationality, or *zweckrationalitat* as Weber called it, gave the institutions modeled after it allowed this particular logic to so dominate the rest that Weber described it as a systematic transformation of society, i.e., rationalization. In this theory, the narrow logic of optimization of material output encompasses the reduction of human labor to a mere factor of production (where surplus value is the *summum bonum*). The process whereby this logic transformed the political arena was most developed in his writings. Weber proceeded to develop an account for how society, through processes of rationalization involving accounting and organization, developed a rational model of governance embodied in the bureaucracy. For example, bureaucratization allows a specific branch of government, e.g., the Department of the Interior, to maximize its specific, narrow objectives, e.g., maximization of capacity of reservoirs and dams, over other criteria such as environmental protection or social values. *Zweckrationalitat*, as opposed to *wertrationalitat* (or true rationality), allows the single-minded pursuit of some prespecified end without so much as reflection on the end itself. In such a system, measurable inputs to analysis, such as monetary value or energy output, naturally hold sway over other, incommensurable considerations such as aesthetics, morality, or community. Weber's theory was also significant in pointing out that such processes worked out not only on the material plane, but in the very meanings attached to human activity. For example, he illustrated the link between religious systems and the rationalization of society (Weber, 1864).

It was in the 1930s and 1940s that an extensive effort to further develop these ideas arose in the Frankfurt School, who counted among its ranks Adorno, Fromm, Horkheimer, Marcuse, and others. In a series of related, though disparate, treatises, the members of the Frankfurt School proceeded to extend the concepts of Marx and Weber to all facets of modern-day life, including art, advertising, consumption, and education. They also attempted to further these theories to encompass political events of their day — including the experience of the two world wars, the onset of advanced or late capitalism (in Western Europe but, increasingly, in the United States), the rise of fascism, and the socialist experiment of Stalinist Russia.

In *Dialectic of the Enlightenment*, Horkheimer and Adorno portray the process of rationalization as the Homeric myth of the Odyssey (Horkheimer and Adorno, 1972). They picture Odysseus as the archetype of the modern condition, which is the submission of society to the narrow, technological mastery of nature. It is symbolized in his refusal to succumb to the enchanting music of the muses, choosing instead to fasten himself to the mast of his ship. When Odysseus orders his crew to plug their ears and steadfastly row on to their objective, Horkheimer and Adorno draw a parallel to the present-day human condition in which people are enslaved to production, which is none other than technical mastery over nature. Odysseus upholds the myth of individuality and technology at the expense of nature and authentic needs and desires, and his lashing himself to the mast is symbolic of processes of alienation, whether these be the labor contract, bureaucratization, or other. In turning away from the myths of tradition and superstition, we choose to widen the separation between subject and object (or nature) by objectifying the world around us. This means treating nature, resources, beauty, and places as mere factors in our modern drive toward maximum instrumental gain. This separation, in turn, has a dehumanizing effect on us, to the extent that we end up objectifying ourselves in the process as well. In Horkheimer and Adorno's depiction, the rational ideal of the autonomous, rational individual is itself a myth that succeeds in treating the person as a utility maximizing machine or, as one author put it, rational fools (Sen, 1970). In so doing, the Enlightenment succeeds in ingraining yet another mythology.

This myth of technical reasoning is also taken up by Marcuse in his portrayal of the modern-day human as the one-dimensional man (Marcuse, 1964), reduced to an automatonlike existence in the present capitalist industrial age. Though disparate and often conflicting at times, the works of the Frankfurt School develop the same basic point, which is to show the degree to which human thought and institutions have been captured by the primacy of the individualistic, utilitarian, technological, and positivist.

These writers also draw liberally from Nietzsche, who posited that all our social institutions are designed upon one implicit objective, which is the furtherance of domination. That is, institutions such as the school, government, and the market all are meant to extend the control of the powerful over the masses, something that Nietzsche attributes to the basic human "will to power" (Nietzsche, 1967). This necessarily questions the neutrality of systems of thought and associated practices (e.g., the neutral accounting stance of decision theory). This same theme was developed by the more contemporary sociologist Foucault in his historical accounts of the development of modern-day institutions such as the clinic, school, prison, and others. Foucault carefully traces the evolution of these institutions and shows how their design draws from the same basic principles of surveillance, mensuration, and control (Foucault, 1977). Most importantly, however, he develops the notion of the infinitude of the spaces of domination, ranging from the structural, which Marx and others wrote about, to the most intimate relations between individuals, within households, and in the everyday practices of the person. In fact, domination is all the more perfect in situations where control is implicit, nonphysical, and internalized. As an example, he cites Bentham's idea of the futuristic prison, the Panopticon, in which each cell would be built to face a central observation tower and fitted with one-way mirrors such that the prisoner could be seen but not able to see anyone else. The mode of control here is a perfect one that need not even require the presence of prison guards or routines for monitoring the prisoners. Instead, each prisoner is disciplined simply by the possibility that, at every moment in time, whether true or not, someone may be observing him or her. This analogy can be carried over into any social practice — for example, the creation of a daily retinue or quotidian regime of scheduled TV programs to which the viewer responds by dutifully sitting in front of the set in a semitrance can be seen as a form of discipline. Related notions can be read into the concept of the code (Baudrillard, 1994) or habitus (Bourdieu, 1990).

The critique pertains to the model of reasoning and, as importantly, to the subject at the center of the model of rationality, as well. The members of the Frankfurt School rejected ontologies of the subject as the liberal, atomistic, self-seeking individual, or objectified as the stimulus-response machine of the behavioral model. Others, who would constitute the field of feminist theory, rejected the masculine conceptualization of the subject. In particular, Gilligan discussed how the subject of the liberal model corresponds to the masculine archetype (autonomous, competitive, utilitarian) as opposed to other value systems that might be characterized as feminine (the relational, caring, integrative, ecological). In this, she posited new value systems that pointed to the need to reinstitute the feminine in male-dominated institutions (Gilligan, 1982). We return to her ethic of care in chapter 11. Another important system of critique stemmed from rejecting the implicit assumption of the subject of history as Western (or Occidental) and the parallel positing of the Eastern (or Oriental) as peripheral — so-called postcolonial studies (e.g., Said, 1993). For example, the European movements known as the Enlightenment and Renaissance are portrayed as turning points for the human species, forgetting profound revolutions in art, philosophy, and culture that occurred much earlier in Asia, the Middle East, and others. Most immediate of our concerns is that each of these critiques points us to horizons that lie beyond the rational model (in its Western, masculine, and technological sense). More broadly, hegemonic practices or bodies of thought operate by constructing the "other," i.e., people, groups, or places that constitute the periphery, and proceeding to systematically create a privileged position for them in the center of policy, discourse, and practice.

While, as we saw in the last chapter, some of the critiques ultimately came to rest in various forms of relativist thought (e.g., Lyotard and his total rejection of grand narratives), by and large, members of the Frankfurt School did not espouse the relativist. Yet, after some had begun to move beyond the positing of the protelariat as the revolutionary subject of history, there remained the absence of the alternative. This has direct implications for methodology, inasmuch as we are left with little guidance as to what to substitute for the *summum bonum* of the classic model. Certainly, if we understand analytics to mean the search for truth, knowledge, or purpose, then what is to result from analysis? As we see in the next section, we realize that the critique can be the analytic itself.

Analytics

Probably the most extended treatment of methodological considerations resulting from the Frankfurt School is to be found in Adorno's negative dialectics (Adorno, 1973). In this work, Adorno posits an epistemology that revolves around the uncovering of inconsistencies and fallacies in systems of thought. In doing so, he offers up an analytic that is encompassed in the critique itself. To quote:

> The critique of every self-absolutizing particular is a critique of the shadow which absoluteness casts upon the critique; it is a critique of the fact that critique itself, contrary to its own tendency, must remain within the medium of the concept. It destroys the claim of identity by testing and honoring it; therefore, it can reach no farther than that claim...It is up to the self-reflection of critique to extinguish that claim, to extinguish it in the very negation of negation that will not become a positing...it does not mean to have escaped from that context. Its objective goal is to break out of the context from within...It lies in the definition of negative dialectics that it will not come to rest in itself, as if it were total. This is its form of hope.
>
> Adorno, 1973

In it, Adorno chooses not to "posit" or to solve; rather, it suffices only to critique self-absolutizing systems of thought (or, in our terminology, the mythological). This is not a form of relativism since he maintains hope in breaking out of false modes of thought. However, his analysis is content merely to defeat these systems of thought from within. Where we proceed from there is left for the emancipated to work out over the course of history.

As a system of analysis, we do find an outline of a methodology here. To work it out more substantively, we have to begin with the central notion that the negative dialectic strives to negate: so-called identity thinking (Horkheimer and Adorno, 1972). The claim of *identity* or *equivalence* is the mythological positing of attributes to some entity — to the extent that the latter is reified as the attribute. We will easily recognize the fetishization of labor as the claim of identity (in this case, identifying labor with market value). We recognize the claim of identity in any analytic that reduces all phenomena to a unidimensional field (e.g., utility, power, matter). Decision theory is an example of the equivalence principle, which reduces every consideration to a uniform unit of analysis — utility.

Adorno's method is to show the inconsistencies within the identity, i.e., to negate it "from within." For example, he illustrates this with the labor example. One of the claims of liberal philosophy and the market narrative is that it is through the free market that individuals can attain autonomy and equality. Adorno would counter, however, that contrary to these claims, the capitalist economy reduces the worker to a servile cog in the wheels of industry — with no choice but to sell one's labor to the dictates of the market. Rather than experience equality in the marketplace, the worker feels devalued. Consider the plight of the coffee plantation worker who lives in a place and time where one can work ceaselessly in the field for 12 hours each day and still not earn enough to satisfy his or her children's hunger or basic need for shelter. In other words, the negative dialectic examines the claims or underpinning assumptions of a system of thought and proceeds to reveal internal inconsistencies in its logic or in a gap between its claims and reality.

Let us try to systematize the method to whatever extent we can. We might posit the process as consisting in the following steps.

1. Reconstruct the foundational assumptions on which the theory, concept, or policy rests, or the fundamental claims that are made by its proponents.
2. Test these assumptions or claims for internal inconsistencies. An example of this is when the set of assumptions or claims are not all compatible with each other.
3. Test them against reality, checking for conditions that are not consistent with the theory's assumptions or outcomes of the policy that counter the claims made for it.
4. Propose alternative assumptions that are more logical, consistent, or realistic.
5. Seek out elements of the program or policy according to central themes of critical thought, including domination, reduction, alienation, and reification.

The last element of the analysis simply involves analyzing the program according to central themes that have been developed in critical theory. As an example, consider the evolution of participative methods of planning and program implementation, which were designed to undo the paternalistic, technocratic, and dominating practices of experts. In a twist on the use of critical theory, some practitioners used some of its concepts to analyze participative practices themselves (e.g., Cooke and Kothari, 2002). These critics suggested that participation, as a *raison d'etre* can have hegemonic elements itself — as in the hypostatization of a unitary community when, in reality, a town may be characterized by deep stratification, exclusions, and power-ridden relations. Or, by freeing the state of responsibilities for local communities, decentralization might result in a further burdening of these communities, in contrast to its stated goal of local empowerment.

For students of program evaluation, there is much in the previous method that matches the process of evaluation, which is often exactly the testing of claims against outcomes. In this regard, we find it useful to use some of the methods developed in the field of program evaluation. For example, it is often the case that one of the early steps in the process of evaluation has to do with reconstructing the program logic that underpins the program (e.g., see Weiss, 1998). Sometimes, this can be done by the analyst in isolation, but much of the time, it is constructed in conjunction with stakeholders. The program logic is none other than the laying out of the mechanisms, logical sequence, or train of reasoning that lies behind a program or policy and leads from its inception to realization of its goals. This can help us in our critique inasmuch as it affords us a tool for constructing those underpinning assumptions that provide justification for a program. An example of a program logic is shown in Figure 6.1.

In the example in Figure 6.1, we depict some lines of reasoning that portray how the program, in this case universal preschool, will work. It is part of the public discourse that legitimizes the proposed policy. In this case, there is a further reason for laying out the logic of the program in such a detailed manner. Here, we are analyzing a proposal to make preschool (for children under the age of five) available to all children and, furthermore, publicly funded. Its ultimate goals are to foster the development of creative, responsible, and productive adults who will strengthen the workforce as they add to its numbers. Note, however, that these outcomes (productivity, employment) are so distal that they cannot possibly be monitored as part of an early analysis of such a program or proposal. For this reason, we need more intermediate or proximal objectives (or steps in the train of logic) that we can test. The construction of program logics, policy narratives, and other modes of legitimization are important for critique.

We may choose to test some of the intermediate nodes in the logic diagram. For example, our analysis may focus on the second step in the logic diagram, which is the assumption that parents receive timely information about the program. For them to receive it, we might suppose that the information might be in a form that is most conducive to them receiving

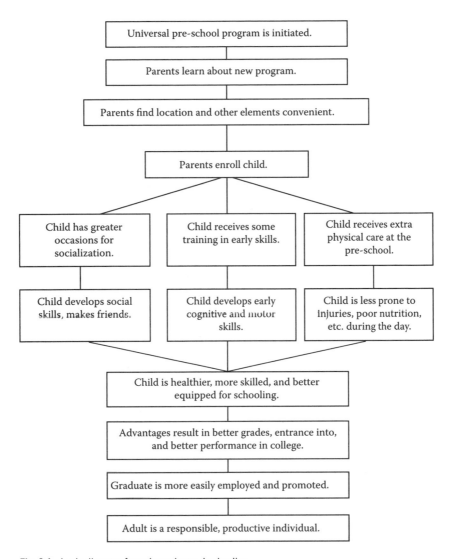

Fig. 6.1 Logic diagram for universal preschool policy.

and digesting the information. Is there an information campaign underway? Is the information packaged in culturally appropriate ways (e.g., in some communities, there may be need for bilingual program material). Are the messages and signals that are being received by the parents positive ones? Perhaps the message alienates certain sectors of the community. At any rate, the critical analysis aims to test the assumption to judge whether it is realistic or even plausible.

We illustrate the negative dialectic in the following case study.

Case Study: Emissions Trading in Southern California   In 1994, southern California embarked on an ambitious program to attempt to meet its air pollution reduction goals. The idea was to create a regional market in emission credit, wherein the rights to emit a certain pollutant (in this case, nitrogen oxides, NO_x, and sulfur oxides, SO_x) could be bought and sold among air-polluting industries. The marketable emissions program, the Regional Clean Air Incentives Market (RECLAIM) was instituted in 1994 (as Rule 2001) by the South Coast Air Quality Management District (SCAQMD). The SCAQMD is an air pollution control district delegated by the U.S. Environmental Protection Agency (USEPA) to implement the Clean Air Act in Los Angeles, Orange, Riverside, and San Bernardino counties, an area of about 30,000 square kilometers and home to more than 14 million people. SCAQMD develops plans and programs for the region to attain federal standards by dates specified in federal law. The agency is also responsible for meeting state standards by the earliest date achievable, using reasonably available control measures. In 1993, SCAQMD proposed a bold initiative to create an emissions trading program for NO_x and SO_x in the South Coast Air Basin (SCAQMD, 1993). This study focuses only on the NO_x program because the SO_x trading program has been considerably less active. A total of 390 large emitters of NO_x were included in the trading regime, which allocated initial credits to each firm based on their historical emissions. After setting the initial allocation of NO_x credits, SCAQMD allowed trading to begin with the requirement that all original credits be scaled down over time until the program achieves a total basinwide reduction of 80 tons per day by July 2004.

The concept of emissions trading (or marketable discharge permits) is illustrated in Figure 6.2. In the figure, we consider a regional air quality agency that has set a goal of reducing total emissions of pollutant P in this area by half. We then posit two firms in this simplistic example, each with differing costs or emission reduction, and two regulatory options: (1) command-and-control, which in this case, we assume to mean mandating that each firm reduce its emission of P by 50 percent, and (2) emissions trading, which we will assume means allowing the firms to buy and sell rights to emit P among themselves. In the upper half of Figure 6.2, we illustrate the case where each firm incurs the cost of reducing its own emission of P by half. In contrast, the lower part of Figure 6.2 depicts the case where only Firm B reduces its emissions but to a degree that its reductions equal the total areawide emission reduction goal, thus exempting Firm A from needing to reduce its own emission.

Why would Firm B agree to undertake extra reductions in emissions under emissions trading? Simply put, it would if A paid B to do so. As

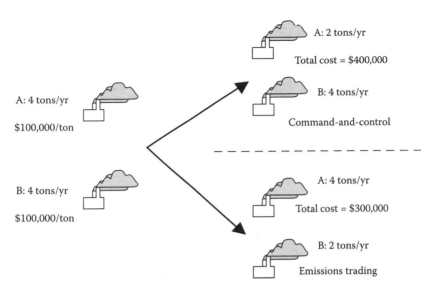

Fig. 6.2 Command-and-control vs. emissions trading. (From Lejano, R. and H. Rei. 2005. *Environmental Science & Policy* 8:367–377.)

illustrated in the figure, there is a side payment from A to B. The amount of the payment is enough to compensate B for the latter's making further reductions in its emissions — in fact, even a little more. Both Firms A and B are better off with emissions trading than they would have been under command-and-control. Firm A pays B an amount that is less than A's cost of reducing its emission. Meanwhile, the payment to B exceeds B's additional costs to make the extra emission reductions. The emissions-trading regime is said to be more Pareto efficient than command-and-control.

However, a closer look at Figure 6.2 shows that the spatial distribution of emissions changes greatly when we move from command-and-control to emissions trading. Essentially, under the emissions-trading regime, a much greater portion of the regional emissions are coming from Firm A. This suggests that we ask whether the population living around Firm A is not hurt by this change in distribution. Perhaps people are being hurt by this change in policy. For a policy to be institutionalized and effectively implemented, it needs legitimacy, and part of this means being able to address questions such as these. That is, some narrative needs to be developed and maintained that rationalizes the existence of the policy. To justify emissions trading, a number of conditions have to hold, some of which we discuss below.

Assumption 1: There are no local impacts from trading pollutant P.

The first requirement is that the buying and selling of P should not create any hotspots of unhealthy air around Firm A. Other conditions have to hold for this to happen. First, we might suppose that pollutant P disperses so rapidly into the bulk of the air basin that no local hotspots form. Another alternative condition that would ensure this is that P is not a toxic pollutant on its own. NO_x, nitrogen oxides, fits this description because nitrogen oxides participate in the formation of ozone, which is a chemical reaction that occurs over the time scale of hours. Thus, the effects of NO_x are felt only long after the pollutant leaves the smokestack and disperses into the upper atmosphere. Moreover, there is assumed to be no toxicity from NO_x to the residents immediately surrounding Firm A. The first possible rationale posits that no hotspots form, while the second maintains that even though local hotspots form they are nontoxic.

> Assumption 2:   It is possible to turn pollutant P into a commodity that can be separated from other goods and bought and sold on its own.

This assumption states that when Firm A buys an amount of pollutant P, it should not also be buying, along with P, some of pollutant Q or R. For this to hold, pollutant P needs to be separable, not just mathematically but physically. The other way of saying this is that there be no externalities associated with the trade, where an externality is defined as an effect that is not taken into account by parties when they negotiate the transaction. In this particular case, the externality is the presence of pollutant Q or R that, though not considered in negotiating the trade of P, is bought and sold unwittingly or unknowingly by the parties along with the transfer of the commodity, P.

> Assumption 3: The market for P approaches the ideal for a perfectly competitive market with low transaction costs.

We also assume the existence of a well-functioning market. The ideal is that of perfect competition, and most important for this analysis is the assumption that there is a sufficiently large number of sellers and buyers such that no one firm can influence prices. This also requires that there be no collusion, i.e., no coalition formation. The other condition for a well-functioning market is that there be no barriers to participation. Participation, in reality, can involve modes of action other than the simple participation in the market, of course. The assumption of low transaction costs has been dealt with elsewhere, with some researchers positing that these costs may be significant enough to hinder trades (Hahn and Hester, 1989; Atkinson and Tietenberg, 1991; Stavins, 1995).

This case study illustrates how to test whether air quality can be commodified and treated as a market good, or whether, in fact, there are irreducible public, nonexcludable, or incommensurate features of air quality that cannot be completely captured in a trading regime. This has potentially great consequences for an agency that is struggling to rationalize its operation vis-à-vis charges of environmental injustice. Previous treatments of the distributive impacts of air quality in the southern California air basin have suggested that the maldistribution of air quality is significant and systemic (Szasz et al., 1993; Boer et al., 1997; Lejano et al., 2002; Morello-Frosch et al., 2002).

The logic behind this critical analysis is a simple one. We seek out key, underpinning assumptions that validate or justify a proposal program, and we then test each of these assumptions for how realistic or justifiable it is. We admit that longer experience and much more information is needed to be able to assess conclusively how RECLAIM has fared and whether, on balance, its institution is justified. The critical analysis consists in showing how key assumptions can be tested and how an evolving program can be subject to ongoing assessment.

To test the distributional impacts (Assumption 1), we model differences in *local* air quality that result when we move from command-and-control to emissions trading. The results of the air quality modeling for the year 1996 (just after initiation of the RECLAIM program) are shown in Figure 6.3 in the City of Wilmington, one of the more polluted areas of southern California. As we see, local concentrations of NO_x in the vicinity of large emitters in Wilmington actually exhibited an increase after RECLAIM commenced. The figure points to the impossibility of dispersion being so efficient that the emitted NO_x is almost completely mixed into the atmosphere, creating uniform concentrations of NO_x throughout the area. The maximum NO_x concentration at ground level in this area with RECLAIM was found to be 694 $\mu g/m^3$. In contrast, the without-RECLAIM scenario only had a maximum NO_x concentration of 552 $\mu g/m^3$. What is the import of this finding?

Consider, for a moment, if the NO_x were mainly present in the form of nitric oxide, NO. While the concentrations shown in these figures do not violate any acute toxicity criteria for NO, the question is whether there might be potential for chronic effects. Researchers have begun uncovering some evidence of the toxicity of NO (Last et al., 1994). Some animal studies do suggest possible toxic effects even at these NO concentrations. For example, Mercer et al. (1995) show lung impairment to laboratory mice

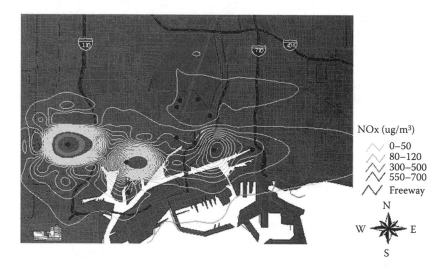

Fig. 6.3 Change in NO$_x$ concentrations due to RECLAIM. (From Lejano, R. and H. Rei. 2005. *Environmental Science & Policy* 8:367–377.)

at NO concentrations of 0.5 ppm (approximately 620 μg/m³). What this suggests is that there is some possibility of local health impacts from NO$_x$. Moreover, these impacts would be exacerbated, significantly so, by RECLAIM.

Perhaps more significantly, we then test Assumption 2 and ask whether there might be a possibility that, rather than simply purchasing a volume of NO$_x$ credits, one is also implicitly gaining the right to emit other constituents, namely air toxics and particulates? One way to begin inquiring into possible relationships between the emission of NO$_x$ and other constituents is to examine individual firms. As discussed previously, since other SCAQMD control programs are in place concurrently with RECLAIM, basinwide or industrywide reductions in other emissions vis-à-vis NO$_x$ emissions may reflect the effect of these other programs and dilute the observable effect of RECLAIM. The proper analysis is to look at one industry at a time. We illustrate this by examining the emission patterns of Firm U and Firm B over time (Figure 6.4a and b). In these figures, we represent total emissions of air toxics as an aggregate toxicity index (i.e., in the case of a carcinogen, the mass of a constituent multiplied by its unit risk factor). Firm U had a sudden drop in its emission of chromium between the years 1996 and 1997. Whether due to a control measure or change in monitoring regime, this sudden change needs to be factored out to assess any movement of air toxics vis-à-vis NO$_x$. If we remove the effect of chromium, we obtain the aggregate toxicity emission curve (without chromium) as shown in Figure 6.4a, which shows the total toxicity of the emission expressed as an equivalent benzene emission, with chromium factored out.

Figure 6.4b shows a similar trend for Firm B. Here, we show the trend for the main toxic pollutant found in Firm B's emission, nickel, and see that it also goes up and down along with the NO_x emissions. What Figures 6.4a and b suggest is that the pattern of emission of air toxics follows that of NO_x over time. The implication of this is that trades in NO_x

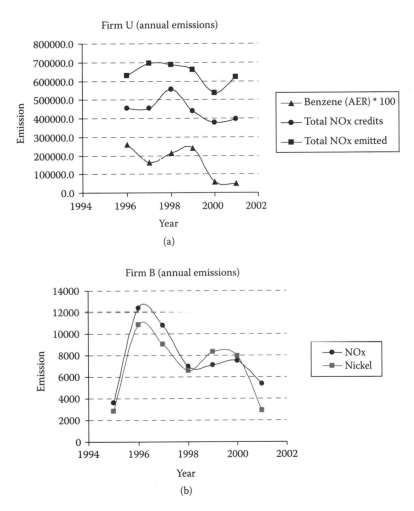

Fig. 6.4 (a) Historical emission patterns (Firm U, Wilmington, California). (b) Historical emission patterns (Firm B, Wilmington, California). (From Lejano, R. and H. Rei. 2005. *Environmental Science & Policy* 8:367–377.)

may be accompanied by unanticipated "trades" in air toxics. That is, if a firm purchases rights to emit additional NO_x, it is also unknowingly obtaining the ability to emit more air toxics as well. This is a reasonable proposition because if a firm is able to increase its stack emissions as a result of NO_x credit purchases, the additional amounts emitted through the stack will contain not just NO_x but other constituents as well. In physical terms, we cannot treat NO_x as an isolated commodity because trading NO_x means trading other pollutants as well.

The third assumption that we need to question is that of the marketlike conditions that are assumed to prevail in the RECLAIM program. Regarding the assumption of a thick market, it is noteworthy that to stabilize recently surging unit prices of NO_x credits, the SCAQMD recommended removing electric utilities from the RECLAIM market, leaving an even smaller number of active firms (SCAQMD, 2002). What led to this action was that prior to 2000 many firms were not greatly affected by RECLAIM because they had excess credits to give up as the agency began ratcheting down on credits. For many firms, this excess was finally depleted in 2000, at which point they realized a need to purchase additional credits. The shortage of credits was exacerbated by the energy crisis in California, which forced utilities to increase electricity production in its existing plants. This sudden increase in demand, coupled with the large purchasing power of the utilities, caused the price of NO_x to shoot upward (SCAQMD, 2001).

The historical trend in RECLAIM unit prices for NO_x is shown in Figure 6.5. The large swing in price was completely unanticipated. While previous studies predicted a movement of the price to $11,257/ton by 1999 (Johnson and Pekelney, 1996), the actual market price for credits jumped to $45,609/ton in 2000. This is far higher than the upper limit of $12,700/ton for the most expensive selective catalytic reduction control technology (e.g., as reported in http://www.epa.gov/EPA-AIR/2005/May/Day-12/a5723a.htm accessed December 14, 2005), which indicated that the long-run investment in pollution control as not occurring as the market model had conceptualized. The degree to which the California energy crisis and subsequent deregulation, as well as the sudden increase in demand for NO_x credits from the electric utility sector, affected prices suggests that a few firms can drive prices in this market. All this suggests an evidently thin market, wherein a few large traders held inordinate sway over the price of NO_x credits.

Another aspect of critical analysis involves analyzing the program with regard to certain themes that have proven central to the task of critique. Take, for example, the exclusion of the "other" as a symptom of hegemonic practice. In the case at hand, we can recognize the other as those communities

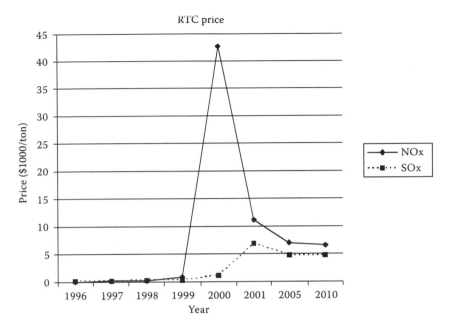

Fig. 6.5 RECLAIM market prices for emission credits. (From Lejano, R. and H. Rei. 2005. *Environmental Science & Policy* 8:367–377.)

that exist in the periphery of the urban universe — those places where the dirtier industries and lower-income households are relegated. In this case, exclusion can mean the neglect of these communities' concerns in policy-making. The emissions-trading program can be portrayed as exclusionary for a number of reasons. The most immediate one concerns the cognitive act of taking the entire region as the unit of analysis. That is, the market is set up so as to reduce total (or average) regional emissions. When the analysis is done on a regional basis, however, it washes away differences between specific places in this region. The act of setting up such a regional market is tantamount to reducing the analysis of air quality impacts to a likewise regional, average basis. This allows previously dirty places to become even dirtier after commencement of the trading program, even though average emissions over the region may have dropped. The institution of a regional market essentially removes the local from consideration.

Policy Reflection

We have discussed how the critical endeavor is not at all an exercise in nihilism or a type of relativism. Rather, it can be an essential step in institutional reform. The task of critique is to lay bare the inconsistencies or internal fallacies of a policy or program. This is accomplished not by directing critique from outside the object of criticism, but beginning within it. The ultimate objective, however, is to break out of the false construct and exceed the bounds of it and the critical analysis itself. We are not given any directions for how to go beyond the limits of the negative analysis, however, but some of it can be found in the critique. In the case study, we saw how a number of key assumptions were not entirely realistic. The prescription for institutional reform can begin exactly where these assumptions break down. For example, reform can mean bringing attention back to local concerns as opposed to a completely regional outlook. If prices of the good are too volatile, then it may be that some controls may need to be built into the program.

The task of critique can be seen as central to our stated aim of bridging the gap between the text and context of policy, or between concept and practice. The critical element lies in showing the degree of divergence between the two sides. Critical analysis can also clarify at what points in the policy narrative the greatest divergence occurs. What elements, assumptions, or claims are most problematic? As important, how do these divergences come about?

However, we keep in mind that the methods in this section mainly aim to undo falsities in thinking. It is, after all, a negative dialectic in which we simply tear down the illusory. What we put up in its stead is another question. It is left to other modes of analysis to posit ways to bridge the gaps. That is the topic that we take up in Part III of this book.

CHAPTER 7

Ethics

Introduction

In chapter 1, we discussed the foundations for much of the theory that underpins policy. As early as the days of the Enlightenment, in the midst of the contending schools of thought that arose around the utilitarian-empiricists and the rationalists, one of the most resonant voices was that of Immanuel Kant, whose moral philosophy informs much of what we discuss in this chapter. This is not merely a philosophical matter, inasmuch as this very debate resounds daily in the political sphere.

Perhaps it is most fitting to begin with an actual situation, and see how these theoretical considerations manifest themselves in real and immediate ways. Not long ago, some students took to interviewing residents from a housing complex that was adjacent to a vigorous and particularly noisy construction project to expand the complex. In these interviews, the researchers sought out the residents who lived closest to the construction site and spoke with them about the nuisance that the construction posed to their daily life. More than this, they spoke about the good and bad, as well as the right and wrong of the project — in other words, they sought to have the residents form judgments.

Here are two excerpts from the resident interviews.

> ...So, it is not like I am bearing the burden now so I can reap the rewards later. I am bearing the burden now so that I can bear the burden now. There is not victory for me. I don't get to reap any

benefits from the construction at all. It is not like — OK, you put up with the construction like in the case of maybe they are building a movie theater right next door to your house. The value of your house will go up. Usually what is the case is that more construction means that the value of the area is going up. Well, that doesn't matter to me at all. I won't even be around in three years.

…The problem now is that I get angry when I hear it and that it brings out emotions and maybe it is even worse than the first time I heard it. Because now, every time I hear it, it is just like me feeling powerless because I cannot stop the construction and when I try to sign a petition it has almost no effect. So I think the real problem is that I feel unlistened to. And if the university had handled it in a way where I felt like we were making progress and it was really getting quieter or the hours were getting better or they were just far more respectful, then I feel like I would almost be OK with it. But now it is even worse because uh, because it makes me so angry to hear it, so I play music.

As can readily be seen above, both statements can be classified under the category of judgment; however, they are also strikingly different. The student should try to plumb the nature of their difference. Is it merely in terms of grammatical form, emphasis, accent, or emotion, or is there a fundamental difference in the ground of their substance and their very logic?

In fact, we can recognize in the first statement that same ethic, cognitive framework, and logic that we encountered in the utilitarian model. What is the nature of its logic? As we had discussed before, we find unmistakable elements, including comparability, choice, and commensurability. The last element is the most obvious. The student, at this point, is asked to hold out both hands, palms out, and pretend that she or he is comparing the weight of, on the left, a grapefruit, and, on the right, a small coconut. Now imagine the mental equivalent of this exercise — whenever a person does this mental calculus, we are well inside the territory of the utilitarian. Note, too, the ever-present element of choice. By itself, a situation, e.g., things as they are, goes nowhere in an analysis. What is needed is something to compare it against and to spur a choice. When this happens, the situation becomes an alternative, and we are well on our way toward the maximizing (or, as some philosophers might say, optimific) the operation of choice.

Now, consider excerpt number two and ponder how fundamentally different this type of statement is. The student would do well to begin, even at this point, sketching out the elements found in these types of statements correlative to the elements (such as comparability) found in the classic model. Comparative analysis begins by getting a deeper sense that two things are indeed different. The second step involves judging how different they are and considering the different reasons that they seem fundamentally different. Personally, I favor the use of the mental exercise. Whereas in the classic model, we find the analyst imagining the balancing exercise, what sort of exercise is the analyst doing in the second case? Try this mental picture. In the second case, the analyst is not juggling the grapefruit and coconut, trying to sense which one impresses on one's hands more than the other. The analyst is not, with eyes closed, trying to simply compare the pressing of fruit upon palm, left versus right. I say, with eyes closed, deliberately to make the point that to do this comparative exercise one need not even look at the fruit, or smell or taste them, or even know what they are (which we would not if we closed our eyes). The only relevant dimension is that single one — the pressing of weight upon our palm.

In the second situation, I picture the analyst as taking a completely different stance. Here, the analyst looks at a fruit — and, in this case, there is only one of them — not just from one vantage point, but from every which direction. She tastes it, inquires about it and basically tries to understand the nature of that fruit. What is the analyst doing, and why this studious reflection? Basically, the analyst needs to attempt to thoroughly understand this object, in whatever way seems meaningful because the operation is no longer a simple comparison but a rendering of judgment on the object as it stands on its own. To be able to judge an object in absolute not comparative terms, we ought to understand it.

Coming back to the interviews, we might say that some of the ways that the second excerpt differs from the first include the following. First, the nature of the operation is not that of comparison, and hence choice, but one of moral discernment. If there is some lingering sense of comparison, it is not with equals but with some external, absolute measuring stick. In simplest terms, whereas the first operation involves descriptives like "better" or "worse," the second involves notions such as "right" or "wrong." Whereas the relevant dimension of analysis in the first case is simply whatever the plane of comparison happens to be to the exclusion of all else, in the second, the relevant property is the nature of the phenomenon itself. There is another fundamental difference. Utilitarianism is a consequentialist mode of analysis that seeks out what end results occur as a result of an action. In contrast, the second mode of thought, which we refer to from this point onward as ethical, focuses on the action or object itself as being right or wrong.

Which of these models one chooses to employ has great policy implications. As a practical matter, in the housing example, one may be led to a policy of compensated damages on the one hand or toward absolute damage avoidance on the other. The ethicist will claim that some situations are inherently right or wrong, while the utilitarian will posit that everything is commensurable, that, at some point, increasing some dimension of good in one situation (like compensation) can eventually allow one alternative to overtake another on the calculus of merit. "Everyone has their price," as they say. We do not question which mode of judgment people employ — evidently, as evinced in the housing interviews, people are seen to be employing all of them. What is more relevant for us is to ask which mode of analysis suits our policy analytic.

As a way of introducing the discourse surrounding these topics, we posit another example and two more quotes related to it. The situation involves what is known as risk analysis, which means judging what — environmental or other — risks to human health and life should be allowed. Consider a more specific situation involving the decision of a transportation agency whether to raise the speed limit to 80 mph. If they do, then experts predict that an additional 20 lives a year will be lost as a result of collisions. At the same time, however, the same experts predict that the decreased travel times will save society $2 billion a year throughout the state. Now, consider two contrasting rationales used to argue either side of the issue.

Life cannot be priced.

Like it or not, we are making a trade-off.

Rather than having such an argument take place for as long as the parties are willing to argue, perhaps it will help to recognize that the two statements above constitute two very different modes of reasoning. Recognizing this, we wonder whether it is futile to allow people have such an argument given the possibility that there may be no way to reconcile these two modes of reasoning, to fold them into a common plane of understanding, or to judge which one is more correct.

Foundations

Deontology
We briefly return to Kant, who in large part, wrote in response to the empiricists of his day. Among these empiricists were strong proponents of consequentialism, including Locke, Hume, and Bentham. Kant forwarded a notion that we have by now covered in various ways: There is something

about an act itself, irrespective of its consequences, that speaks to the rightness or wrongness of it. That is, normative ethics must be able to judge an action in and of itself. However, what determines the normative or moral worth of an action? According to Kant, it is surely not the pleasure produced by its results because examples abound where the sum total of pleasure fails to erase the immorality of a wrong action.

Rather, rightness derives from the maxim or principle on which an action is based. This leads us to the secondary, but equally important, question of what maxims are right? For some, moral rightness derives from the norms or standards for behavior and thought that evolve in a time and place — they may be specific to one's generation, place, or culture. To Kant and other deontologists, however, the right maxims depend on one's ability to universalize them. That is, if we can find those founding principles that can be adopted by all reasonable people, then these are maxims on which to base our decisions. For Kant, this was expressed in the categorical imperative, which he provided in three different forms, but all of which basically recommended a principle only on condition that it be something that might be universalized or extended to all. Thus a white lie, though temporarily wrong, that can bring about a large temporary gain, might be rejected by the deontologist on the ground that to allow one to break such a principle could not be universalized because if everyone were free to break the principle of truth telling at will, then the entire system of communication and integrity of communication would break down. The white lie would not work since there would be no foundation of credibility within which a white lie could possibly take effect (because to be a white lie, it must be believable).

At any rate, the deontologist posits that behavior should be based on a system of rules. Consider the departure from the utilitarian model, in which the determinant of action is to be found in some measure of value, which one seeks to maximize. In the normative realm, rules are not subject to valuation, such that a rule might be "overruled" by some good of great value. Some posit the absoluteness of rules, but many ethicists do not maintain strict absoluteness. However, the point is that rule-based systems are not subject to the same weighing operation that we find with value-based systems. The question here is the compatibility of an action with a rule. Perhaps, in some cases, we can think of degrees of compatibility, but this is a secondary point. The main question is whether our thoughts and actions are deliberately in alignment with moral principles. The focus of the deontological is on the nature and motivation of an act itself in contrast to the teleological (e.g., utilitarianism), which focuses on the end result of an action.

How do we recognize a moral principle when we encounter one? One simple way is to judge whether a statement can be phrased in the form of a classic if–then syllogism, although moral principles cannot always be put in this form so easily. With regard to the previous examples, we posit a few:

> We cannot trade away life for income. Accordingly, if the proposed speed limit will result in any additional loss of life, then we must reject it.
> No citizen must be excluded from the right of suffrage. That is, if a person is a citizen, then she or he must be allowed to vote.
> Everyone must get water of potable quality. That is, if a person receives water from the public utility, then its total bacterial count must be below the cutoff.
> No person must be treated as merely a means to an end. That is, if someone is a person, then she or he must be afforded an absolute dignity that is priceless.

The last statement, which is a restatement of the categorical imperative, illustrates how awkward it can sometimes be to insist that we state a principle as a syllogism. However, it is useful to be able to use the form of the syllogism because it readily allows the positing of conditions. Whether we maintain a rule as an absolute or not, every rule applies to a set of conditions.

In a classic decision situation, rules are used to drive the decision makers to the right answer. These are of immediate application to innumerable situations, but some fairly common ones include:

> Decisions regarding human health or life
> Decisions regarding quality of life or standards of living
> Decisions regarding basic rights

These decisions are, so far, all fairly standard areas where one might expect moral arguments to hold sway. However, what about the more mundane, and common, instances of policy — situations such as the siting of a new correctional facility, the design of a flood protection system, or electricity rate restructuring? Consider the example of water supply provision. Surely, a reasonably capable community would insist that the water supplied be of such a quality as not to make anyone sick. However, the water supply provider insists that determining the "healthiness" or lack thereof of water is not couched in absolutes. There is a sliding scale of quality of water within which a treatment plant may choose to operate, a reasonably large range of which almost no one would ever conceivably get seriously ill from drinking the water. The water purveyor will also say that no matter how great a treatment system is built, someone, somewhere, sometime will inevitably get sick from the water. In this situation, the provider would say that any of a large range of choices would still basically comply with the principle of keeping people healthy and still not tell us what exactly our standard should be. In these situations, the utilitarian model has more obvious answers to this problem since it is inherently based on gradations of value and comparing even the finely differentiated. Normative ethics, on principle, does not work by such systems of valuation.

Toward the end of the chapter, we return to the question of commensurability, inasmuch as utilitarians would object to rules as being essentially absolute goods, and many people would object to the existence of any absolutes. We take this up at a later point and discuss how, even if the absolute primacy of a rule were not maintained, this need not be an insurmountable problem for policy analysis.

However, for now, we comment that normative ethics still has a wide range of applicability, even in the gray areas of policy. It is clear that a principle, no matter how noble, will be broken in situations where society could not possibly meet it. This need not be limited to matters of earth-shaking proportions. For example, I do believe that every student in my department deserves her or his own office and computer — believe me, I really do. However, my department, which I equate with society in my myopic universe, cannot afford this at the moment or, possibly, at any foreseeable moment this century. But the question becomes, what is the best we can provide even with the resources we have at hand? What sort of rules might result from a normative approach? In the case of the water purveyor, it might consist of so-called defeasible rules, or rules that are subject to particular conditions that, though not universal, allow one to make moral judgments that hold in particular contexts. Again, using the form of the syllogism, a system of defeasible rules might appear as follows.

If we cannot supply water that is 100% clean, 100% of the time, then we can at least postulate the following system of secondary rules:

1. If we can build a system to prevent, all of the time, fatal illness so long as it is run properly and environmental conditions are normal, then we should provide this without hesitation.
2. If we can create a fund to deal with disease outbreaks, in case these occur, and some insurance fund for caring for anyone shown to have gotten ill because of the water supply, then we should do so.

3. If we can create a system for monitoring both customer health and satisfaction and for allowing periodic forums within which we can confer with the customers regarding the level of service, then we should do so.

This then leads to further systems of defeasible rules. For example, rule 1 might translate to the employment of, just for example's sake, a multistage filtration and disinfection system that, in all the laboratory tests done with it, has never been found to allow potentially fatal waterborne vectors of disease to get through. Doubtless, some microbiologist could easily make the claim that under some conditions, sometime over the next hundred years, some vectors will get through just by sheer probability. However, we are not necessarily dealing with absolute principles anymore, and normative ethics merely motivates us to search for reasonably practical principles that allow us to maintain the spirit of even higher-order (if not absolute) rules that can work for specific times and places.

Virtue

Aristotle and some later authors espoused a different type of normative ethic altogether. In his formulation, what mattered was not so much the nature or even consequence of an action, but rather the nature of the actor herself or himself. The focus of the analysis is that of the policy agent, specifically the characteristics of some standard of moral or other personal development or, in Aristotle's terminology, *eudaimonia* or human flourishing.

> We may remark, then, that every virtue or excellence both brings into good condition the thing of which it is the excellence and makes the work of that thing be done well: e.g. the excellence of the eye makes both the eye and its work good; for it is the excellence of the eye that we see well…Therefore, if this is true in every case, the virtue of man also will be the state of character which makes a man good and which makes him do his own work well.

> Aristotle, 350 B.C.

See Hardie (1981) and MacIntyre (1983) for a related discussion.

In contrast to deontological or teleological theories, virtue ethics focuses not on the action but on the agent of the action. The motivation for noble action, then, according to virtue ethics, is not primarily the happiness to be derived from it, not primarily the obligation one has to do it, but rather, the positive nature of the quality of nobility itself. We do noble acts to be noble.

Virtue is actually a strong component in policy discourse, though it may be masked as other things. First, we note that just as one can seek virtuous qualities from an individual, by extension one can seek other virtues from groups of individuals, organizations, even programs. The extension is not a simple expansion of the virtue to encompass the group, however. Take, for example, the common store of charity that one finds in individuals and families, whether it is charity to one's neighbors or to the stranger, and contrast this with the self-seeking behavior of nation-states that represent these same magnanimous individuals. The nation-state, even when engaging in acts of charity, very often does so with self-interest in mind. While the virtues may differ when we change our scale of analysis, the operation of virtue ethics moves the same way. We can posit qualities that desirable institutions should have, and these can and do have a great sway on policy decisions. Contrast the dichotomy that new institutionalists sometimes foist in front of states when calling for reform (Table 7.1).

The discourse goes on to posit reform as an embedding of the characteristics in the right-hand column (or, perhaps left-hand column, depending on one's ideological leanings). This is exactly the operation of virtue-based ethics where rather than focus on programs and actions, one begins with the idealized qualities of the desired institution. The list in Table 7.1 is quite commonly found in the development field. As another example, Schneider and Ingram discuss how, increasingly, institutions can and should be deliberately designed to exhibit greater degrees of democracy (Schneider and Ingram, 1997).

The question is: How do we employ these virtues in the everyday decisions that confront policymakers? How does a consideration of long-run characteristics help us in short-run decisions? The first thing we should note is that these virtues, whether personal or organizational, can translate into practices. Just as the goal of charitable behavior gives us guidelines for everyday actions, so too does the institutional virtue give one an agenda for decision making, even in the short run. We observe how each of these

Table 7.1 Dichotomy of institutional types

State-Centered Institutions	Decentralized Institutions
Top-down	Bottom-up
Authoritarian	Democratic
Technocratic	Participatory
Secretive	Transparent
Hierarchical	Entrepreneurial

virtues (left-hand column) readily leads to corresponding norms (right-hand column):

Participative	Empowerment
Decentralization	Capacity building

which then readily translate into sets of practices. For example, within the theme of capacity building in the case of, for example, an urban nonprofit service organization, the following tasks, among others, might follow: organizing skills development, computer literacy, paralegal training, accounting, and administrative training. A focus on virtue-based criteria can often translate very readily into programmatic details. To take another example, consider the recent attempts at building transnational institutions around transboundary issues such as pollution, trade, labor, and others. One author posits the virtues of transnational institutions shown in Table 7.2 (Benvenisti, 2002).

These institutions might, in turn, lead to very specific directions in everyday policymaking. For example, consideration of new information database systems might be delegated to the national or local information management agencies to design, in accordance with a principle of subsidiarity. In marine protection programs, decisions on requirements for improved fishing gear for the artisanal fishers might lead to establishing direct links with local fisher's groups and a call for dialogue on policy options.

The danger, in fact, is in reifying norms such that one posits actual material resources that may or may not really exist. Consider the virtue of

Table 7.2 Characteristics of effective transnational institutions

Subsidiarity	Delegation of responsibility to the lowest possible institution in the vertical hierarchy of institutions
Autonomy	Ability to engage in deliberation, analysis, and policymaking independently of the participating national governments
Supremacy	Legal primacy of international conventions and agreements over domestic policy
Information sharing	Capacities for joint data gathering and dissemination
Participativeness	Existence of linkages with other levels of governance, particularly from civil society and local communities

Adapted from Benvenisti, Eyal. 2002. *Sharing transboundary resources: International law and optimal resource use.* Cambridge: Cambridge University Press.

community, a reified notion in itself, which translates into a notion that strong community links might create a store of so-called social capital. Social capital, in this author's view, is most properly understood as a virtue, but this too easily translates into a norm that may be reified into some idea of actual, usable capital. It is almost as if, through communitarianism, a store of almost bankable capital were created. However, the virtue of communitarianism is valued in and of itself, not with an eye to an end such as, in its bluntest form, capital formation. In one recent project, the author was surprised to learn that in a dense lower-income community that lay within not even a square mile more than 20 NGOs (nongovernmental organizations) existed. Surely, this was a strong indication of social capital and moreover, a store of endogenous wealth that a project proponent might utilize. However, we saw, at the same time, that community ties notwithstanding, the community was wrought with institutional and infrastructural breakdown, local experiments at cooperative income generation had ceased, and civic pride was long since gone. An attempt at a community sanitation program was met by some residents with unbridled derision. This experience reminded us that however positive community ties were, they were not enough to pull a poor community through hard times. It may or may not constitute a store of potentially employable resources that the community might actually utilize. It was not, most of all, capital as commonly understood.

In the real world of policy, of course, form and content are impossible to separate. In choosing a different mode of deliberation, the very content of what constitutes ethical judgments will invariably change. To change our focus from rule systems to that of program characteristics may allow us to broach a discussion of policies not in terms of which rules are most correct, but to the question of whether a program, as presently defined, adequately captures who a group understands itself to be. This can allow a broadening of the scope of the policy question beyond the specifics of its operative rules to that of the integrity and meaning of the program *en toto*. Thus, the group may find itself in a position to begin discussing whether its very functions are the right ones to be pursuing, i.e., moving from the question of "Are we doing this right?" to that of "Is this the right thing to be doing?"

The notion of virtues is mirrored, to some extent, by the early phenomenologist's theories of value (Husserl, 1900; Scheler, 1957). To these phenomenologists, personal cognition of good in things in this world reflected objective qualities of goodness that inhered in these things themselves. However, our approach to the realization of goodness stems from an integrated experience of these moral judgments, entailing intuition, desire, affect, and attitude. Though these inclinations may register as subjective phenomena, they nevertheless point to an objective content of goodness that the person can recognize but does not create.

Contrast this to the Kantian notion of the normative as stemming from pure formal considerations — in other words, the legislative function of rules that act regardless of the content of the application. In the Kantian formulation, rightness originates precisely apart from the action of inclination and, even in a phenomenological sense, is most recognizable in those circumstances when the juridical most completely deviates from the attitudinal. Whereas Kant posits the universality of a rule as the very origin of ethics, the early phenomenologists recognized universal acceptance as the consequence of will being closely aligned with the objective nature of goodness. When the phenomenologist is confronted with the apparent subjectivism in this position, the question is resolved by appeal to a teleological personalism that posits the existence of an ideal for personhood. While phenomenologists would agree with Kant in the notion of the person as an ultimate end in herself or himself, this ultimate dignity inheres not in the person's rationality but in her or his unique personhood. Morality then consists in the person responding authentically to the core of values found in his or her very being — an ideal that is necessarily hidden. It is only when one insists on constraining value and good to the unidimensional plane of the intellect that this equates with a Kantian insistence on the universalizability of any ethical rule. For the phenomenologist, goodness is something that we continuously strive to become, without undue concern that this notion of the ideal community of persons or good be something that we might actually define, but instead, merely experience.

Is there any hope for agreement on our normative ground? For the phenomenologist, this is about as possible as that of all persons being able to attain some ground of authenticity. But there is room in this construct for dialogue. To later writers like Levinas (1961), influenced by phenomenology, morality originates from each person having to respond authentically to the other's moral claim on one's self: Without recognizing the other person's necessary incursion into my personal freedom, I realize a moral requirement to respond to the other person.

Unlike the requirement of strict deontological universality in the Kantian construction, there is an easier connection between this sort of teleological perfectionism to working practices in the policy realm. Freed from the formal requirement to universalize, the policy maker is allowed to pursue evolving sets of norms that are compatible with the inclinations of diverse sets of stakeholders without bearing the entire weight of universal assent. Unlike Kantian ethics, however, this comes up against the strong notion of policy as rulemaking or the creating of blanket prescriptions that are, by design, to be universalized. To focus upon some hidden essence of virtue instead of systems of rules is to pursue policies that tend toward reasonable directions — these policies may be types or sets of rules rather than specific rules themselves, which can be problematic in a policy setting in which policy is understood as regulation. Policy might even be construed not as rule systems but as ideal characteristics that leave their exact translation into specific prescriptions undefined.

Though not formally related to the phenomenological school, feminist ethics, like the phenomenologists, involves a focus on the attitudes found in the person. In particular, by contradicting the strong dichotomous logic of rationalist theories (including Kantian ethical theory), feminist theories undo the rigid structuring of the subject–object duality. What this means is movement away from deontological systems with their rigid rationalist–universalist system of rules, which amount to an objectification of a community of persons into passive bearers of justice. In the deontological system of ethics, one is often led to a strongly allocative notion of justice. In feminist theory, on the other hand, equity is embodied not in an impersonal system of rules but in an ethic of care — i.e., an attitudinal predisposition of a person to establish and nurture relationships with others (persons, nature, etc.). By eschewing the juridical, feminist ethics tend less toward allocative logics and more toward a virtue ethics that places primacy on the denial of formal division and structuration with the aim of establishing interrelational patterns of caring, pathos, and integration. The notion is that structuration, and its rigid divisions, engender domination (since hierarchization necessitates a top and a bottom). One cannot comment on the feminist ethic of care without noticing at least some connection to phenomenological (specifically Heideggerian) ontologies of being as caring — i.e., the consideration of the potentialities of relation between self and things in the world that constitutes the structure of understanding or disposition toward others (Heidegger, 1927). Heidegger, unlike the earlier phenomenologists, did not eschew the Kantian notion of subjecting one's self to the primacy of the law as an ultimate realization of independence or being, except that this results not from a need for rationality but from the authenticity that comes from a proper consideration of being as caring (Heidegger, 1927). At any rate, caring, whether in the feminist or phenomenological mold, involves the nurturing of proper relationships between self and others and the world.

Virtue ethics involve more than a simple enumeration of virtues but an explication of how behavior and institutions should be arranged in accordance with these virtues.

Justice

Justice is most commonly understood as the notion of "just desserts" or the bestowing on a person what he or she deserves. Furthermore, "dessert" may be understood as constitutive, i.e., being a member of society or some other grouping, or as a result of some notion of merit. In general, dessert is operationalized in terms of either membership in a group or community, or through an action by the potential recipient or other agent linked to the recipient. This, of course, gives rise to other questions regarding how one defines a community or how one determines membership. The underlying logic, however, is one of similitude: Things that are alike should be treated in like manner, and, conversely, things that are different should be treated differently. This then ripples outward onto further questions, such as what dimensions of "likeness" are morally relevant versus inadmissible or how is likeness defined and operationalized.

Part of the answer is that, more often than not, we cannot simply resolve to find absolutes but rather perhaps context-specific or even contingent "absolutes." Consider the issue of suffrage, a right that has been bestowed according to membership in relevant groups, but the relevant categories are those which are morally pertinent to the generation in question. When we consider how only recently (i.e., twentieth century) the right to suffrage has been extended to groups such as women and people of color in countries such as the United States, we realize the need to reflect on the moral underpinnings of society. The realization by society that the present way is more morally just involves a claim that, gradually, society has opened up to deeper truths. However, standards may not be considered absolute either. It may well be that a generation from now society may come to realize that an even broader definition of membership may be recognized (e.g., extending suffrage to youth, which is found already in some countries or to noncitizens who contribute to society, etc.).

What is most important for this chapter is when and how considerations of justice can be explicitly brought into policy deliberations, and the instances or situations wherein the notion of justice as dessert can come into conflict with other normative constructs, such as a deontological fashioning of human rights. For example, associating admission into primary school with some merit-based criterion such as performance on standardized tests immediately violates societal norms of the basic human right to education and equality of opportunity.

How can standards for claims of justice be determined? Ostensibly, but not simply, through broad, open discussions, a community should hope to approach some understanding of what standards or rights the society identifies itself with. Note the use of the word "to identify" and the deliberate avoidance of the phrase "to opt for" since it is not clear that the issue of determining standards for justice is a choice as classically understood. It may be better described as a translation of the term as we understand it in our persons and society into rules and institutions. By developing a notion of a universal right to education, we express our self-understanding as persons of inherent dignity, wherein dignity extends to the development of our capacities. By developing standards for progression along a professional path that are based on criteria for dessert (such as productivity), we express our self-understanding as autonomous agents who have the freedom to actualize goals and aspirations or to seek further progress along an individual path. Some have equated this process with choice, however. In particular, Rawls posits a choice by a reasonable individual from the so-called original position (Rawls, 1971). From this position, we transpose our social position into a stance set behind a veil of ignorance, behind which we do not know what our eventual position will be in the ideal society that we are imagining. From this original position, we are then to ask about the structuring of institutions so as to bring about the state that is most desirable to us. In a sense, this is an attempt to combine the notion of preferences from Bentham and the notion of universalism from Kant. At any rate, Rawls contends that from this accounting stance, the individual will opt for a social contract that is protective of the least well-off in society because there is a real chance that the individual may end up being the least well-off. There is also, strongly implicit in this judgment, a notion that we are fundamentally risk averse (such that the negative prospect of being the CEO of the world's largest software firm is outweighed by the negative prospect of possibly being the stricken refugee from a war-ravaged society). From this position, the contract is said to consist of the following:

1. The establishment of rights and liberties to the maximum that can be extended to all
2. The arrangement of institutions so as to result in the greatest possible benefit to the least well-off, a solution concept reminiscent of von Neumann's max–min rule

The point to made, however, for policy deliberation, the deliberate focus is on the eventually agreed upon principles and not a consequentialist focus on the end results. It should be sufficient to recommend the principles in and of themselves. Otherwise, it is possible to merely utilize the principles, or to fashion them deliberately simply to bring about a desired end result such as the maintenance of the status quo. How is one to avoid the recursion into consequences? Ironically, in many cases, it may require the explicit consideration of consequence. Rather than avoid talk of end results and to attempt to have these determine the policy discussions "on the sly," the more effective deliberation may require the direct consideration of consequence. The reason for this is, that everyone should engage in the discussion in full awareness of its possible results and "misconstruals," and, moreover, that outcomes do matter and do bring dimensionality and substance to our understanding of a normative claim. It is part of bringing squarely into the analysis considerations of the here and now, the immediacy of action, and the corporeality of change.

In addition to these ethical theories that we have discussed, there are several others that should be noted. Elsewhere in this book, we encounter the work of Gilligan and others who have studied an alternative mode of ethical reasoning based on the ethic of care (e.g., Gilligan, 1982). Gilligan, herself, couched her original work as a response to the strongly deontological model of moral reasoning used by Kohlberg and others (e.g., Kohlberg, 1981). We also note a body of work on communitarian ethics (e.g., Walzer, 1990), which poses a strong counterpoint to the radically atomistic concept of the utility-maximizing individual, especially as found in the liberal model of the person.

Policy Application

In previous chapters, we have seen how classic policy analysis has created systematic methods for constructing alternatives and making choices between these same alternatives so as to routinely allow both programmatic and project-specific judgments. There is, of course, some advantage to the rational model's ability to discern values to any exactitude required. In contrast, rule-based or virtue-based ethical approaches tend to maintain some level of generality. After all, a rule is meant to be applied with some generality, otherwise it would not be a rule but an idiosyncrasy. The policy analyst may wonder how does positing the normative standard of egalitarianism help her or him divine how much to budget for recreation and how much to budget for street sweeping next fiscal year? The movement from the realm of principle to that of the particular may not be an obvious one.

However, normative systems have advantages as well. Rules and virtues can embody in their substance real practices that can lead to institution building without having to focus on results that, in the case of programmatic actions, may be impossible to predict anyway. Consider the prospect of creating fundamental changes in curricula in public schools, e.g., a new series of courses on civic mindedness, and then consider the impossible task that the utilitarian faces in trying to divine the consequences of different decisions over the succeeding generations. In fact, consequences in this case are unfathomable, and a strict utilitarian analysis is impossible. And yet, these types of programmatic decisions are readily and, we might suggest, necessarily treated in normative terms. Standards allow for consistency and, more than this, a consistent normative foundation that longstanding institutions eventually develop. In contrast, standards are not even possible, strictly speaking, under classical theory because consequences of institutional qualities are case-specific and so can only be evaluated on a case-by-case basis.

Normative approaches can be useful even in the classic situations that seem to be inherently suited to decision–theoretic analysis. Take the case of designing a new public transportation system for a city. The rational model would posit a range of alternatives, evaluate each for performance vis-à-vis a number of key outcomes such as cost and travel time, and come up with summary valuations of each alternative. This procedure is intimately connected with the process of choosing one alternative public transport system. However, normative considerations can help a polity decide on a suitable public transportation system as well. Community norms would be proposed that directly rule out some possible modalities and direct society toward other specific solutions. As an example, we might find the following norms to emerge from the process:

Standard 1: All families below the poverty line should have access to public transportation.

Standard 2: No individual should need to walk more than 15 minutes, one way, from their home to the depot or waiting shed.

Standard 3: Frequency of service over different areas of the city should be proportional to the density of the customer base in these different areas.

Standard 4: No person should have to wait more than 15 minutes at a bus stop.

In fact, these types of norms can have an exceedingly large amount of input to offer the policy process. In many cases, the process does not even need an exacting comparison of alternative solutions. As discussed previously, in the majority of cases, the operative question is really not which one specific alternative is the best, but rather whether we can come up with a solution that gives us what we need, will last indefinitely, and will satisfy most or all of the customers. In fact, an inordinate focus on maximization of some value through choice may preclude the necessary attention that should be paid to setting up the conditions (public receptivity, financial sustainability, etc.) that will ensure the longevity of any solution on the ground. It may be that the major portion of an analysis may, as it turns out, only need to be devoted to establishing principles and norms for program design.

Yet, we have to address the question of how one goes about constructing systems of standards and norms by which to design an institution. They do not, of course, emerge like a rabbit out of a top hat. Neither can we assume that they lie in dormant state because latent principles that are embedded in the life of a community need only be unearthed by the policy process. In general, we desire to establish deliberative systems in a policy context within which explorations regarding community norms might be conducted. Would norms then emerge from this process in the manner of a negotiated result or as a compromise resulting from a process like mutual partisan adjustment, wherein policy actors engage in a multidirectional tug of war, and through their individual bargaining efforts, move the ring toward some happy mean. This may be so. In general, however, we can understand deliberative systems to be those forums within which a community of policy actors can learn, jointly, which values, priorities, and understandings they have in common, and work out reasonably adequate resolutions even in those areas where people may differ. The result is a set of principles that the community of policy actors has committed to keep. The questions asked are: What do we stand for, or what can we resolve to stand for, even provisionally? It can involve the realization or, in other cases, the working out of the meaning and vision of a community.

The question may come up, however, that, "Yes, it is all well and good to agree on what we stand for, but tell me, what do we do exactly?" This last question does bring up a real issue in that often we may find ourselves short of a program. Consider the, by now, familiar mantra of participation. When construed as an organizational virtue, we do understand it as a desirable thing in and of itself. However, when posited as not just a virtue, but the basic teleology of the organization, i.e., participation is the goal of the program, then we run the risk of falling into the trap of pursuing form over substance. The goal of a participative community planning program is not merely to attain participation, but to achieve improvements in community life, amenities, employment, and others. In fact, treating some such virtue as participation as the holy grail of a program can lead to converse results (Cooke and Kothari, 2002). When engaging community in a process — for example, a collaborative workshop, focus group, or design charrette — this teleology can result in the analyst's sole preoccupation being the participative. Moreover, this too easily leads to an obsession with the idealized pure form of participation, which is never seen in actual practice and which is often merely a discursive device. Every now and then, I come across a community process wherein the organizers bemoan eventualities like sparse attendance, a low ratio of women to men, a predominance of representation from one income or age bracket, or the absence of youth, leading those who actually took the time to attend to wonder whether they were, indeed, chopped liver. In such a situation, the hegemony of the formal notion of a virtue like participation has succeeded in, ironically, alienating and disrespecting the community that participation was supposed to engage in the first place. In this manner, a focus on virtues instead of actions can too easily lead to a predilection for the formal as opposed to the actual. However, virtues are realized not in form, but in action. In similar fashion, a focus on rules and standards can lead a community to the merely formal assemblage of principles without thought to actual practice. However, rules and standards are meant for translation into real practices in real instances and, in fact, are not meaningful outside the discerning lens of action. It is in this spirit that our analysis must maintain its footing in the here and now — in other words, in policy action.

As a set of analytics, normative considerations leads to a number of questions that the analyst should bring into a situation. The following is an example of a structure of policy questions that can be used to drive the analysis.

1. Standards

   Does the policy have elements within it that can be considered in the light of providing a minimum standard of quality for those affected by the policy?

   Can we begin discussing what levels of quality the policy can ensure at this point in time and what degrees of quality we can aspire to in the future?

   Can we express these standards in the form of rules?

   Can we have a discussion of how these (explicit or implicit) rules might be constructed?

   Is there a hierarchy of values that the policy needs to consider, and how are different values prioritized in this situation?

2. Distribution

   What is the distribution of costs, benefits, opportunities, obligations, and others, associated with the policy?

   Are burdens and gains inequitably distributed?

   Should the policy have a redistributive component?

3. Structural Relationships

> Does the policy foster a structure of sociopolitical relationships that privilege some groups or individuals and systematically marginalize others?
>
> How does the policy create this structuring?
>
> Does the policy undo existing social structures and privilege the presently disenfranchised?
>
> Does the policy give enough consideration for the situation of different stakeholders?
>
> Does the policy reflect virtues of care and empowerment?

4. Process

> Does the policy allow access of all concerned to the policy process?
>
> Does the policy create additional support for participation or representation of the traditionally underrepresented?

Compare the previous set of analytic questions to the one-dimensional focus of rational model, the latter being summed up in the one question, "Do benefits outweigh the costs of a policy?" In other words, while the sharp analytic of the rational model leads easily to a systematic operational definition of efficiency, the less sharply defined model of ethics provides a richer analytic ground of policy questions around which to focus the analysis. Consider, also, that the previous framework can lead to further questioning. For example, the question pertaining to possible needs for ordering values (or hierarchization) is one possible way of systematically addressing conflicting priorities. In an examination of a university's affirmative action admissions policies, for example, we will find ourselves having to grapple with a number of overlapping, sometimes conflicting, value considerations, for example:

> The value of formal or procedural equality in the admissions process
> The value of substantive equality of access to education
> The value of redress of historical or societal misdeeds
> The value of education as a way to empower the disenfranchised
> The value of social and intellectual diversity on campus

Normative deliberation entails asking questions to discern the nature of a group of individuals or an organization, i.e., what do its members and the group stand for? This can lead to a kind of deliberation that is foundational in the sense that the members find themselves engaging in discussions regarding the very identity of the group or program. The practical question is whether this might not, in fact, preclude the consideration of specific actions. When a discussion entails the virtues of an open and civil society, at what point can people actually take up specific yet important matters such as the purchase of ballot boxes for the upcoming election? If, at every meeting, the neighborhood committee decides to waffle tirelessly about the universe, will anybody ever move onto deciding whom to hire to trim the hedges? The point we should make is that deliberation need not devolve into sloganeering. At this point, we need to bring in a distinction between the ethical discourse we are considering and the phenomenon that constitutes the endless committee. The difference is that normative thought is not, by definition and certainly should not by practice, be divorced from action. Whether one engages in rulemaking of the deontological type or character building of the virtue–ethical type, rules and norms are meant to be immediately relevant and perceptible in the plane of action. The question then becomes: What actions and programs cohere with our system of values, virtues, and morals?

There is another reason why normative talk need not devolve into endless generality: Rules and norms embody in their very nature thick sets of practices. This is the reason why the notion of "grassroots" empowerment is not merely a slogan but a directive for a complex set of actions that follow suit from this primary virtue. In a sense, normative concepts are carriers for entire sets of practices. It can be, in fact, an efficient way of communicating and encapsulating a whole system of actions and programmatic activities. We have used the notion of risk to introduce various ethical concepts because risky situations almost always immediately lead to ethical considerations. Let us illustrate this with a case study on the same theme.

Case Study: Environmental Justice and Regulatory Reform Over the last two decades, a coalition of civil rights, environmental, and community-based groups in the United States has gathered around the campaign to challenge the phenomenon of environmental injustice, i.e., the coincidence of residential communities of color with environmentally undesirable land uses. For example, some earlier analyses of this issue began with tracing the locations of landfills and incinerators vis-à-vis minority communities (see USGAO, 1983; UCC, 1987; see Been and Gupta, 1997 for a more recent account). This systematic pattern of coincidence of people of color in zones affected by these types of environmental risks continues to this day despite a complex set of environmental regulations designed to reduce the exposure of people to risk. This has led to various initiatives to begin to reform both the regulation of risk and the very analysis of it. One such initiative was begun in 2003 by the U.S. Environmental Protection Agency (EPA), when it sponsored the formation of a Working Group on Cumulative Risk. In the way of a background to the movement, we trace its discourse to the language of both the environmental and civil rights movements. In the United States, the latter draws mostly from the experience of the southern black movement led by Martin Luther King and more regional movements such as the United Farm Workers movement of Cesar Chavez, Dolores Huerta, and others in California. Accordingly, it starts out with an ideology but does not remain there inasmuch as it also responds to both experienced and measured health and other outcomes that do point to real injuries to communities. By injuries, outcomes such as acute and chronic illness as well as occupational hazards come to mind, but they also include disenfranchisement from avenues of commerce, redlining of neighborhoods, and stigmatization in the public sphere.

The normative tenets embedded in the environmental justice movement involve concepts drawn from all three conceptual bases discussed herein. There is, first of all, a strong call for justice, understood both as dessert and inclusion in the process. The most obvious manifestation of environmental injustice has been the disproportionate exposure of minority communities to undesirable land uses. This notion of disproportionality has, before anything else, strong elements of the discourse of justice. However, it is not the only embedded ethic in a movement that, despite efforts to unite the front, is proving more multiplex than any one set of discourses will allow. There are commonalities even in the midst of the diversity. Another strong ethic is that of a fundamental upholding of the dignity of traditionally disenfranchised communities, not just in the sense of equality before the law, but in a stronger sense of empowerment, which means allowing the disenfranchised increased opportunities to close gaps, seek redress, and have communities progress in accelerated fashion. Strongly embedded in many of these discourses is the theme of territory inasmuch as, more than anything else, it is in the aspect of place that the disenfranchised and excluded seek to express their dignity. This is one reason that community mapping has proven to be a powerful tool in the movement. In Figure 7.1, we see one graphic illustration of how maps have been used as graphic tools to convey some of these narratives.

There are other reasons why mapping is becoming an important tool. One salient feature of it is that digital mapping allows the user many options for showing what are, more than anything else, normative claims. How are normative claims structured? We have seen some of the ways — deontological rules, for example. In most cases, these structurings can be understood as institutional gaps. For example, considerations of fundamental human rights or basic needs translate (or should translate) into standards for quality of life. Considerations of proportional justice should translate to manifestations of equitable treatment, whether in government services, opportunities, measures of quality of life, etc. In all of these, a powerful method for expression of these normative elements is to posit the

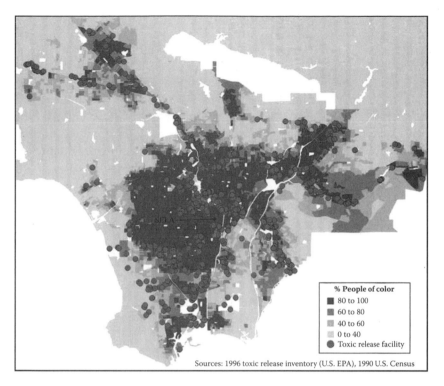

Fig. 7.1 Mapping of toxic facilities vis-à-vis demographics (Los Angeles County). From: Bansal et al. 1998. *Holding our breath: Environmental injustice exposed in southeast Los Angeles.* Huntington Park: Communities for a Better Environment.

standard or rule, analyze the existing situation or institution for the status quo, evaluate the discrepancy between the status quo and the norm, and illustrate this by various means. When these gaps manifest themselves spatially, then graphical devices like mapping can prove to be useful. As in Figure 7.1, we see that these maps are not so much representations of valuative considerations, such as utility — the layers on the map are not meant to combine like utility (i.e., one does not simply add up layers of poverty with environmental quality). We cannot conclude that these representations are simply textual devices to carry a discourse because the mapping is also a representation of fact and events that are unfolding in real time. In the way these devices are used, we could say that what the representations are speaking to is actually graphic expressions of the normative. The map in Figure 7.1 illustrates this and shows how one can utilize our cognitive ability to understand the dissonance in institutional and normative phenomena (e.g., Festinger, 1954) by graphically portraying it. In the figure, the striking counterposing of areas shaded dark gray (communities of color) and their relationships to undesirable land uses vis-à-vis other, unshaded areas and their relative dissociation from these land uses points to the lack of complete equity, as the latter would be seen by the mind's eye as a uniformity in spacing, shading, and other parameters. So the use of alternative devices for cognitive representation is one way by which normative claims can be made, especially since the valuative (e.g., utilitarian) modes of analysis have dominated traditional expert agency processes. In addition, these alternative modes of representation should be amenable to showing qualitative information because maps are particularly well suited for this task.

Another tool for normative policy analysis involves a prescription for reform, embodied in the same forms discussed earlier — rules, rights, norms, and virtues. In the case of the EPA-sponsored Working Group on Cumulative Risk, the task was to find ways to reform a long-established mode of environmental analysis. Much of the discipline of risk assessment is embodied in the positivist but, more to the point, in the same language and analytic as expected utility. In this case, risks are understood as probability — recall the conceptual tool of the lottery in chapter 3 — and outcomes are understood as expected utility, which is none other than the product of probability and utility. First of all, the policy analysis had to go beyond the structures of this analytic since one of the main contentions of the movement is that the sole reliance on it has helped disenfranchise entire communities. As we have seen before, part of the reason is the predilection of the analytic for the quantifiable, and because most environmental agents have not been studied enough to yield strong quantitative estimates of harmfulness, they end up not being included in an analysis. More to the point, many of the effects of injustice just may not be expressible in these analytic terms. We have discussed this already, and one should realize that if we ascribe to deontological reasoning, then this *a priori* is not amenable to expression in positivistic terms, e.g., recall the discussion on the valuation of human health. Probabilities, or other modes of measurement, may never be adequate to express the normative.

There are other groups studying how to address the problem of cumulative risk (e.g., USEPA, 2002). The recommendations that came out of the EPA and other committees' work can be portrayed as a set of principles, which, while one can take them at face value in merely generic terms, should lead to very specific sets of actions that stem from these principles. The recommendations are not mere goals but prescriptions for specific policy directions and should be understood as carriers for entire sets of practices that can flow from these. The recommendations from various working groups are condensed and summarized in Table 7.3.

Table 7.3 Recommendations from working groups on cumulative risk

Decisions should be based on vulnerability, defined as the susceptibility or sensitivity of communities and their differential exposure, preparedness, and ability to recover from environmental risk.

The framework for analysis, along with methodologies, should be drawn from the area of community-based participatory research.

Action should be proportionate to the needs of communities.

Qualitative information should be deliberately used in analysis and decision making.

Actions should work to also address capacity issues in communities.

The EPA and other groups should maintain a preference for action in the light of uncertainty.

These recommendations are none other than a policy analysis framed in the form of rules, norms, duties, and virtues. One way to understand this is that these policy recommendations form a framework for the reform of institutions and practices. Perhaps a more direct way of describing this type of analysis is that these normative statements are meant to embody entire sets of practices. In fact, embedded in these recommendations is a strong set of typological reforms that are should result in the practice of risk assessment and in agency decision making. Granted, the specifics of these reforms are not explicitly found in these prescriptions, but there is enough grounding in the latter to lead to real changes in practice. Perhaps a useful methodology for proceeding along this mode of analysis can be summarized below.

1. Assess the group's or community's normative foundations, and seek out common ground and important areas of differentiation in these normative foundations.

2. Express these normative foundations in narrative, descriptive, graphical, and other forms so as to encapsulate the important elements of the structure. Investigate the use of multiple modes of representations for these elements.

3. Assess the present institutional structure and the status quo vis-à-vis the normative stance and assess the degree of disparity between the status quo and the norm.

4. Create sets of recommended policy changes by seeking to "fill" in the institutional gaps wherever they are identified. The directives and prescribed measures might directly address the specific areas that the current institutional framework deviates from the desired.

5. Seek to identify and create institutional mechanisms by which these policy actions might be initiated, enacted, and made to move in the desired directions.

The last step is a crucial and often neglected one. It is a necessary element in the policy analysis and is an acknowledgment that institutions cannot be effectively changed overnight, and oftentimes the crux of the issue is how to redirect present-day institutions in the right direction and how to create possibly new mechanisms to apply a directive force to institutional change. Note that this analysis, while intimately cognizant of outcomes, is not operationally a consequentialist one. The most important task is to the creation of mechanisms for reform to be sustained and embedded in the enduring reality of a context.

The postconstructionist sentiment insists that there be, deliberately, a direct linkage of the policy analysis to action. We see some of this sentiment expressed in the normative stance represented in Table 7.3. This linkage to action first entails grounding the analysis on real situations and community experiences — hence, the employment of narrative histories and testimonies. However, it also often begs the attention of policymakers toward consideration of new institutional modalities, whether in the form of new measures to act upon or new modes of organizational interaction. The test of the analysis is that if the effort does not include deliberate attention paid to possible specific avenues for action, then perhaps the level of analysis is too monodimensional or the level of generality needs to move within a greater range. In the work of the Cumulative Risk Working Group, some specific actions are to be found even within the normative analysis. These include actions such as the identification of at least five areas to attempt to reform and the modification of the predilection for action involving a kind of grounded research that employs learning in the midst of intervention (Strauss and Glaser, 1967).

Another kind of analysis along these lines is seen in the increasingly employed instrument of sustainability indexing, which is, most often, an initiative from community groups to create new measures for assessing where a community is at and where it is going. This is also a response to agency-driven analyses that do not seem to capture the experience of the community at hand. Often, this involves discussions over what types of changes or community elements are most important or cherished by the community, and then to create systematic indices or methodologies to track these elements over time and space. Their employment as monitoring tools is itself an action. Oftentimes, however, the construction of these new indices becomes the end of the effort itself. The most common end result is that the community group mounts the indices on a Web site or publishes them in a report, but this in itself does not lead to any continuing action. To be meaningful, we must insist that the analysis deliberately enter into the identification of institutional mechanisms by which the knowledge gained through this monitoring be explicitly ingrained into mechanisms for institutional change or as new input into existing mechanisms for policy making and programmatic action. The insistence on the explicitness of the linkage to action is not a disavowal of the profound changes that can result from the very discovery of new ways of understanding or in the creation of a new way of talking about a situation. However, change also comes about through strategic intervention, and a grounded, in fact postconstructionist, mode of analysis must insist on a strategic element. In the case of community indices, the stakeholders might seek out ways by which such information be included, in a deliberate, systematic, and transparent way, into an agency's decision process. This means that it not be enough for an agency to respond by acknowledging the verity of the knowledge and resolving to make use of it. Rather, it requires an identification of mechanisms that the agency can follow to ensure this. For example, these indices might be part of a new element that is made requisite in environmental impact analysis, or part of the formal agency record in budgetary hearings, or in other ways. The important thing is the explicit identification of the mode of action. It is in this manner that normative considerations not be simply "statements of principles" but directives for action.

Further Notes on Comparability

Lastly, let us reconsider the issue of comparability. Neoutilitarians contend that, by the very fact that we make choices everyday, we implicitly assume and understand everything to be comparable. That is, when an ethicist states that there are some principles that cannot be broken, or values to which no price can be attached, the utilitarian will counter that the proof of the converse can be found in actual practice. For example, consider the principle that human life is priceless and is not subject to any compromise. Utilitarians will maintain that, even in this case, society exhibits choices that reveal some finite, commensurable valuation that people actually attach to the value of human life. What choices are these? A budget is one example. That is, the contention is that when society or its legislators pass a budget, they are actually making choices that limit expenditures on public health and other issues related to preserving human life or, similarly, avoiding the loss of life. However, budgeting is an act of distributing a finite amount of revenue among a number of issues and not sinking the entire amount into any one thing. While much will be spent on public health, emergency services, and accident prevention, not all of a budget will be spent on life-preserving issues. Instead, some of it will go to education, some to parks, and some of it to street landscaping. By this very act of allocation, society is said to be attaching some finite value to human health and life — otherwise, none of the budget would be spent on non–health-related items. At that point when society is deciding to spend no more on health and to distribute the rest of the money to other issues, it is at that marginal point that we are said to be revealing the exact monetary value that we attach to human life, and it is evidently a finite sum. In other words, there is a real trade-off being made with regard to human life and other goods, including money.

Chang generalizes the contention in this manner (Chang, 1997). Regardless of whether one is explicitly trading off money for life or some other ostensibly priceless thing, by the very act of choice, we exhibit comparability. It need not be stated in monetary terms at all. The important thing is that, when confronted with two situations, one of which might involve a priceless thing such as life, a person will always be able to make a choice by the very fact that one cannot enter into two different futures — only one scenario can come true. The individual is able to make such a choice by essentially comparing two alternative situations according to some so-called covering value. One can say that there is no comparing a painting by Van Eyck with a sculpture by Rodin but, if one were to come into a sudden horde of money and wanted to spend it, one can always decide to buy one of these. By this action, the person is said to be comparing the two works of art not in an absolute sense, but only in the limited sense of how they register on the dimension of money. The very act of choice reveals that there is some covering value by which any two situations, goods, or phenomena can be compared.

What does this do, then, to moral principles, some of which purport to be absolute? Take the principle of holding human life sacred. The budgeting example suggests that however we may consider it sacred, we will and do trade off human life for some finite amount of money. Does this negate normative ethics altogether and reduce us all to utilitarians? Some will say yes, but let us point out some reasons to think otherwise.

First of all, it is one thing to project two situations onto some plane of comparison (or covering value) and yet a very different thing to contend that this comparison pertains to their whole nature. We can compare a dross of platinum with a brick of gold according to the covering value of weight and decide that one outdoes the other, and yet it would not be saying that one is more valued than the other. To take another example, one could compare Toscanini with Rubinstein according to the speed with which either can play the minute waltz and yet have no wherewithal to judge who might be the better pianist, at least not in an absolute sense. The comparisons we make are, at best, limited, temporary comparisons made according to some provisional reason. We might want to buy one CD, and cannot buy both Toscanini's and Rubinstein's. Yet, this is not the same as saying that we actually are able to compare one pianist against another. The comparison is a tentative one, perhaps even an arbitrary one. Suffice it to say that the comparisons we make most often only look at a small aspect of a thing and not the whole thing altogether and so we really are not attaching or valuing the thing as a whole.

But what about the contention by some ethicists (but not all ethicists) that some things, like life, are priceless? Does the budgeting example suggest that nothing is an absolute good? First, it may well be that nothing is treated as an absolute in practice. Certainly, examples abound of some people's eager willingness to trade away some other people's health and lives for money — muggers do this everyday. But would any trade away their own lives? This latter question may be essentially, for most persons, an absolute good. Absolute goods are not limited to our own lives. That martyrs and saints have walked this earth attests to the fact that, for some, love of country and of God can be absolute. But this may not hold true for all. The easiest way for the ethicist to argue against the utilitarian perspective is to say that even if it were true that a person held no good to be absolute, this does not equate with comparability or commensurability either. Just because people may be willing, out of desperation, to give up a good that they would call priceless or break a moral principle that they would call paramount, as in scenes of destitute individuals willing to fight with their neighbor for a scrap of bread, does not mean that one consciously carries out the mental calculus of constantly trading off amounts of friendship for corresponding amounts of income. No, perhaps they are merely substituting one rule for another in a hierarchy of rules. The system of rules might look something like the following:

Loyalty to one's friend is a rule that should not be broken.

When, and only when, one has to break a moral rule in order to literally survive, then and only then can one consider breaking a moral code, such as loyalty to a friend.

This is a system of rules, entirely consistent with a deontological system of ethics that is entirely different from a notion of comparability (and commensurability), which involves a radically different operation, as follows:

Loyalty to one's friend is a good to which a person attaches a value equivalent to a thousand dollars per broken friendship.

Just because a rule is not absolute, or is embedded in a complex system of defeasible rules, does not mean that the operation of comparability holds. In fact, as in the previous example, it seems highly unlikely for a valuational system to have much application here. Rules can be contingent, multiplex, defeasible, applicable to certain ranges of action, hierarchical, or overlapping, without at all being subject to an operation of valuation. Recall, from chapter 2, how commensurability requires perfect comparability, i.e., the ability to compare two things regardless of how fine the comparisons were.

Policy Reflection

The recognition of the normative and moral as a fundamental basis for policy making is an important step forward in our deepening of the analytic. It allows us to explicitly tap into the most basic motivations for human thought and action.

Moreover, consideration of these dimensions helps us explain certain social phenomena. For example, Olson, in his portrayal of collective action, asks the question of why is it, given the marginal benefit a person gains or contributes through participation in a collective activity such as voting, that some people continue to participate? Using a rational choice model, Olson concludes that there must be other individual benefits from joining a group, which he calls "solidary benefits" (Olson, 1968). However, this is not a strong explanation for this type of behavior, and certainly not something that most people would point to when queried about their participation. What is missing is the normative dimension. That is, some people continue to vote — or join civic organizations, turn lost items in to the lost-and-found, recycle paper, give up their place in line, and a host of other acts — because, simply, it is, for them, the right thing to do. This is something that is not expressible as an individual benefit, except only in the most awkward way (since, sometimes, people give until it hurts and, even when it does not, individual pleasure in most of these cases is a poor descriptive for what actually happens internally). Now, some choose to expand the notion of utility to capture everything that we might identify as good — even morality as discussed previously. But this actually reduces the notion of utility to something trivial, i.e., it is whatever we maximize whenever we do anything or, in other words, if utility is everything, then it really is nothing.

The most straightforward, and probably truthful, way of handling questions of right and wrong, is to simply recognize the dimension of right and wrong explicitly. It is one of the most powerful motivations that guide human behavior (along with maternal love — but this is perhaps why

we sometimes think the latter also belongs to the moral dimension).
Clearly, policy analysis would be inadequate without a treatment of this
dimension.

So, why is it most often missing from analysis? One reason is that it
is contentious. The most moral questions are also the ones that people
disagree over the most vociferously. Perhaps partly because of the positivist's
claim to neutrality, the analyst often consciously avoids these moral traps
and keeps the analysis on the plane of "something we can all agree on."
However, this would remove that dimension of the policy question that is,
at times, the most important. To repeat: Ignoring the normative or moral
dimension in policy analysis is sometimes tantamount to reducing the
analysis to the least significant denominator. If one were to return to the
United States of the 1960s, how would one reason or carry out a public
discussion about civil rights without considering the moral dimension?

At this point, we raise one practical difficulty with analyzing along the
normative dimension. This is that we have, since Kant onward, associated
the normative with rules. That is, we would try to capture this dimension
through the specification of a rule, or if that does not suffice, an entire
suite of rules. And yet, we often find that the rules do not serve as a complete
enough guide and that no set of rules can possibly capture the complexity
of many social situations. What does it mean to be a good parent? Well, a
parent would answer, where would she or he begin? And where to end?
Positing rules can sometimes be creating an artificial plane of formal
juridical structures that we can build a policy or institution around. But
real moral reasoning can be more complex than this. In a sense, positing
absolute and rigid sets of rules is creating a mode of thought that is
removed from practical moral reasoning — i.e., mythologizing. We take
up this matter further in Part III where we attempt to create new descriptives
that might provide us with more options for portraying the normative and
other dimensions.

Part III
The Postconstructionist Sentiment

CHAPTER 8

Background: Grounding the Discourse

We started the book with a brief account of how analysis can lead to the mythologizing of policy. Often, this can be described as a gap between theory and practice. Perhaps more apt is a dramaturgical analogy, where the gap exists between libretto and opera (or, linguistically, between langue and parole, as Saussure might put it). We also have occasion to see this in the distance between the formal and the everyday — that is, the terrain that the analyst travels upon may not be the same landscape that people walk every day.

It is most useful for this discussion to simply describe the gap as a separation of text from context. This is illustrated in Figure 8.1, which portrays policy as a text that is constructed by authorities, power wielders, and decision makers. This policy text, which can literally be text, as in a new statute, is crafted in some locus of decision and then imported into different situations and implemented. In this logical process, text is created far from the context of its application.

The separation of text from context is problematic in many respects, but most centrally, we realize that one could not possibly construct a text that remains the same in every place and time. Surely, the contingencies of context must matter. In other words, what is missing is a mechanism by which the consideration of context can influence or guide the formulation of the text. Taking as an example a new regulation (which begins as text or words on a page) that provides start-up funding for microlending programs in rural, lower-income parts of the world, we realize that not

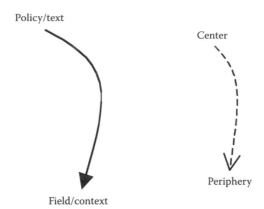

Fig. 8.1 Policy as text.

every community is ready or able to promote microlending among its members.

Institutions can be thought of as text, too. As another example, let us take the institution of a nation's constitution. In fact, we might as well use the U.S. constitution as an example. Here, some might say, is an example of a body of text that is universal, i.e., is applied everywhere across the nation, and timeless, and so, it has resisted change over time. As an institution, it has somehow fit every time and place in which it is enacted. Is it true, however, that the constitution has remained intact and unchanged? There are, of course, a number of amendments over time, but largely, the actual text has remained intact. Or has it? The constitution, if we ponder it for a while, has evolved just like any other institution. Even when its words have remained unchanged, what the words mean is a matter of constant interpretation and reinterpretation. In fact, the judicial system is one venue in which the words of the constitution are reinterpreted every day, and the interpretation may have evolved into something quite different from the original. Not only its legal meaning, but the actual, everyday sense of these words is in a state of constant flux. We might consider, for example, that in Jefferson's time the word "equality" meant something very different than what it means today. These changes are necessary so that the institution remains vital and meaningful in different times and places.

We see the gap between text and context manifested in numerous instances. For example, take the model of state-centered governance that in its modern-day form is none other than the regulatory model of government. In this model, we posit a central locus of decision making (the state) and a peripheral locus of implementation (the field). Policy, in this model, need only be crafted at the center and exported (like text) all throughout the field and simply enacted. The notion of regulation, in fact, has its roots in the leveling of the field so that the entire jurisdiction is brought in line with the central design. This notion of governance is radical separation of design from action and neglects the possibility that design might evolve from action or that the peripheries might have a hand in policy formulation. Rather, in the model of the regulatory state, control is absolute, and the state is omnipresent, much like the universal condition evoked by Joyce in a memorable passage:

> ...Snow will be general
> All over Ireland
> Falling on the churchyard
> Where lies Michael Furey's grave.
> Lying thickly upon the crooked crosses
> And on the headstones,
> On the spears of the gate,
> On the barren stones.
> Softly falling through the universe
> Softly falling upon our bed...

> Joyce, 1916

However, constructing a policy that is portrayed as a blanket, uniform piece of text that need only be subsequently brought into every context and enacted denies the importance of context. This has roots in our most fundamental epistemological assumptions. The subjectivist model of the *ratio* posits that reality is simply a subjective concept that we impose upon nature. In this case, the text is a construct, classification scheme, or theory that we impose upon nature. This operation is carried out regardless of the extent to which nature may or may not fit the construct. On the other hand, the most complete form of objectivism is found in the positivist insistence that reality is something we simply observe and, in fact, measure. In this case, the text (or analytic) that we impose upon objective reality is the plane of analysis upon which we make all things commensurable. In the natural sciences, this involves measuring those characteristics for which we have measuring devices. In the social sciences, however, we deal with phenomena such as trust, hope, greed, imagination, and other things that are innately immeasurable. These realities are not just observed but experienced and interpreted. In this case, the positivist insists on finding dimensions of measure that can translate these phenomena into physically observable and measurable things. In a utilitarian scheme, the unit of measure may be utilities or willingness-to-pay. But is this so very different than a postpositivist approach wherein, as in a critical framework, the primary descriptive may be that of, say, power or domination? In either case, we are left with an irretrievable loss of dimensionality, which is reminiscent of recent attempts to describe and, indeed, measure the social capital of a community, a notion originally posited by Bourdieu (1977) but one which he proposes without any evident intent to interpret within a positivist framework. Whether we maintain a strongly subjectivist or objectivist stance, the rigid assumptions made concerning both the subject and object work to widen the rift between text and context.

In this last part, we focus on approaches by which we begin to bridge these gaps, whether we focus primarily on the separation of theory from practice or policy formulation from policy implementation. This entails, at least to some extent, closer attention to not just how policies and institutions are conceived but how they are practiced. Perhaps a useful place to begin is a look at the notions of the so-called pragmatists of the last century. The first definition of the pragmatic point of view was given by Peirce:

> Consider what effects, that might conceivably have practical bearings, we conceive the object of our conception to have. Then, our conception of these effects is the whole of our conception of the object.

> Peirce, 1905

That is, for Peirce, we are to understand phenomena only through the effects that these have in the practical realm. The difference between this and a positivist-empiricist scheme can be traced to the fundamental conceptualization of reality. For the positivists, reality was the sum total of our observations. For Peirce and other pragmatists, reality is not captured by our observations, and we are forever caught in somehow trying to obtain a better understanding of it. Epistemologically, while positivism aspires to be a theory of truth, pragmatism is better understood as a theory of meaning. That is, the way we can best judge whether an interpretation of a phenomenon is good or not is through the practical effects it has. The use of the word "interpretation" is deliberate and meant to draw a distinction between pragmatism and empiricism. Pragmatism, at least to Peirce, James, Dewey, and other colleagues, is not a materialist system. James's restatement of Peirce's maxim interprets the word "effects" as the experiences we have of the object of discussion and the reactions we have to it. This includes purely subjective experiences and reactions. The pragmatist is a realist in the sense that she or he does not deny the existence of an objective reality but does deny that our thought can ever hope to capture reality, in its utter complexity and opacity.

Of course, one can critique the pragmatist method as being at least prone to empiricism because the test of practical significance is most easily interpreted through the empirical. But we can learn from its basic appreciation of reality and its concept of theory. In James's words, "Why may not thought's mission be to increase and elevate, rather than simply to imitate and reduplicate, existence?" (James, 1975). That is, pragmatists reject the notion of theory as an attempt to produce a conceptual copy of knowledge. The modern philosopher who most closely echoes this is probably Rorty, who dismisses the idea that science is fundamentally a mirror of nature (Rorty, 1980). Thus, for James and others, whether we suppose that the Sun revolves around the Earth or the reverse, whether we assume the Earth's orbit to be a circle or an ellipse, the fact is that none of these is, in fact, reality, but only scientific approximations of reality, e.g., there is no such thing in reality as a perfect ellipse. Dewey provided a more instrumental version of the pragmatic maxim, in that the better theory is that which allows us more effective use of it. That is, Newton's theory of gravitation and physics provided us with a set of ideas that allowed us to make powerful advances in mechanics. Later on, we would find these ideas to have limitations — for example, such as explaining subatomic phenomena or light — for which Einstein's theory would prove to be more useful (not more true, merely useful). This means that the way we resolve arguments and conflicting theories is not through observation and empirical measurement, but rather through discussion. Dewey would propose a criterion of warranted assertibility, in which we might come to some agreement over a better theory through the test of argument and practical effects. Rorty goes to the further extreme in stating that there really is not assertibility, only conversation, which really leads to a social constructionist view of reality. In large part, pragmatism meanders somewhere in between the empiricist and constructionist universes.

These pragmatic considerations can allow us some useful notions for analysis. For one, it provides some relief from the strictures of ideology, which can bind up a discussion (or policy analysis) without ever reaching a point where we consider effects on people's everyday lives. The question is most often not so much whether one espouses one party or another, but what programs one supports. The question that really confronts policy is not, the market or the state? but rather, what kind of market? and what kind of state? The pragmatic turn toward the place where things really count, where the rubber meets the road, etc., provides the analyst a greater chance to encounter real context in its everyday, complex, multidimensional sense. The turn toward the "new institutionalism" (e.g., North, 1990), which has as its basic proposition that "institutions matter" gets closer to this. What these writers are proposing is that institutional details, the finer points of design that one encounters after getting past the formal, are what makes these institutions effective or not. It is not a matter of instilling democracy in every place — rather, it is in the particular design of democratic society that evolves in a place or is most suited to it. We are allowed to leave, if only for some period, the plane of ideology, and get onto that plane where people and society function, which is the realm of practice. The test of an idea is whether it helps us get along in our daily lives.

This leads us to search for better ways to describe and analyze "practice," i.e., the ways that people understand things and carry out tasks in real life. To understand practice is to realize, for example, that many poets do not imagine poetry in their minds and then proceed to put this image down on paper. Rather, poets will think of an idea or a phrase, test it out on paper, reflect on these first few words, think again, then test some more words on paper, in a process that others call a "mixed scanning procedure" (Etzioni, 1993). Practice is that element in secondary-school education characterized by alternating and intertwined periods of interest, tedium, hormonal change, learning, and indignation, and not just a period in a young person's life in which more advanced concepts such as literature, mathematics, and civic responsibility are instilled. What we might characterize as years of progressive learning, can and should also be characterized as long periods of looking out the window daydreaming, doodling, listening, falling asleep, waking up, exchanging notes, and many other activities that really make up the hours spent in the classroom.

Why is it that the pendulum seems to oscillate between the purely objectivist and subjectivist notions of reality? According to the critical realists, it is because we fail to realize that reality is stratified and that we are able to access the different strata in dissimilar degrees (Bhaskar, 1979; Bunge, 1979). They point to three primary ontological domains: (1) the empirical, consisting of things we experience; (2) the actual, consisting of events that happen whether we observe or recognize them or not; and (3) the real, consisting of generative mechanisms that give rise to events. For example, though gravity is a real force that is constant and inexorable, it will be manifested in an event only when such expression emerges from the complex of generative mechanisms at play (i.e., an apple will fall only when friction, cohesion, and other mechanisms allow it to). The problem with empiricism is that it reduces reality to the observable. According to these theorists, although there exists an objective reality, our knowledge of it will always be fallible. This does not degenerate into relativism, however, since they maintain that knowledge can have differing degrees of fallibility. The play of generative mechanisms is important to this theory's approach to learning. Over areas of time and space, some mechanisms may come to dominate and others remain hidden — these mechanisms give rise to partial or demiregularities that we need to explain. The partial nature of these patterns and the assumption of multiple generative mechanisms lead the researcher to complex explanations. This, in turn, leads to a penchant for multimodal research designs, including what these theorists call "intensive" (e.g., case study) methods combined with "extensive" (e.g., comparative and statistical studies) methods. The critical realists also reject the constructionist notion that knowledge can be reduced to what we can say. In fact, our actions are influenced by and embedded in a deep context of history, culture, and relation so that social phenomena are much more than whatever we can work out discursively. Much of this, as Bourdieu suggested, shows part of itself in the intricate and ineffable logics of practice.

The pragmatic and realist (even critical realist) outlooks suggest that we take a closer look at the dimension of practice, i.e., the arena where events and actions are worked out. It will help us, in our attempt to deepen our analysis, to be cognizant of modern theorists of practice. Inevitably, recognition of the universe of practice entails rethinking the radical separation of subject from object. Another way that this is portrayed is in terms of rethinking the dichotomy of structure and agency. A theory of structure posits that individuals are carried by a tide of social phenomena or laws that determine how society functions. In this conceptual system, the analyst can simply focus on these broad, systemic processes to the exclusion of considerations of the individual. Theories of agency, on the other hand, focus on the motivations and actions of the free individual — as in the liberal notion of the atomistic individual freely choosing according to whatever moves him or her (be it acting according to moral principles or maximizing one's own utility). In rethinking these dichotomies, theorists are forced to come to grips with the complexity and multidimensionality of practice. For example, in his theory of structuration, Giddens posits the individual as acting and being acted upon by broader institutions in their social context, and the institutions as being both the medium and outcome of individual action (Giddens, 1984). The relationship between individual and structure is a reflexive one. For example, in his analysis of rebellious middle-school youths, Giddens sees their nonconformist behavior in school as mirroring larger structures of their society in which labor is divided into the specifically skilled and a large pool of less narrowly trained working class. However, the actions of these youth are necessary to reproduce or transform social structures. The agent retains the power to act but within loose and fuzzy constraints set by the agent's social reality.

In Bourdieu's theory of practice, the constraint is portrayed as the habitus, a patterned set of admissible responses from the individual that is built into the history, patterns of life, implicit meanings, explicit signs, and even unconscious drives that make up a person's context (Bourdieu, 1990). While Giddens's structural field concerns movements in society at large, Bourdieu's structurings are more contextual, individual, and possibly higher in dimensionality. It is still possible, in Giddens's formulation, to specify structural sets such as wealth, education, and employment. In Bourdieu's theory, the habitus is embedded in one's conscious and preconscious reality such that only an aspect of it can be identified. The individual acts within a landscape that is shaped by innumerable and, in fact, partly unnameable influences, histories, motivations, constraints, and understandings that if we needed to find a single word to capture it, we might have once used the word "culture." We might contrast this to the unidimensional explanatory variable of utility. However, to open up our analysis to understanding individual action through these complex motivations and constraints also requires that we understand and characterize actions and institutions through the more complex and everyday cognition of the agent. If we are to understand how the terrain of social–cognitive context acts on the individual, we need to enter into the cognitive reality of the individual and try to understand how this reality is experienced.

Essentially, this mode of analysis motivates us to find a meeting place for text and context. A textual approach might be understood as the viewpoint of the observer who interprets social reality from his or her particular perspective on it. For example, observations of expressed patterns of ritual kinship might be interpreted by the observer as reflecting a classification scheme or fundamental structures of the mind (Levi-Strauss, 1968). However, that might not be a good account of how these social practices are actually experienced by the individual in the situation. The problem, as Bourdieu explains, is that analysis is done from a vantage point that is completely divorced from practice. From the observer's point of view, events that are spaced over a long period are taken in all at once, juxtaposed, and condensed into a pattern when, in reality, these things are experienced in their sequence. Moreover, the logic of a sequence of events derives from the fact that they have to be performed. For example, the pattern of grant funding received by a nongovernmental organization (NGO) might be interpreted by the analyst as an ideological shift toward a certain direction when, in reality, the NGO is simply responding to its own shortfall in funds and applying for whatever happens to be available at the time.

The sentiment that this chapter, and book, reflects is a renewed concern with the manifold and complex nature of experience, the necessity and overriding role of context, and the realm of practice. In the following chapters, we outline some approaches that attempt to capture these notions. In chapter 9, we deepen our interest in experience and suggest how we might provide richer or thick descriptions of experience. More to the point, we develop analytics that allow us to more directly link experience, whether personal or collective, to policymaking.

In chapter 10, we turn to the complex yet real dimension of context. If we are to bridge the gap between text and context, then we must be more careful not to assume away the latter in the search for universal policy prescriptions. A turn toward contextuality requires, however, analytics that allow us to more carefully trace the connection between context and policy or institutional design.

In chapter 11, we return to the dimension of practice and illustrate how being more attentive to the rich and sometimes ineffable logics of practice can provide us cues for how to more richly describe policy situations and design institutions. For now, we simply point out that, for the analyst, entering into the world of practice entails being open to understanding a practice for whatever it is. That is, to some extent, the analyst has to be able to forego, at least temporarily, strong presumptions that may have been brought into the analysis. There is a phenomenological component to the understanding of practice.

The task that remains for the analyst is to increasingly reduce the cognitive distance between the policymaker and those for whom and around whom policy is being made. If we are to understand why it is that some policies seem to work and others do not, or why a policy seems to work sometimes and not others, we have to more seriously endeavor to enter into the world of those people for whom the policy is being crafted. The populations of concern, which in some circles is known as a "target population," cannot anymore be treated as a passive recipient of policy. People may experience policy in ways very different from that assumed by the policymaker. They are affected by their specific circumstances and situations in richer ways than we can conceive of, perhaps in a manner very much as portrayed in Bourdieu's notion of the habitus. Lastly, people bring policy to reality and whether deliberately or not, are coconstructors of policy. We have to find ways to narrow the gap between policy design and policy action. In the following discussions, we take up the notion that these very people who otherwise could be treated as passive, target, policy recipients, might very well help solve policy dilemmas by participating as authors of policy.

We can also recognize that espousing these modes of analysis is also an unmistakable turn toward complexity. This is, in many cases, unavoidable. The motivation for us is the realization that policy problems are utterly complex. Reforming Social Security is something that defies solution, at least within one term of office. Solving global warming will become increasingly intricate and problematic the more we get serious about it. In fact, for many policy situations, true solutions may only evolve over time.

Part of the solution is to somehow find ways to match the complexity and multi-dimensionality of a policy problem with our policy responses. Dealing with high fertility rates in the developing world is something for which, we now recognize, unimodal policy prescriptions simply will not work. Whatever strategy might prove to be effective, it will need to combine multiple dimensions including education, social security, livelihood development, human rights, primary health care, and international (or other) aid. It will need to address multiple aspects of the policy situation, including the ecological, cultural, religious, economic, and political. The turn toward dimensionality will, in practical terms, move us to go beyond unimodal analytics. This is why, in leading the reader to this point in the book, we needed to cover some terrain that others have already walked. The reason for critiquing the model of policy as decision is not to leave it behind but to seek ways to increase its power to inform our analysis. Part of the postconstructionist sentiment of this book lies in the realization that these analytics do contribute to the thick description of policy.

CHAPTER **9**

Experience

Introduction

We began with an account of how analysis can mythologize policy. Part of this problem lies in the gap that we generally find between analysis and its field of application. The result of this is a policy analytic that can be abstract, reductionistic, simplistic, and devoid of context. Our response to this is to insist that we chart ways to ground our analysis in the context and complexity of real policy situations. This is not simple realism; to quote one writer: "although we can never represent objective reality literally and absolutely, we can assume confidently that it has a consistently identifiable nature" (Morrow, 1994). In fact, a realization that we all come to, sooner or later, is that each of our models of analysis and, in fact, all of them put together, are but partial descriptions of policy situations that are more complex than can be expressed in the different languages of policy analysis.

In this chapter, we present a model of policy as experience. By experience, we simply mean the mode of knowing of the person (or group) embedded in the policy situation. Since it is grounded in experience, this model respects contextuality by definition, and in fact, presumes that there is no analysis outside of context. The hope is to draw from the richness of experience and reflect this in a parallel richness of analytical insight. Since experience is complex and multidimensional, so is our analysis. When we understand something through experience, we do so on many levels, including those that we might never find a way to express. Moreover, the model is utterly respectful of the knowledge, sentiments, and even moral authority of those caught up in the policy situation. In this model, the analyst is not the thinker, looking down on the ebb and flow of the sea from a lofty perch — rather, it is that of a "fish that swims in the ocean."

We can contrast this model with those we previously discussed. In the rational-positivist model, we encountered a subject (the analyst) who arrived at understanding through careful observation and measurement of a static policy object. In the constructionist model, the subject did not measure but, rather, constructed or authored the policy text. Both engage in the mythologizing of policy. As one author put it, "On the one hand, there is an *instrumental view* of policy as rational problem solving...On the other hand, there is a *critical view* that sees policy as rationalizing discourse...Neither of these views does justice to the complexity of policy making." (Mosse, 2004). In the present model, analysis lies in neither measurement nor artifice, but in experience. The thing that matters most for analysis depends on what model one chooses to espouse. In the classic model of rationality, we attempt to understand everything in terms of value. In a constructionist mode of analysis, what counts is the power of a policy narrative. In this model, the criterion is that of authenticity — i.e., how true our rendition of a policy situation is compared with the real experience of policy actors.

It may be useful to use a geometric analogy. In Figure 9.1, we picture an object. It is a complex one that has many facets, undulations, and sides. If we use this as an analogy for experience, we can similarly think of the latter as something characterized by multiple dimensions (e.g., sensory, normative, emotional, etc.), angles, and particulars. Real policy situations, by analogy, are also impossibly complex, to the extent of precluding complete description. Also depicted in the figure is the projection of the object onto a flat plane. Policy analytics often work this way, i.e., by taking a situation of sheer complexity and simplifying it to fit a preexisting construct. In the figure, this is akin to projecting the complex figure onto a flat surface, the result of which is a simple geometric figure (an ellipse). Now, this is not to say that the ellipse is a bad representation of the complex body — just that it is a partial one. The *lingua franca* of each policy lens is like the plane in the figure. In the utilitarian model, everything is reduced to the plane of utility. In some critical theories, everything is understood in terms of power and domination. However, experience is a manifold thing in which we might recognize each of these aspects and yet much more. This is not to say that the model of experience is atheoretical — only that it is a grounded theory in which we aspire to move away from the plane of reduction and closer to the complex body of experience.

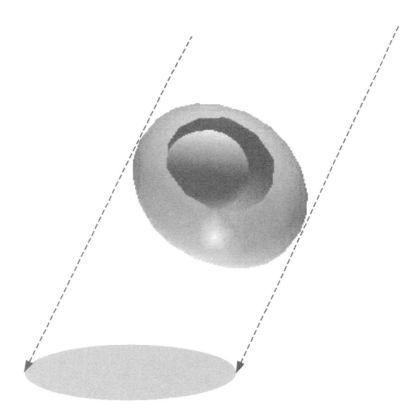

Fig. 9.1 A geometric analogy.

In and of themselves, these policy analytics are fine, as long as we admit the possibility that these are but partial descriptions. However, within these analytics, there is always the danger of inauthenticity and misrepresentation. During the civil war in Rwanda, there were accounts in the press of the situation through a profound detachment or, in a way that seemed to support non-intervention (see Fair and Parks, 2001 for an analysis of the coverage). In this way, a narrative of the fighting was constructed that seemed to suggest that the matter would best be left alone, that international efforts were already adequate, etc. Now, years later, we realize the situation for what it was — one of the most murderous, genocidal periods in recent history — and the failure of the international community to respond in any substantial way is a dark blemish in the history of the world.

The analytic can be a wonderful tool, as tools go, but can also be used in a way to misrepresent a policy situation. This would be akin to someone using their hands to make shadow figures of a dog (or a duck) onto the flat plane. Now, some depictions of policy do subscribe to the notion that it is primarily a contest of whose shadow figures are the best or most convincing. There is always that aspect to analysis. However, in this chapter, we encounter a model in which the main criterion is that of authenticity.

In the previous chapter, we spoke of how policy analysis often operates by separating text from context. This rift has deepened from a notion of the policy process as involving two separate stages: that of policy formulation and policy implementation, in that sequence (as in Pressman and Wildavsky, 1979). The resulting policy can fall short of the kind of relevance that makes for effective intervention in a situation. Let us take the example of music piracy and suppose that an agency decides to make this the focus of the present administration. The agency tells its field operatives that, starting this year, their new policy is "an immediate ban on music piracy and an employment of agents in the field to enforce the new policy." Well and good, but this simple directive lacks the wherewithal to deal with the ubiquity of the problem, its existence as a form of counterculture, the extent to which this practice has been integrated into the everyday round of college students, and simply the profound revolution that has characterized this new digital milieu. The policy directive does not speak to how the agency might begin a conversation with youth, how it might begin to more deeply understand the phenomenon of music file sharing, and how it might begin to dissuade organized proponents of music piracy.

In the mode of analysis that follows, we aspire to find procedures for discovering different aspects of a situation and integrating different kinds of knowledge. In a phrase, what we aspire to is "thick description." We also realize that policy is what emerges from a process and is not prior to action (or implementation). Policy formulation occurs in the midst of action in a type of grounded learning. This merging of policy formulation and implementation is probably better described with the term "policy action." In this chapter, we discuss a mode of analysis that emphasizes: (1) the uncovering of different aspects of policy situations which make up experience, (2) their integration into a coherent body of knowledge, and (3) the linkage of policy prescriptions and action to this thick description of the policy context.

Foundations

In the first half of the twentieth century, there arose a view of being and learning that was primarily phenomenological. Proponents such as Brentano, Husserl, and Heidegger claimed that the essence of meaning was to be found not in observation of the object by subject, as is in classical analysis, but in experience (Brentano, 1874; Husserl, 1913; Heidegger,

1927). Husserl, in fact, pointed to a "bracketing of existence," setting aside the question of objective reality and focusing entirely on experience, cognition, and impression. This did not allow for the formulation of the world according to rationalist conceptions, nor the empiricist penchant for aggregation of measures (and its tendency to objectify things in the world). Rather, the essence of phenomenology was the edict, "to the things themselves." In this mode of thought, experience is everything, and correspondingly, the analyst needs to strive to enter into pure descriptions of the experience, whether the observer's or the participant's. Rather than seeking the *summum bonum* of the rationalists or the utilitarian-empiricists, the phenomenologist seeks the pure description of everydayness — the authenticity that one seeks by reflecting on one's relationships with entities in the world. The essence of analysis, in the phenomenological context, is pure description. This is not constructionism, either, since it is based on real encounters with the world.

Closer to the realm of practice were the writings of John Dewey, of the so-called pragmatist school, who created an epistemology in which learning came out of the person testing and developing understanding by practical engagement with the world (Dewey, 1925). There is no consequentialism here, in that learning, preference, and value only came out of the active engagement. Like the phenomenologists, Dewey decried the dichotomization of subject and object. Rather, learning occurred from the testing of abstract notions and the progressive grounding of the person in his or her environment. Unlike the phenomenologists, Dewey was less essentialist; for him, truth and knowledge were always provisionary — always subject to testing in the smithy of experience. This had implications for education, in that Dewey espoused a regimen that was based not on the mere transmission of prepackaged knowledge, but the construction of settings for engagement with the real world, out of which came knowledge.

Paolo Freire, the Brazilian pedagogue, sought to reverse the traditional directionality of education, which was that of:

Expert → lay person

which also takes on, in various modalities:

Technocrat → peasant

First world → third world

and others, and instead, build in the following, richer modality:

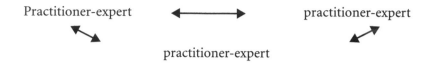

in other words, building a community of grounded experts or indigenous educators. This search for a reversal of the classic mode of education prefigures later sentiments from Lyotard who critiqued the scientific mode of knowledge transmission. This mode necessarily requires a credentialing of the expert who alone can transmit the store of knowledge to the exclusion of more traditional, narrative modes of transmission, which does not privilege any actor and, instead, allows speaker and hearer to be both competent in the transmittal of knowledge (Lyotard, 1979). Freire's conceptualization greatly influenced the field of learning and, moreover, other areas such as development theory and research, and gave rise to present-day practices in policy formulation and project development that go by the names of "participatory rural appraisal," "participatory action research," and others.

This is immediately relevant to the policy model presented in this chapter for a number of reasons. First of all, it acknowledges that learning and policy must be grounded in a situation and so is less enthusiastic about the model of the policy analyst as a neutral observer removed from the policy context.

Here we treat policy contexts as phenomena that can only be understood by someone who has experienced it. Note that this is entirely compatible with this book's postconstructionist leanings — although experience allows us different modes of access to it, there is, nevertheless a reality to be accessed. The phenomenology of insight and learning is not simply alternative constructions to be employed as in mere discourse. Rather, this experiential knowledge is reality itself. What is needed, it follows, is an analytic that can bring out the diversity and richness of this experience and firmly link it to the policy process.

Even the notion of the expert can be modified to more closely fit this conceptualization. Rather than do away with the notion of the outside "analyst" altogether, policy analysis has been influenced by descriptions of the researcher as more of an ethnographer than an objective observer. The analyst aspires to more closely enter into the experience of the person through opening up the analysis to different knowledges and representations, without pretending to ever have the complete competence of being a "native." Here, "competence" means entering into different experiential worlds by approaching them through different means, e.g., by interviewing, researching written artifacts, participant–observer techniques, etc., to such a point that the analyst might finally learn the significance of what, in objective terms are exactly the same operation, distinguishes a wink from a blink (Geertz, 1973). A similar definition of this mode of learning that is closer to the policy field is found in depictions of it as learning-in-action (Schön, 1983). This mode of policy analysis would require methods for reflection in the midst of engagement in a policy problem. This is a distinct movement away from the classical, Cartesian separation of mind from nature, subject from object, and onto a kind of subjectivity that realizes itself only in relation to others and its environment.

Analysis

We remind ourselves what the objectives of the model are.

1. To aspire toward a thick description of policy situations. This requires that we seek out different aspects, perspectives, and dimensions of a policy situation. This, in turn, motivates us to find modes of inquiry that allow us access to these different forms of knowledge.
2. To integrate the different pieces of information into a possibly coherent policy account.
3. To create opportunities for knowledge, and policy, to emerge from a process that is inclusive of action. This motivates us to design policy forums that allow for the merging of perspectives, including and especially that of stakeholders directly affected by the policy. This also requires forums within which the process of policy design might take place.
4. To create policy prescriptions that respect, and perhaps emulate, the complexity and contextuality of policy situations. This requires the consideration of multiple strategies, hybrid policies, local solutions, and innovative practices.

The need for thick description is driven by the notion that for policy prescriptions to be effective, they need to respond to how the situation actually is, in all its complexity. The policy situation is treated as a phenomenon that, rather than being beheld through a preformulated analytical template, is understood as something that reveals itself in the process of analysis. In this manner, any policy recommendation will derive directly from a description of the issue — allowing the design of policy actions to be more closely patterned to the nature of the situation. The notion can be depicted as follows:

Phenomenon → Response

Simply to seek out differing perspectives, different aspects, and particularities to a policy situation seems simple enough. It can seem like nothing more than throwing out theory and method and allowing for a free-for-all process wherein anything and everything counts. The analysis of experience is anything but impromptu, however.

First of all, it requires that we employ multiple policy "languages "or modes of description, but more specifically, that we employ those modes that best fit the policy situation. One could not conceive of a comprehensive analysis of corruption within a government agency without considering the extent to which a rational choice model might explain patterns of behavior. On the other hand, one could not possibly attempt to understand the debate about stem cell research without listening to moral or normative aspects of the discourse. With each policy lens that is employed, the need for methodological rigor does not decrease but, in fact, remains. More than this, the analyst needs skills in bringing out and using policy lenses or languages that are "native" to the situation. A situation often needs the employment of the modes of description and, in fact, actual language employed by those in the middle of the situation to better understand it. For this reason, the analyst needs some skills in discerning particular ways of knowing and, to some extent, "interpreting" this to a larger policy audience. We want to seek out modes of description from those directly affected by the policy if we are to understand some element of their experience. For this to happen, we need to be skillful in creating avenues for drawing out these perspectives. To a large extent, the analyst needs skills in designing and, perhaps, managing participative processes. The demands on the analyst are greater, not less, in this mode of analysis.

There are some rules of thumb that guide the analyst in structuring these processes of analysis and codiscovery:

Rule 1: Policy actors need to have the freedom to provide their perspectives without undue structuring from the analyst (or moderator) and others in the process.

Rule 2: Avenues for joint reflection need to be designed into the process so that these multiple perspectives are assessed, compared, and perhaps integrated into a coherent policy narrative.

Rule 3: Policy actors should have multiple avenues for presenting their experience, thus allowing for emergence of different facets of the experience.

Rule 4: At some point in the process, policy actors should be engaged in a process by which knowledge that is generated is linked to action.

Perhaps a good example of this pertains to how one might structure an interview with a stakeholder. If we were to conduct a different approach, i.e., a decision theoretic one, our interview would be a highly structured one where the respondent might be queried on their subjective estimates of utilities of different consequences of different policy alternatives. However, in the model of experience, the interview would be more like the open-ended, unstructured type. The analyst would start the interview by simply allowing the respondent to speak, encouraging her to add more to the response when desired, but taking care not to structure the responses. One might ask the person how she feels about recent changes in Medicare policy, but not how enraged she is about it. In the beginning of the interview, you would not even ask the person what solutions she might offer if she has not identified the situation to be a problem. At some point in the interview, after a sufficiently rich account has been given by the respondent, the analyst might then engage her in a process of reflection. Here, they jointly go over what has been said and ponder on further implications, what all of it means taken together, or why the respondent understood or chose to describe a situation one way and not another. Meanings would be clarified, and the significance of various statements judged. The respondent may even walk around the community with the analyst in order to provide a richer perspective on her reality. Lastly, if there were additional time or patience, the analyst would engage the respondent in a discussion of what actions these considerations might or should lead to. Later on, when reporting about the discussion, the analyst should try to be faithful to the words of the respondent, perhaps quoting her verbatim when appropriate.

In the suite of tools at the analyst's disposal, a number find greater use in an experiential model of analysis:

- Participant-observer techniques
- Personal narratives (through interviews, testimonies, etc.)
- Participatory research
- Multimedia techniques

We quickly realize that the experiential model demands a certain methodological syncretism from the analyst. It is not just a matter of assembling diverse bits of information and simply squeezing them all into one package. What is required is an element of integration — that is, the operation by which different knowledges are made coherent. That is, the analyst has to take the entire stock of knowledge and make these different pieces fit together. It is an act that attempts to recreate the integrity of a person's experience, not in different parcels of information or in separate planes of information, but as one coherent whole. One does not separately perceive

the rosy light, the waning of the tumult of the day, and the gathering cool-
ness of the air, and then remember a similar day in one's distant past —
rather, one simply experiences a sunset. Integration is a facet of analysis
and, in general, can come about through a number of different approaches.

- Metanarrative: This entails searching for a higher, encompassing narrative that combines and contains the different pieces of knowledge.
- Composite: In this mode of integration, a suitable medium is found
  or constructed in which the different knowledges are presented
  together as a unified whole.
- Triangulation: Different types of bodies of knowledge may overlap
  and corroborate the same conclusions in a process often known as
  "triangulation."
- Testimony: This entails a reflective assessment of a policy actor who
  is caught right in the middle of the situation.
- Action: The different knowledges can be used to support routes of
  action. Action can result from a consideration of all the relevant
  knowledge.

Some explanation is needed concerning how these modes of integration
can happen. In some cases, we aspire toward a relatively complete (or
global) integration of the different bodies of information. One way we try
to do this is by constructing a metanarrative or a depiction of the policy
situation that encompasses and is consistent with the store of knowledge
— in this case, the challenge is to try and construct something coherent.
The second way is more like assembling a pastiche of perspectives and
information in the situation, but this requires some ability on the part of
the researcher to summarize, link, and otherwise create a sense of the
whole. The third, triangulation, is a reduction of the multiple lines of
knowledge onto the common elements that they all corroborate. Areas of
contradiction or noncommonality are left in the background in this mode
of integration.

The last two modes of integration need some elaboration. By integration,
we mean the process by which different aspects of a situation and different
forms of knowledge are considered as a whole and used to make sense of
the entire policy situation. However, we are reminded that experience itself
does not occur as an assemblage of different knowledges but as a coherent
whole. Thus, one way to get a sense of how everything fits is to probe
directly into the perspective of one who is caught in the middle of a policy
situation and for whom the phenomenon is experienced as an integrated
whole. Most often we cannot capture the experience in words, with any
integrity. However, the testimony of the person can give us glimpses of the

whole. A similar thing can be said for action. In a sense, when a group of people attempt to use the entire store of knowledge to identify directions for action, they are performing an integrative act. The integration, in this case, does not occur as a synthesis of the knowledge per se, but folding them all into a strategy for action. The action itself reflects the knowledge that has generated it.

Integration requires reflection, whether by the group of policy actors or by the analyst alone, on what the store of knowledge means when taken together. What consistencies can be found across the different pieces of data? What insights do they support as a group? What areas of inconsistency appear across the assemblage of knowledge? What might be the reason for these inconsistencies? What new knowledge do we gain from each single piece of evidence? Can we tell a story that links the entire collection of knowledge? Most importantly, do these stories strike policy actors as authentic, i.e., true to their experience? The reflective process is necessarily a circular one. It is possible too that the analyst finds that a coherent narrative cannot be created that is consistent with all of the information. If the reality of the situation is itself incoherent and fraught with contradictory elements, then so will the analysis.

At this point, we need to see how these elements play out in a real example, which brings us to the next case study.

Case Study: Participatory Action Research for Health in Southeast Los Angeles
In this case study, we describe a project wherein the analyst teamed up with a community group in designing a process to (1) enter into the experience of community residents and capture the multidimensionality of the phenomenon of health, and (2) link intervention to these thick descriptions of the situation through a participative process.

The project began when a community-based organization, Communities for a Better Environment (CBE), approached university researchers with the idea of initiating an investigation of the causes of environmental health problems in Southeast Los Angeles. The notion was that the problem of air toxics in this area was complex enough, and the sources so numerous, that the community needed a richer understanding of the phenomenon in order to begin designing intervention programs. The area is interesting in and of itself, being characterized by a land use pattern that is unusually dense and heterogeneous. The community is largely Latino and low to middle income. The area had, beginning in the 1960s, lost much of its large industrial base, which was subsequently replaced by a large number of smaller, light industries. Many of these were suppliers, waste haulers, and other businesses associated with the nearby I-710 freeway and Alameda Street, which were the main corridors to and from the Port of Los Angeles.

To deepen the community's understanding, the research coalition sought to design a two-year process in which different perspectives on the issue would be sought, along with information from a number of different sources. The group had hoped that rich insight would be forthcoming from residents who knew the area intimately, and so the process used the model of participatory action research (PAR), a community-based process of reflective inquiry that draws its roots from Freire and subsequent development practitioners. The role of the analyst in this project was to help structure the process and guide the community through a series of workshops in which the entire group would collectively share, discover, and disseminate knowledge about problems in the area.

The very first workshop involved a cognitive mapping session in which residents simply drew their renditions of their neighborhood onto a large sheet of paper. Two things emerged, quite clearly, from this process and ensuing discussions:

1. Environmental health problems in the community occurred on many dimensions, including air emissions from small, previously unstudied sources, congestion in schools, poorly maintained apartment buildings, and transportation-related hazards. The degree to which these sources of risk agglomerated in Southeast Los Angeles seemed remarkable.

2. Industrial sources of risk (or, as identified by the residents, "nuisance") were more ubiquitous than realized by the researchers. These included traditional sources of air toxics but, more ominously, small, unstudied sources of risk such as truck depots, fast food restaurants, markets, auto body shops, and other land uses that were tightly embedded into the fabric of the residential neighborhood.

The bewildering mix of land uses required an extended period of research. In a related endeavor, researchers took information on possible sources of air pollution in the neighborhood and used computer modeling to simulate levels of air toxics and resulting cancer risks in the area. The resulting graphical representation of risk is shown in Figure 9.2.

The figure shows a number of distinct peaks, corresponding to the handful of larger point sources (or clusters of point sources) in the study area. However, what is more meaningful is that even when we ignore the peaks (or assume that regulatory action will eliminate these), the rest of the vicinity is still generally characterized by "hills" and elevated plains all throughout the landscape, particularly with regard to the risk map shown in Figure 9.2. Even if we removed classic sources of pollution (i.e., large

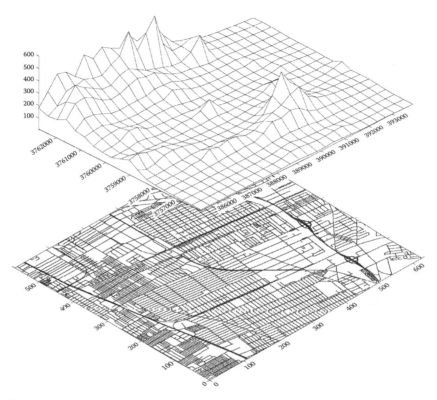

Fig. 9.2 Mapping of cancer risks in Southeast Los Angeles. Source: Lejano and Smith (2006).

factories) from our model, the resulting "topography" of risk would essentially remain as shown in Figure 9.2, which suggests that the origin of risk is broadly dispersed and evidently due to the cumulative effect of many sources. It suggests that the pattern of land use that leads to such a profound buildup of risk is a systemic one that occurs over most of the area of Southeast Los Angeles. Early on in the process, the group realized that CBE's traditional advocacy process wherein they would conduct short, intensive campaigns aimed at protesting a single large polluter did not fit the situation in Southeast Los Angeles where sources of risk were ubiquitous and intimately integrated into the community. Said the southern California director of CBE,

> …the cumulative impact problem is very complex…You're talking about gas stations, dry cleaners, small chromeplaters — this is where people in the community work, this is intertwined in people's lives. This is not something we can go to (the agency) and simply say, we need a cumulative impact rule next week, it is

> something that requires a lot of participation by the commu-
> nity...I mean how would the community define cumulative
> impact?...And they participate through this process of defining
> the problem and finding the solutions. So that develops the
> capacity of the community to find solutions, from things like cor-
> relating pollution to health outcomes, to learning to interact with
> policy decision-makers...

The notion, even early on in the project, was that the problem was complex enough that deeper insight needed to be gained on the sources of risk
and, importantly, patterns of movement and daily life that made residents
in this community particularly vulnerable to exposure to these risks. This
promoted the idea of using a grounded, participatory research design. In
the following sections, we characterize the process, outcomes, and mode of
integration of the research in Southeast Los Angeles. To underscore the
characteristics of the experiential model, we contrast this with a second
research project that occurred around the same time, but one that was
based strongly on the classic, positivist model of measurement and statistical
analysis. The latter was a two-year epidemiology study in a part of Southeast
Los Angeles that established correlations between asthma and proximity to
the transportation corridors in this area (Delfino et al., 2003).

The Process In Figure 9.3, we compare process diagrams for the experiential model, which we have labeled PAR in the figure, and the positivist
one, which we have labeled Epidemiology. A number of important distinctions are seen in the comparison.

1. Logic: The positivist model is characterized by a highly linear process,
   which proceeds from hypothesis setting to hypothesis testing. In this
   case, the analyst constructs the hypothesis in isolation from the case,
   imports the hypothesis into the situation, and proceeds to test
   whether real data fits the supposition. This is an operation that is
   akin to projecting the phenomenon onto a plane of analysis. In contrast, the experiential approach is highly nonlinear. Here, hypotheses
   emerge from a circular process wherein a group of stakeholders
   share knowledge, reflect on it, and begin integrating the information.
   It is a grounded research in which theory emerges from practice
   (Glaser and Strauss, 1967).
2. Knowledge: The experiential model brings in multiple ways of
   knowing, which means that different types of information are sought
   out. In the Southeast Los Angeles example, this involved at least
   three different types of data: qualitative testimonies from residents,

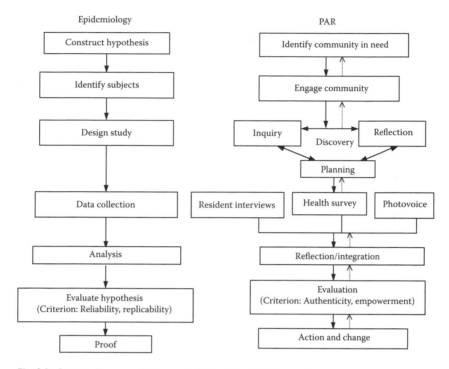

Fig. 9.3 Process diagrams of the experiential and positivist approaches.

health survey data, and photovoice, which are photographs taken by residents and subsequently annotated with their impressions, reflections, and other notes. In contrast, the positivist model confines knowledge to one narrowly defined type — in this case, statistical data collected in standardized format in a formal survey.

3. Analysis: In the positivist model, reality is tested as being in or out of conformance with the analyst's hypothesis. The end result is a yes/no proposition (does correlation exist or not). In contrast, in the experiential model, analysis means integration, i.e., the merging of different lines of information to give a more complete picture of the whole. The criterion used for analyzing the information also differs, wherein the positivist model it is that of replicability and confidence, while in the experiential model, it is authenticity of policy description to experience.

4. Objective: The goals of the exercise are also quite different in each case, which perhaps partly explains why the processes involved look so different. In the positivist model, the ultimate objective is that of statistical proof; for the experiential model, the objective is action.

For the analyst, the type of policy recommendation that comes out of the process can be every different.

5. Mode of learning: The positivist process, possessing a linear logic, constrains learning to a predetermined mode, i.e., hypothesis testing through measurement of the object of study. In the experiential model, learning involves discovery of new, unthought-of hypotheses, sharing of knowledge, and reflection. Importantly, it also involves learning-in-action, which means that the analyst studies how a program is implemented, brings this back to the hypothesis stage, and so on, in a circular process that some have labeled "double-loop learning" (see Argyris and Schön, 1974).

The kinds of information brought to bear in an experiential analysis ranges from the positivist (i.e., measured statistical information) to the subjective and qualitative, as in the excerpt shown below (taken from a transcript of an interview with a community resident):

Los umm … para los niños de la escuela cuando vienen esta pasando el tren se me hace como muy peligroso. Y hay unas fabricas que estan … hay unas fabricas que estan ahi que su … yo pienso que son dañinas para … por los humos que salen para los niños, pa' la salud de los niños … O si, este … pues, yo pienso que el polvo de las telas o algo sale … yo pienso. Que eso puede ser algo … Ay si, porque a veces cuando yo paso ahi, siento que me da mucha toz.

(Translation: The umm … for the children of the school when they come the train is passing, it seems like very dangerous. And there are some factories that are … they are some factories that are right here and that their … I think that they are hurtful for … because of the fumes that come out for the children … for the children's health … Oh yes … well, I think the dust from the fabrics or somethings comes out … I think. That could be something … Oh yes, because sometimes when I pass by, I feel that I cough a lot.)

The Outcomes We should also be able to compare the outcomes of the experiential and positivist models, specifically, what constitutes knowledge in each. In Figure 9.4, we diagram the research products of the PAR and epidemiological approaches. The most distinctive contrast is, of course, the manifold nature of information generated by PAR: photographs, testimonials, statistical data, and others. The health survey itself gave multimodal results, as suggested in Figure 9.4. The data includes standard health outcomes, e.g., a prevalence of childhood asthma of 16.7 percent was found in Southeast Los Angeles, as compared to 6.5 percent over all of Los Angeles County. The data also include other types of information, such as on environmental perception, problems with health care and qualitative text on individual priorities for health and intervention. For example, 11.7 percent of heads of household reported that they had no regular health care provider, and 21.8 percent reported transportation a major barrier to health care access. Thirty nine percent thought that poor air quality contributed to poor health in Southeast Los Angeles. Lastly, the results also provide qualitative accounts of residents' priorities for health research and action. Dealing with such a complex array of data was a challenge for the community group and university researchers. In contrast, the epidemiological results can be summarized in simple statements as shown on the bottom of Figure 9.4.

Integration The multimodal nature of knowledge in the experiential model brings up the element of integration and, ultimately, linkage to action. In contrast, epidemiology does not require an explicit integration and intervention stage. This is because integration occurs much earlier, when the epidemiological model is adopted, and data are constrained to the unimodal form that the epidemiological method can treat. In contrast to the assumed objective nature of epidemiological data, knowledge in PAR is subject to reflection and interpretation.

How did integration happen in this particular project? One mode is through triangulation: the different types of data can overlap and provide common accounts of a phenomenon. For example, the results of the health survey were mapped on GIS and verified results from the photovoice, resident interviews, and secondary data that there were hotspots of vulnerability. One such hotspot is the northern portion of Southeast Los Angeles. Another mode of integration lies in construction of a metanarrative that, in this case, was a thick description of the phenomenon of vulnerability. Here vulnerability is the heightened susceptibility of residents to injury from air toxics and is revealed as a prevalence of asthma, lack of health access, proximity to sources of air toxics, and qualitative, personal opinions on quality of life. The multidimensionality of the picture of health, including quantitative and qualitative information, narrative, and visual elements, is the result of this integration. In Figure 9.4, for example, note the rich insight that narratives can provide. We can summarize the metanarrative as an account of how residents in Southeast Los Angeles are vulnerable because of the overlap of phenomena such as incompatible land use,

1. PAR

Community health survey
Health outcomes: e.g., childhood asthma prevalence of 16.7% (29 out of 174 children). Environmental perceptions: e.g., 39% of respondents link poor air quality to health outcomes. Health care: e.g., 11.7% of surveyed households have no regular health care provider. Qualitative: e.g., "Freeway noise is a main cause of migraines..."

Reflection ⟶ Action

Photovoice

Storage tanks...

Resident interviews
"A mi me da miedo porque cuando vienen los niños de la escuela y pasa el tren, digo, a veces unos son previdos y se andan subiendo alli arriba – bueno ya unos niños mas grandes."
Translation:
I get scared because when the children of the school come and the train passes. I mean, sometimes some are cautious and they are climbing there on top–well, the older kids.

"Cuáles son las dificultades que enfrentan los padres en este vecindario? ... Pues las clinicas, no ay clinicas donde uno pueda decir, oh voy y me atienden a mi hijo en ese momento... la clinica esta bien lejos de donde tu vives y tienes estar manejando, y los que no tienen carro pues batallan mas"
Translation:
What are the difficulties that parents face in this neighborhood? ... Well the clinics, there aren't clinics where one can say, oh I can go and they will attend to my child at that moment... The clinic is really far from where you live and you have to be driving, and those that don't have a car, well, they struggle more.

2. Epidemiology (Delfino et al., 2003)

Odds ratio (95%CI) = 1.83 (1.18, 1.89) for bothersome or more severe asthma symptoms per increase to mean concentration of PM_{10}.

Odds ratio (95%CI) = 1.44 (0.98, 2.10) for bothersome or more severe asthma symptoms per increase to mean concentration of o-xylene...

Source: CBE (2005).

Fig. 9.4 Comparing outputs of the experiential and positivist models. Source: Communities for a Better Environment. 2005. *Children's health and environment in SELA: A participatory research project.* Huntington Park, CA: Communities for a Better Environment.

poverty, lack of access to health care, poor municipal infrastructure, lax enforcement of environmental regulations, and others.

Integration may also occur in the linkage of knowledge to action. In this case, specific interventions are triggered when the information is deep and convincing enough to spur action. In the case of Southeast Los Angeles, intervention can be considered that responds to those elements of vulnerability that were identified. For example, since a lack of transportation is identified as a barrier to care, the option of community members organizing car sharing or a dial-up van service can be considered, beginning with key hotspots.

Moreover, the multidimensional, unbounded, and complex array of information produced by the PAR process seems to be what is needed to attain a thick enough description of similarly multidimensional, complex phenomena such as vulnerability and cumulative risk — for example, the picture we obtain by combining indications of elevated asthma prevalence in children of ages 0 to 5 with hotspots of perceived exposure to polluting factories and to transportation and other barriers to health care access. These phenomena could not be comprehended through unimodal kinds of information such as that produced by epidemiological studies, but rather require the mix of information sets such as that portrayed in Figure 9.4. To some extent, the different knowledges were integrated — the concentration of asthma cases, pictures of incompatible land uses, and residents' complaints about noxious light industries in this area — and give us a thick description of vulnerability.

Perhaps the most important result of the experiential process is a strategy for action, i.e., a policy recommendation that is high in dimensionality and relevance. This results from linking policy proposals to the experience itself. From the kind of ubiquitous, embedded nature of health risk portrayed in Figure 9.1 to the multidimensional and complex information illustrated in Figure 9.3, the notion is that the complexity of experience, when linked to routes for action, produces a parallel complexity in policy recommendations. In the case of the Southeast Los Angeles project, the reflection workshops produced an array of measures, including:

Initiating a joint project with various environmental agencies and the community to create a comprehensive, easy-to-use Web-based mapping tool for different people to exchange information, share insights, and to generally link residents to agencies (The Regional Geographic Initiative).

Holding a health fair in the park (or other public place) in which the study team and community group could reach out to residents and initiate a healthy neighborhoods campaign.

Plans to engage households with the most vulnerable children in order to ascertain exactly where, when, and under what conditions they are most exposed to toxins and asthma triggers.

Initiate a three-year pilot phase where interventions would be tested and assessed against impacts on the exposures of the most vulnerable children.

Promotora-based health education programs. (Note: A promotora is a roving community health professional.)

This wide-ranging approach is perhaps aligned with the insights of Foucault, who pointed out that the iniquities of society occur across an infinitude of settings, in all sorts of social arenas, from the microspaces of personal relationships to macrospaces of social groups. As a result, policy action must, likewise, attack the problem from an infinitude of directions through a rich diversity of actions. This caused a shift in the strategy of CBE, which traditionally concentrated on classic forms of protest (after Alinsky, 1972) to a more grounded type of research that required more sustained, careful, critical inquiry (after Freire, 1973). It is a type of analysis that is grounded in experience and geared toward action.

Policy Reflections

The experiential model provides the analyst with a powerful lens with which to formulate policy that is responsive to real conditions, immediately applicable, and respectful of the particular circumstances found in a policy context. It is not easy to provide a definitive template for this model. Truth is, the specific design of the analytic process changes with each situation, and a study conducted in Southeast Los Angeles in the early 2000s might be designed in a different way from one implemented in Beijing or Prague in the 2010s since the objective of the analyst is to understand the problem as it is, where it is. In fact, the process may change considerably depending on who in the community is able to participate, what specific community issue is being addressed, and the resources the group has to use for the process.

In this chapter, we took up a case study in which the analyst had recourse to participative forums within which to access the experience of the policy actor. While participation is most often a goal of this type of analysis, it is not always an option for the analyst who, at times, must craft policy analyses alone and under tight time constraints. Whatever the actual process that is used by the analyst, the basic steps of the analytic are the same:

1. Seek out different aspects, perspectives, and dimensions of the policy issue.
2. Integrate the different types of information into a thick description of the issue.
3. Link policy recommendations — and action — to such thick description.

The question of resources is not a trivial one. An analysis that uses elements of experience is bound to be longer, more labor intensive, and perhaps more data rich than traditional models. Consider the case of the Southeast Los Angeles project and that while the study design in the epidemiology study took perhaps three months, the participatory action project took about a year. Formulation of research questions, which is relatively straightforward in the epidemiology project and which requires only the analyst pondering the situation, in the other project this occurred over a series of about five workshops with community residents.

The demands can be even greater on the analyst. Consider the kind of commitment required of the analyst when he or she makes the decision to conduct research as a participant–observer. In this mode, experience and integration might occur in the analyst. While this mode of analysis has become quite common in areas such as anthropology and pedagogy, for the policy analyst, the prospect of this grounded type of study can be daunting.

The analyst will also struggle with how to present the analysis. In what format can the analyst present such a rich aggregation of knowledge? Again, this requires something extra of the analyst. Imagine a policy report with chapters entitled, "Costs and Benefits," "Narrative Descriptions," and "Visual Images" all contained in the same volume. Or, imagine a policy report with sections pertaining to reconstructed narratives from interviews with different sets of policy actors — each section presenting perspectives from a different policy group. This task requires skill on the part of the analyst, not to mention a little bit of courage.

CHAPTER **10**

Coherence

Introduction

In many respects, this chapter follows closely upon the previous one. We begin with the realization that policy, at least the kind that effects change, does not simply land upon a latent field from above. Rather, policy evolves on the ground, within and part of a context. In this manner, the solution might stand some chance of matching the breadth and complexity of the policy context, which involves real communities, contingencies, and dynamic processes. The other way of understanding this is, if a policy solution is to be effective and be maintained in a situation, then it must, somehow and in different respects, "fit" that situation. This chapter entails analyzing policy through the notion of institutional "fit" or, as we hereon refer to it, "coherence."

The first notion that motivates this kind of policy analysis is the simple fact that a new policy does not simply touch down upon a situation like some alien ship and then proceed to colonize the surroundings. Rather, policy must find linkages to the existing patterns of governance, to social structures, and to the community itself. Coherence, then, describes the extent to which a policy initiative can or has been incorporated into the manner of things in a place. One aspect of this is the linkage of a proposed, or ongoing, policy to governance structures already in place. Yet another aspect concerns how a policy coheres with and into people's daily life, i.e., their everyday lives and patterns of commerce. For this reason, we focus not just on the formal but also on the everyday institutions of a place. One caveat is that, to some extent, a new policy can be worked into a situation so as to make the latter correspond to the policy. That is, if we imagine the policy field to actually be a field, then we can rework the landscape to some extent to make the new policy fit. This is possible, and the analysis should also consider ways by which existing institutions might be reworked or new ones initiated so as to allow more coherence with a proposed initiative. It is also possible that, even if a policy does not quite cohere, that the surrounding society will eventually adjust to it and fit the surroundings to the new institution. In the following discussion, we sometimes interchange the word "policy" with the more general word "institution."

To better understand what we mean by fit or coherence, let us take up a simple example. The author, while driving around the city, sometimes goes through a particular intersection where it is observed that there is often a man who sells oranges to motorists while they wait for the light to turn green. He has evidently settled on this particular spot as his area of business, and he apparently is there almost every day of the week. Now, realize that even this simple example can be thought of as an institution — that is, a practice that has grown habituated in some context. Now, for this practice to last in this place, it has to somehow "fit." What does the notion of fit mean in this particular case? Well, certain things have to be true for this man to be able to sell oranges day in and day out. For example, there has to be a demand for the service, meaning that there should be a steady stream of motorists who crave oranges, that there is place to buy them easily around that area, and that the man's prices are low enough to entice people to actually buy. This particular district has no local ordinances prohibiting vending in this area, or if there are, the authorities choose not to enforce it. There are even more rudimentary things that are required — for example, the timing of the traffic signal has to be such that it stays red long enough for people to roll down their windows and actually buy oranges. All of these are part of the local conditions, local circumstances, and local institutions that have to be compatible with the new institution (that of a "man selling oranges"). Analyzing coherence is nothing more than this mode of reasoning.

The other notion that lies behind the idea of analyzing coherence has to do with the state of institutional analysis over the last decade or so. There has been, for some time now, the notion of institutions (and we should infer policy) as social constructs (see Hannan and Freeman, 1977; DiMaggio and Powell, 1991; and Berger and Luckmann, 1966 for early treatises on social constructionism). That is, institutions can be thought of as ideas that groups in power or other stakeholders support, maintain, and advance. The emphasis of this literature is on the concept that emerges from a policy discussion and on the subsequent employment of this policy from situation to situation. Policy and institutions, then, are to be understood as text that can be interpreted and reinterpreted to serve the needs of the reader or writer. More importantly, they are text that can be brought wholesale from place to place and incorporated in every situation. So being, institutions should then tend toward isomorphism, i.e., they should, after a while, look pretty much the same everywhere (DiMaggio and Powell, 1991). The idea of coherence stands partly opposed to the social constructionist view of institutions and maintains that policy and institutions are not just text that one can employ from place to place. Rather, they need to find coherence with the real, constructed or not, patterns and institutions of each context. Coherence means that, to some extent, the original text would be adapted to each place. Essentially, then, while policy is, after all, text and it is, after all, taken from place to place by power-wielders, it still requires physical enactment in each place and this, by virtue of the requirement of at least some measure of coherence, means that the policy will not be identical in each situation. That is, engagement of text with the real induces real changes in the way policy is enacted. What results is not isomorphism, but polymorphism. In other words, if an institution has been able to fit a particular context, then it should exhibit (possibly subtle) differences from another institution that has evolved in a different context. Studying different contexts, we should find some diversity in the design of these institutions.

This brings us to a third important notion, and that is the idea that to attain coherence, policies must be, to some extent, fashioned and instituted in a place using some resources of the place. The model is that of an improviser who fashions a program out of the materials at hand and finds ways to make those pieces fit. The improviser, having to work with locally available materials, finds the form of the resulting program to be inherently dependent on local context. Now, we replace the notion of one agent-virtuoso and instead conceptualize a locus of creative genius that is, at times, located in a central agent, perhaps in a group of agents, and perhaps in a dynamic social process that allows collaborators to pool their motivations and invention. In the absence of the universalizing influence of the state, and because of the great influence of local context in supplying the raw institutional material for the product, we should find programs that display a wide diversity of characteristics and forms, all somehow reflecting the context in which they were formed.

Having been assembled out of context and intuition, the different elements of an institution must have some degree of compatibility to function together. That is, do the pieces fit? Analysis then consists of testing

whether these elements support each other or whether their inherent inco-
herence causes the system to break down at too many points too often.
The main question here is, to what extent does this new program "belong"
to a place or is it too alien to be integrated into the life of this community
without force? This brings us to the need to analyze policy in terms of
institutional coherence.

Though coherence has a self-perpetuating aspect to it, careful analysis
can help greatly. Let us take the example of the new policy relating to the
proposed siting of a new homeless shelter in the middle of a community.
Even if the local government imposed its siting without dialogue with residents, we will find that this siting is not as simple as putting in a new
building. In fact, for the shelter to be maintained in this place, it and the
area around it must adjust to each other. For example, some more critical,
perhaps wealthier, residents may choose to advocate its removal or simply
leave the area. Or, the community realizes that having the shelter creates a
need for other support services in the area. Land use around the new shelter
may change over time. Policy analysis has to consider the context in which
the policy is to take shape, and to analyze ways that the new policy already
fits and the things that are needed to make it fit. At any rate, life will adjust
around this new site. However, responsible analysis should already have
studied, up front, ways to make the adjustment better. A project proponent,
too, should, early on, study ways that the successful enactment of the new
policy might be ensured. In fact, a good analysis might have found the
program to be altogether unsuited for this place. This is what the study of
institutional coherence is all about — it responds to a point we made earlier
that, in many cases, the specific alternative that is chosen is often not as
important as seeing to it that any reasonable alternative is well carried out
and successfully enacted.

What we should find, if we are to take coherence seriously, are several
characteristics of policies and institutions that we study:

- Because policies are enacted in specific places with specific supporting (or opposing) institutions, we should find that, to some extent,
  policies exhibit some degree of polymorphism. This has practical
  consequences for policy since there might exist many more policy
  options than we might otherwise conceive.
- For the same reason, we have to go deeply enough into the rich
  particularities of a policy to find possible subtle differences between
  it and policies enacted in different contexts. At this level of analysis,
  we should find an increased level of complexity. This is part of our
  transition from the abstract level of the policy text to a greater embedding into the rich ground of context. Correspondingly, policy analysis

has to increasingly develop methods for describing and analyzing this complexity. To gain the necessary depth of insight, at least part of our analysis must be increasingly contextual. Otherwise, we cannot understand what elements in a situation can help or hinder a proposed policy.

We have discussed how the underlying sentiment of this book might be described as postconstructionist. This informs our focus on institutional coherence. First, we remind ourselves that institutions are not concrete edifices that just sit on their pediments, as material and social facts. At the same time, institutions should not be understood in solely symbolic terms as text that exists as some ethereal wisp freely floating in some so-called discursive field. No, the conceptualization that most informs us it to be found spanning this range of realizations. Institutions must be maintained by policy actors who have the wherewithal to sustain them, and they must be supported by social and material systems. That is, we should find in the social and material fabric of a situation, niches in which an institution has embedded itself in the everyday aspects of life. We can summarize this model using the diagram of Figure 10.1.

As illustrated in the upper half of Figure 10.1, we can posit institutions as socially constructed, externally crafted, and imposed upon a latent field. However, this does not seem to be, on its own, a complete account of institution building. Specifically, the analysis is greatly empowered when we also consider institutions as ecological phenomena, as illustrated in the

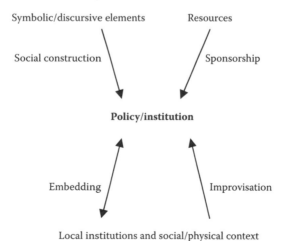

Fig. 10.1 Diagram of institutional coherence. (From Lejano, R. and A. Ocampo-Salvador. *Marine Policy,* forthcoming.)

bottom half of the figure. In this latter model, institutions grow out of a place and, at least to some extent, exhibit features that belong to that context. This ecological effect comes about through at least two processes. First, for an institution to be an institution, it must maintain itself. For this to happen, the institution and its environment must somehow fit together. By environment, we mean the institutions, people, and other features of a place. Second, most often policies and programs are pursued under resource-scarce conditions, and there may not be enough budgetary and other resources to build an institution *in toto*. For this reason, program planners may draw from the resources of a particular place. For these two reasons — the notion of fit and that of improvisation — we should expect institutions to reflect some characteristics that are unique to their particular context. All these overlapping impulses, acting in concert, constitute the model of coherence.

In this chapter, we introduce a type of analysis that emphasizes three basic analytical steps:

1. Studying institutions in enough depth so as to bring out the richness of diversity among similar policies and institutions found in different contexts. This often requires the analyst to find a suitable level of specificity within which programs begin to differentiate.
2. Explaining how these policies and institutions respond (or fit) uniquely to their particular contexts. This involves testing for logical and practical consistency, aided by a grounding in that context.
3. Using these insights to begin predicting or assessing how well a particular policy might fit into a specific context.

We use two case studies to illustrate how this analysis is carried out.

Foundations

Doubtless, one will find, in this chapter, echoes of philosophies that maintain some notion of realism or pragmatism. True, while institutions are not to be thought of as motionless granite edifices, they are not simple social or personal constructs either — they are enacted in real places, and times, by real people. As an example, even the institution of the World Wide Web exists in real, physical terms, as zeros and ones pulsing on and off in a host of computers that exist in real buildings and are switched on and off by real people. As Dewey might point out, our understanding of institutions is to be found, first and foremost, in our experience of them (Dewey, 1925).

At this point, we note that the intent is not to claim that policies and the surrounding context actually establish some sort of equilibrium, but there is some sense that a concept like homeostasis might be useful as a way to analyze social institutions. We might refer to Hannan and Freeman (1977) for an early attempt to treat institutions in ecological terms. In this sense, an institution should be understood as having been designed or having evolved to fit elements in its context. Another way of saying this is that we should find, mirrored in elements or aspects of an institution, determining influences in the surrounding context. For example, a school's organization might exhibit differing degrees of bureaucratization or simplicity depending on the institutional context in which it is embedded (Powell, 1991b).

Also useful are some attempts to address the issue of complexity in institutional terms. Some of this literature has pointed to the need for complexity in responding to situations that demand it or in surviving ever-dynamic conditions in the market or other situations. This, of course, draws from earlier literature on complexity in the physical sciences in which scientists find not-simple patterns in phenomena such as microscopic structures, but do not simply find randomness and chaos either. Rather, this inherent complexity requires new and possibly dynamic modes of description and analysis (Waldrop, 1992). In institutional terms, organizations (e.g., a firm) might respond to its surroundings (e.g., the market) not by settling into an equilibrium, or even a punctuated equilibrium, pattern of behavior, but instead can change continuously in response to the vagaries and dynamism of its environment (Brown and Eisenhardt, 1997).

To the notion of complexity, we add further ideas about the necessary improvisation and desired coherence that we seek in institutions that survive and thrive in a situation. Without engaging in the veneration of the local, we maintain that, if a program is to work well in a place, then to some extent its design or enactment must derive from consideration of what works well in a place or what might be most appropriate. In many cases, it may be that program proponents actually take elements from the institutional makeup of a context, e.g., faith-based approaches to tobacco education, and, in this manner of improvisation, fashion them into elements of the program being designed. To the extent that this happens, then aspects of elements of the new program will reflect elements to be found in that place. Faith-based tobacco education will inevitably inherit some of the language ("you've got to believe"), modes of organization (small sharing groups), media for transmitting knowledge (testimonials), and others, found in the social and institutional context it is embedded in. This is a necessary insight for social scientists. For example, one cannot hope to fully understand the power of the civil rights movement in the

United States without entering, in some depth, into the phenomenon and institution of the Baptist Church in the South. To fully understand the institution of "tree hugging," a social scientist should try to enter into the world of the rural community and the women behind the Brazilian Chipko movement. Policy analysts should be, to some extent, anthropologists — one cannot hope to explain corporate culture without getting inside the recesses of real corporations. To some extent, we need to study institutions and policies in context.

In all of this, there is the strong notion of groundedness of both the analyst and the analysis. The most proper description for such a mode of analysis is not "interpretation" but, rather, "revelation." It is this turn from text to context that characterizes our notion of postconstructionism. It is not just a philosophical turn, and in fact, its primary consequence is a marked shift in the analyst's mode of investigation that stands in some contrast to the reductionisms of classical analysis in the utilitarian mode and the more postmodern turn toward pure interpretation. In our return to the here and now, we emphasize the need to study context and this, in turn, requires employment of different modes of representation in our attempt to better portray the inherent complexity of the policy field.

We note that the notion of coherence employed herein is not about "fit" in the same sense of that of satisficing, as discussed in chapter 2. Satisficing is something that is best understood in terms of attainment of certain thresholds. Coherence, on the other hand, does not employ a notion of threshold; in fact, one cannot even speak of degrees of fit so much as modes of fit (or the opposite). Coherence is not a concept that seems to be well suited to sharp delineation but, rather, multiplex description. As opposed to optimization and satisficing, which are grounded in an ethic of rationality, coherence is grounded in an ethic of sustainability and meaning; coherent institutions are exactly those that endure over time.

Analysis

Institutional Polymorphism

This part of the analysis involves looking at the range of institutional or policy designs that exist in the field and assessing how each fits — or does not fit — its particular context.

The problem with the type of categorization that one encounters in traditional policy analysis, including the rational model, is that the analyst is only able to construct very idealized, abstract types to analyze. Consider an alternative that might be described as "decentralization of service delivery to the local level." The use of the classifier, "decentralization," evokes a false sense of homogeneity when, in fact, there are countless different variations on the modes of decentralization that one might encounter not in the policy books, but in the real world. Policy analysis has traditionally been a reductive exercise, but in the loss of dimensionality of the proposals that we analyze, we also lose relevance. The intent of the analysis is to go beyond categorization, to instead engage in thick description.

The idea is to enter into a concept and dig deep enough into its particularities and the specifics of its enactment until one finds enough diversity of practice. Even after a city council has decided on a ride-share scheme, for example, the analyst should realize that, as a concept, ride sharing is empty until translated into real programmatic features and practices. At that point, the analyst realizes that there are a rich, perhaps innumerable set of options on how one is to design and conduct ride sharing. Would it be imposed or voluntary? What types of incentives might we consider? Would the program occur only during peak hours of the day and in only certain locations? How might we engage the public in this initiative? Should we distinguish special programs such as van pools? Should we require businesses to establish in-house programs? These sources of polymorphism or diversity are essentially where "the rubber meets the road." The failure of ride sharing to make an impact in some cities may be traced not to the essential concept of ride sharing itself, but to these richer considerations.

The process of entering into a context deeply enough to begin to understand the contingencies and uniqueness is aptly described by speaking of cognition using the metaphor of height. From the rarified heights of the simplistic, unimodal perspective of reductionistic analytic approaches, all things can indeed seem the same. From the heights, real landscapes in the countryside can seem like every other landscape. The patches of land that make up Saint Paul, Minnesota, might just as well be Sao Paulo, Brazil. It is only when one descends back to the situation and assumes some cognitive proximity that one realizes the rich particularities that make Sao Paolo what it is and Saint Paul something altogether different.

Analysis then consists of entering more deeply into a concept (or, alternative, if you will) until one reaches a level of diversity at which these specifics start to matter. The first part of the analysis is simply that of pointing out what elements and specifics need to be studied at this deeper level. The second part of the analysis then entails pointing out the range of options that are available or have been attempted elsewhere. This is the range of institutional practices at a level of specificity in which these decisions matter, that is available to policymakers.

The first task is to enter into a concept until one reaches a sufficiently rich ground of program-design elements? What does this mean, exactly?

To illustrate this, we use an example of community-based resource management that is an ongoing experiment in institutional decentralization wherein local communities are delegated with the task of managing and using a local resource (such as a forest or fishing ground). We surmise that this type of program is one where we should find ample polymorphism. First of all, as decentralization goes, what is involved is the transfer of responsibility from the state to local policy actors. This exit of the state leads to a greater tendency toward improvisation — partly because, in many cases, the state devolves without transferring sufficient resources so the local community has to "make do" with the resources at hand. In addition, local actors are free to create new programs of their own design in the absence of a universalizing state that is able to rework entire landscapes to meet its program.

Looking at the literature on community-based resource management, one finds, however, an overly strong tendency to treat this as a homogenous concept. The notion is that this mode of governance is what happens when communities take over, period. This loss of dimensionality is seen in the simplistic characterizations of programs as being either "top-down" or "bottom-up," which, along with the strong directionality of the descriptive, fails to capture any of the inherent complexity of real programs. It is an operation we have seen before in our foray into classical analysis, in the sense that these simplistic dichotomies also transmute actual situations and force them onto a unitary plane of description (be it hierarchy, as in this case, or commensuration as in the case of classic analysis). But classifying every institutional experiment under this catch-all label of community-based or, worse, employing a catchall label even where there is no commonality among programs, precludes our understanding these programs in their richness of practice. This is why, quizzically, analysts struggle to explain why some community-based programs operate in some characteristic ways and others do not. To illustrate the methodologies, we utilize a case-study involving decentralization of coastal management. While the case study derives from coastal communities in Southeast Asia, the method of analysis is quite general.

Case Study: Community-Based Coastal Management Programs   As an example, we look at two areas, quite close together, in which community-based coastal management programs were initiated at around the same time (Figure 10.2). In each of these towns (Mabini and Calatagan in the Philippines), nongovernmental organizations (NGOs) arrived with a plan to engage local residents in establishing programs geared around policing illegal fishing, establishing habitat conservation areas, and providing environmental education. While ostensibly fashioned out of the same conceptual

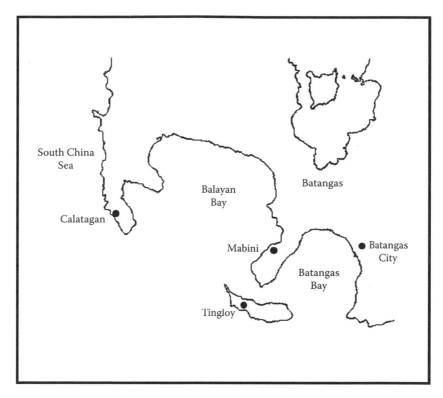

Fig. 10.2 Two community-based coastal management programs.

cloth, we proceed to inquire deeper into the richness of practice found in each program to bring out the areas in which one program distinguishes itself from the other. It is particularly useful to look at these particular examples drawn from a context, the Philippines, that has been the site for a long-standing and profound experiment in decentralization. Being a situation wherein the state has receded to a relative distance, what we should find is local communities having to improvise institutions and programs with the local resources and capacities at hand. That is, if we understand the state as some grand universalizer, then, under decentralization, we should find a fair degree of polymorphism.

Both programs arose out of similar conditions; sometime in the 1990s illegal fishing had been endemic to both areas. In both cases, there arose a plan to organize community members around self-governance of the coastal areas. This required extensive training in the deputization, under the national legal framework, of local fishers and others as patrol officers. In both cases, the process of organizing led to formation of a local planning and action committee with the goal of joint planning and enforcement of coastal management activities. These resulted in two new organizations: MATINGCADC in Balayan (Mabini) and SAMMACA in Calatagan. (Incidentally, acronym wordplay being much in vogue in some circles, we might note that, taking liberties with spelling, MATINGCADC alludes to the Tagalog word, "matingkad" meaning "clear," and SAMMACA evokes "sama ka" which, in Tagalog, means "join us.") In both cases, the organizations were "sponsored" by Manila-based NGOs at least initially: the group WWF in Balayan and CERD in Calatagan.

The two programs had much in common. Both were fashioned after strong notions of grounding governance in the local community. Both were strongly conservationist and employed essentially the same management strategies: deputizing local fishers in the Bantay Dagat ("ocean police") program against illegal fishing, designating areas for marine reserves, and setting up education programs against coral reef harvesting and other practices. Moreover, both are cited for their successes in establishing strong coastal management and enforcement programs in a short time. However, the researchers sank their analysis deeper into these practices until some distinct directions of differentiation emerged. Among these elements of polymorphism, we discuss several to illustrate the analysis: that of organizational structure, manner of enforcement, and issue salience. Snapshots of the analysis are illustrated in Figure 10.3 to Figure 10.7.

With regard to the organizational structure of the program, we can summarize many elements of the analysis using simple diagrams. As illustrated in Figure 10.3 to Figure 10.7, although both programs are based on the same model of community-based coastal management and enforcement, the two programs exhibit some notable differences. First, we note the greater level of complexity in the Calatagan program. The program revolves around an integrative planning body, SAMMACA, which exists as a federation involving a centralized provincial organization and, nested within or under it, a set of local councils. The Calatagan program too is found to have many more external linkages that go beyond the municipality and province. In contrast, the Balayan program revolves around an integrative planning and advocacy body, MATINGCADC. In both places, these bodies (SAMMACA and MATINGCADC) were designed after the same concept: a federated body of collaborating stakeholders.

Figure 10.3 and Figure 10.5 were developed by asking project managers in both sites to sketch the organizational structure as they understood it. There is a phenomenological dimension to understanding one's program, and we have endeavored to maintain the relative spacing, sizes, and configuration of the original sketches. When we analyze these structures, as both the manager and the researcher see it, some distinct differences emerge.

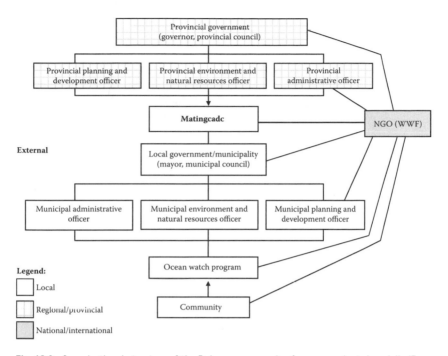

Fig. 10.3 Organizational structure of the Balayan program (performance-oriented model). (From Lejano, R. and A. Ocampo-Salvador. *Marine Policy*, forthcoming.)

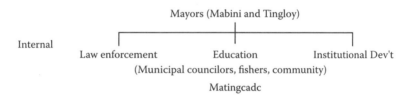

Fig. 10.4 Internal organization chart (Balayan program). (From Lejano, R. and A. Ocampo-Salvador. *Marine Policy*, forthcoming.)

The network of policy actors in Balayan is not as complex as in Calatagan, and the external linkages are relatively less pronounced. In Figure 10.3, we find that in Balayan there is a pronounced focus on the local and provincial. In contrast, in Figure 10.5, one sees a surprising predominance of extra-regional (in fact, national) actors composed of NGOs participating in the Calatagan program.

In both cases, we see the local federated body, MATINGCADC or SAM-MACA, being the central policy actor. However, in both cases we find that there exists a central nonlocal NGO — WWF in the case of Balayan

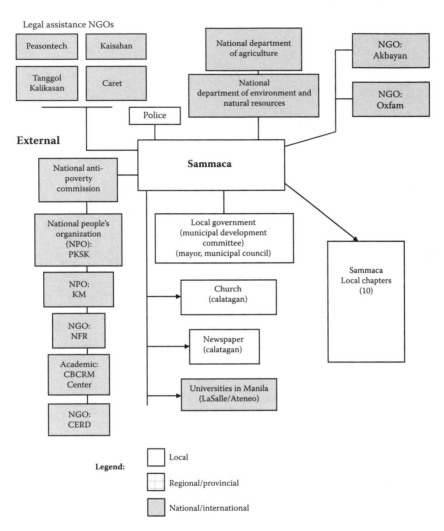

Fig. 10.5 Organizational structure of Calatagan program (network-oriented model). (From Lejano, R. and A. Ocampo-Salvador. *Marine Policy*, forthcoming.)

and Oxfam in the case of Calatagan, strongly supporting the program. However, even here there is a difference in that one sees that while Oxfam merely supports SAMMACA directly (mainly through funding), WWF stands in support of all the participating institutions (supplying both funding and staff).

We also note distinct differences when one enters into the primary organization at the center of the program, seen in Figure 10.4 and Figure 10.6. First, we can compare the composition of each organization. In Calatagan,

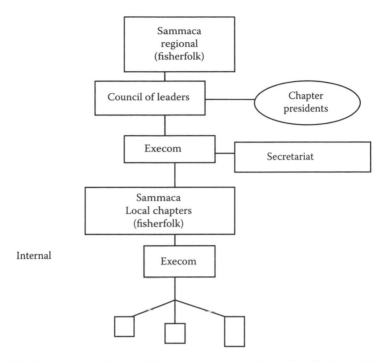

Fig. 10.6 Internal organization chart (Calatagan program). (From Lejano, R. and A. Ocampo-Salvador. *Marine Policy*, forthcoming.)

we find it to be dominated by fishers and, as an aside, notably marginalized fishers who do not own property or have access to private fishponds. In contrast, in Balayan, we see a greater cross-societal mix of policy actors, including not just fishers, but resort owners, local government officials, and other organizations. Thus, in terms of network design, although both programs revolve around similarly fashioned organizations, we see a difference in structure both in the regional and extraregional networks as well as the internal structure of the organizations themselves.

Differences in structure are evident in Figure 10.4 and Figure 10.6, and, in similar fashion, in the regional networks' organization chart the internal organization of Calatagan is characterized by a high degree of vertical hierarchy, seen visually in the number of levels that extend from the central unit. The degree of bureaucratization is also seen in the structural logic of the Calatagan program, which we see in the logical division of sublevels into local community districts. This suggests a strong focus on the formal nature of the organization. In contrast, we find considerably less formal bureaucratization in the Balayan organization, as seen in Figure 10.4.

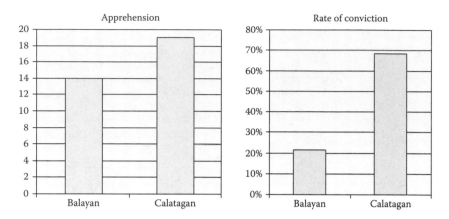

Fig. 10.7 Rates of apprehension and conviction of illegal fishers. (From Lejano, R. and A. Ocampo-Salvador. *Marine Policy,* forthcoming.)

Moreover, subdivision in Balayan is characterized not by formal, political jurisdiction, but along functional lines. In fact, the organization outlined in Figure 10.4 seems more geared toward program implementation rather than organizing or policy formulation.

Lastly, we note the distinct differences found when we enter into the organization of the single organization at the center of the program. In Balayan, we see a cross-societal mix of policy actors, including not just fishers, but resort owners, local government officials, and other organizations. In contrast, in Calatagan, we find it to be completely dominated by marginalized small-scale fishers. Thus, in terms of network design, although both programs revolve around similarly fashioned organizations, we see a difference in structure both in the regional and extraregional networks, as well as internal to the organizations themselves.

Another area of differentiation has to do with the manner of enforcement of ordinances against illegal fishing. Note that both programs basically enforced the same kinds of ordinances through the use of the same model for enforcement (deputized local wardens). At this level, the programs are homogenous. However, the analysis needs to get one level deeper into the enforcement programs (beyond form, that is) and look at their functionality. That is, we inquire into how might these two programs be run or managed differently? One dimension of comparison has to do with the intensity of enforcement, which is illustrated in Figure 10.7. Here, we see a distinctly more vigorous or aggressive enforcement program in Calatagan, both in the frequency of apprehension and, subsequent to apprehension, in the rate of conviction of the violators.

Lastly, we note that although both programs involve very similar types of activities, a deeper, more particular level of analysis will show that the programs "allocate" their time and attention across this spectrum of activities in different ways. Most of MATINGCADC's effort is aimed at enforcement and education. In Calatagan, however, we see an inordinate amount of effort dedicated to external linkages, i.e., networking with NGOs and other policy actors outside the region and even internationally, participating in efforts to lobby Congress for new legislation, and other external activities.

So, just by studying organizational structure and function, we see important distinctions between two formally similar programs. In the following section, we comment on how context and path dependence contribute to bring about these differences.

Ecology

We then proceed to an inquiry into how context (elements of place, demographics, history, etc.) can bring about some of these areas of differentiation. Part of the analysis involves linking features of context to the form and function of the resulting institutions such as those illustrated in Figure 10.3 to Figure 10.6. The intent is not to claim some sort of determinism. In the community coastal management case studies, we would not claim that only a program such as in Calatagan or in Mabini would be ideal or solely appropriate for their respective places to the exclusion of other possible programs. That would be asking too much of an analysis (much like asking a model plane to take us to Rio de Janeiro). When it comes to social phenomena, this author suggests that the reader give up on the notion of determinism. Rather, the analysis of institutional ecology simply posits that some factors, external to the program or policy, support some program or policy designs more strongly than others. The analyst simply endeavors to point out what institutional features are more strongly coherent with elements of context.

For example, let us take Figure 10.2 to Figure 10.7 together. The physical location of the two programs are the most obvious place to start. Note the difference in the coastal environment in both locations. In Calatagan, we see the program sites to be right next to open waters, in fact, the international waters of the China Sea (bordered by Taiwan and other countries). In contrast, the coastal environment of Mabini is more interiorly placed, away from the open ocean and nestled inside an interior bay, although still linked to the China Sea. Another difference is suggested by the composition of SAMMACA versus MATINGCADC. In the first, we find fishers, and historically marginalized fishers at that, while on the other side, we find a more wealthy, economically diverse set of actors. In fact, one notes even differences in the fishers by observing how their very homes look different in the two places — more thatched huts in Calatagan compared with more concrete structures in Mabini. This is also borne out by demographic income statistics. What might be the influence of these elements of place? First, we do not posit that differences in place produce, in deterministic fashion, differences in programs. But we do inquire into how these are consistent with observed patterns. Some areas of consistency are shown in Table 10.1.

The connections are not hard to make. In Calatagan, the greater physical vulnerability of the place and the greater social vulnerability of the organization's membership creates a program that is more wary of the external

Table 10.1 Elements in the institutional ecology of two coastal management programs

Elements of Differentiation	Contextual Support
Calatagan has a more aggressive pattern of enforcement against illegal fishing than Mabini.	Calatagan is more exposed, physically, to potential entrants from other provinces in the Philippines, as well as other countries; and is closer to marine traffic.
Calatagan spends much organizational effort on protest and legal action against industrial and commercial development of coastal areas, much more so than Mabini.	The Calatagan organization's membership is, generally, poorer and historically more marginalized than the membership in Mabini.
The organizational design of SAMMACA is more elaborate and multileveled than MATINGCADC, reflecting an emphasis on organization and empowerment.	Policy actors in Mabini are more multisectoral, while those in Calatagan are mostly traditionally marginalized fisherfolk.
The organizational design of MATINGCADC is more prone to faster and more efficient action. There is less bureacratization and a simpler pattern of communication (i.e., mostly done through WWF).	Policy actors in Mabini tend to be more diverse, and coalition formation is centered around obtaining relatively efficient improvements in resource management. In Calatgan, however, the organization is more based on sustaining a grassroots organization.
The external organization in Calatagan includes more external linkages and a greater emphasis on networking.	The traditionally disenfranchised policy actors in Calatagan are more prone to viewing external linkages as necessary for legitimization and for obtaining external support (e.g., legal assistance, funding, etc.).

and more vigilant against encroachment of industry and commercial interests into their place. In Mabini, there is a greater integration of sectors and a greater ability to focus on the creation of new livelihood strategies, owing to the heterogeneity and social positioning of its membership.

Moreover, the actors that make up SAMMACA are more marginalized than those in MATINGCADC, the former being composed almost primarily of fishers, and the latter including government officials, fishers and, anecdotally, local resort owners. The effect of this can be surmised from the preceding snapshots of these programs. In Calatagan, the emphasis has been on organizing and claiming a political voice. This is why the internal organization of SAMMACA (Figure 10.6) is so much more elaborate than that of MATINGCADC. This is also related to the need in the more disenfranchised Calatagan coalition to go outside the local region so as to enlist the aid, both materially and in policy advocacy, of national groups. In Balayan, in contrast, the emphasis was more on integrative planning and results-oriented collaboration. The focus on collaboration can be seen in the lower rates of arrest and subsequent conviction in Balayan (Figure 10.7). In contrast, in Calatagan, the greatest emphasis has been on enforcement of rights by the traditionally disenfranchised fishers, reflected in greater inflexibility against illegal fishing and emphasis on previous and ongoing legal cases against encroaching landowners.

Even in this brief analysis, we already see important elements of institutional coherence. Each individual program does exhibit elements that do seem to be particular local practices that fit their individual contexts uniquely. The degree of marginalization of the stakeholders that comprise SAMMACA, subsistence fishers, is categorically higher than that found in MATINGCADC. This may help us understand the greater emphasis in SAMMACA on program features that pertain to legitimization of an organization — an emphasis on structure and political subdivision, and a strong focus on establishing complex and far-ranging linkages to external organizations, with some linkages reaching up to Malacanang, the seat of power in the Philippines. In a sense, the structures of both the internal and external organization do display this degree of fit with the program's context, an important element of which happens to be the social and political identity of the program's proponents.

In contrast, the Balayan program focuses less on form and organizational structure and more on functional linkages. This is coherent with context, also, inasmuch as the central point of organizing in Balayan was simply that of resource management needs. In Calatagan, on the other hand, the *raison d'etre* for organizing involved both this same theme of resource management but also a second, equally important theme being that of legitimizing the status, condition, and political standing of the marginalized fishers. One could almost characterize the Calatagan structure as an organization-centered program, and the Balayan as a performance-centered program.

At this point, the analyst might be moved to ask, which program is better? We note that this need not always be a necessary component of policy analysis. It suffices to merely point out that in their different ways each program responds uniquely to elements and demands of their place. The analyst then posits how these programs respond and how they evolve in these conditions. For prospective analyses, the analyst does a similar exercise, but posits how unique elements of a situation might support or mitigate against certain program designs. Note that we use the word "support" and not "determine," where the former is understood as closely related to coherence. Another point we should make at this point is that it may not be possible to decide which is "better" since programs don't fall in easily filled categories (as in "successful" versus "unsuccessful"). In the preceding case study, the researchers found it impossible to judge which program was "better" because in this case, both programs did work to some extent and each could be successful (and even here, defining success is not easy). Both respond to needs of their particular place, as well as local capacities for self-governance. On a policy level, the most important question is not, "which program is best?" which is probably impossible to answer, but "which features of a program seem to work, which don't work too well, and why is this?" and "which program features fit local conditions better, and which would need more extensive work on institution building in the community?" The intent of analyzing institutional coherence is not to engage in categorization, an eminently rationalist exercise, but to instead to study institutions as social phenomena that can be understood through "experience" and need to be studied on the ground. In the next section, we introduce another case study to further develop the notion of institutional coherence.

Institutional Coherence

In this analysis, we look not mainly at physical or even demographic elements of place, but instead focus on the fit of a new policy with the existing institutional, i.e., organizational and behavioral, makeup of a place. The focus is not so much on the features of context as much as on the established practices, which are, after all, what an institution is. To illustrate the analysis of institutional coherence, we introduce another case study, involving the institution of a new regime for managing ecological habitat.

Case Study: The Turtle Islands and Resource Governance   The situation we describe is a particularly salient and moving account of how policy comes about and is enacted in a place. It is also an ongoing and unresolved policy dilemma. The Turtle Island municipality is actually a group of six small islands in the Sulu Sea at the southwestern tip of the Philippines and about 40 km north of Sandakan, Malaysia (see Figure 10.8). The islands range in size from 7 to 116 hectares. The island system is the only remaining major green turtle rookery in Southeast Asia, and several species of turtle nest and breed there, including the hawksbill turtle. While primarily marine, the female turtle returns to land in order to lay its eggs. Egg clutches are small pits, 12 to 18 inches deep, in which the female deposits from 40 to 190 eggs and covers them with a layer of sand. The islands were first settled around 1949 and subsequently incorporated as a municipality in 1959. Beginning in the early 1960s, the sale of turtle eggs has been a source of revenue in the region.

Turtle egg harvesting and sale has long been a practice in the region, but efforts to conserve the eggs and preserve the habitat were formalized under Department of Environment and Natural Resources (DENR) Ministry Administrative Order No. 33, which was issued in 1983 and allowed the local jurisdiction to manage conservation activities. The emphasis in these earlier years was on management. Stemming from initiatives by the local government and the Task Force Pawikan, a small unit created within the DENR, what was negotiated and allowed to evolve is a finely tuned mechanism for controlling the rate of harvest and the allocating the revenues for the same. By the time AO 33 was issued, residents and the local government had already evolved a system whereby harvesters were licensed by the local government and kept within a prescribed maximum level of harvest. Revenues from the sale of turtle eggs were allocated in proportions of 60% to the harvester and associated fees to the municipality, 10% to a conservation fund (the Tawi-Tawi Marine Turtle Conservation Foundation), and 30% reserved for species preservation. Allowable harvest volumes were fixed based on the aggregate judgment of the residents and varied from year to year. During years in which the local management team judged the demand to exceed the allowable harvest, lotteries were held to allocate the eggs above a baseline quota. A fairly thorough set of standards concerning equipment, harvest areas, and harvest procedures were maintained throughout this time.

In 2001, in what was understood as a significant victory for the environmental community, the Philippine congress enacted the Wildlife Resources Conservation and Protection Act, Republic Act No. 9147 (RA 9147), which was passed in compliance with the Philippine government's

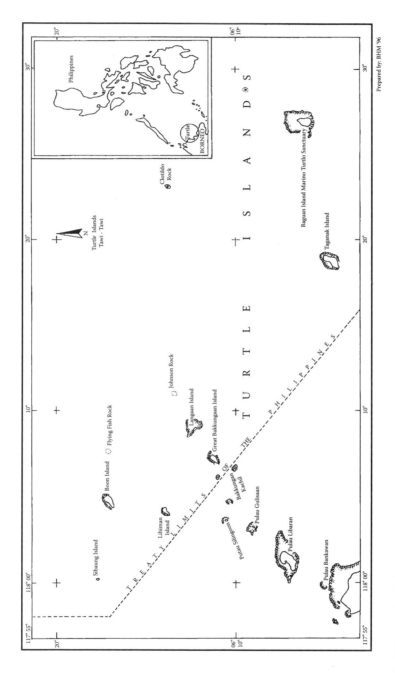

Fig. 10.8 Location of the Turtle Island system.

commitment as member of the Convention on the International Trade of Endangered Species (CITES). This was subsequently translated into actionable regulations by the DENR in its Implementing Rules and Regulations (IRR) for RA 91410. In particular, RA 9147 and the accompanying IRR prohibited the collection of threatened wildlife and by-products, except for scientific or propagation purposes. This directly affected the harvesting of eggs from the green turtle, an endangered species. RA 9147 superseded DENR Ministry Administrative Order No. 33, which had been regulating marine turtle egg collection in the Turtle Islands from 1983. Under RA 9147, there is now a total ban on the collection and sale of marine turtle eggs in the Turtle Islands. The effect on the turtle conservation program was stunning. Almost overnight, the program unraveled. The harvesting of turtle eggs continued, but this time at a greater pace because the situation turned into what was essentially an open commons regime. Most importantly, conservation of turtle eggs halted almost immediately — i.e., the community stopped the practice of reserving 30 percent of the eggs for preservation, and the 10 percent that previously went to a community conservation fund also ceased. In 2003, the Municipality of Turtle Island adopted a resolution assuming the entire authority for managing the habitat and turtle egg resource, effectively denying the authority of the national government. By this time, physical threats to DENR personnel had caused their periodic visits to the islands to cease completely.

The analyst's role is to explain why policy fails when it does and what features of policy might work to prevent its (in this case, catastrophic) failure. The notion of coherence can be a powerful tool in such analysis. We illustrate this for the Turtle Islands case in simple ways. One is to consider the notion of institutional support — that is, what institutions (in the context being studied) would support or help maintain the proposed policy and what institutions would hinder it? The focus then is on the compatibility of the proposed policy with life on the ground, in both the formal and everyday sense of institution. We summarize some findings of such an analysis in Table 10.2, where we describe institutions that support or hinder the establishment of the ban on turtle egg harvesting.

Table 10.2 illustrates the type of analysis required, which can be relatively simple. It may involve identification of exogenous institutions that support versus hinder the proposed policy or, as in Table 10.2, the analyst need not classify the external institutions as "supporting" or "conflicting" since these categories are less important than an explanation of how these external institutions may potentially be related to the proposed policy. It is also possible to add a third column to Table 10.2, in which the analyst

Table 10.2 Elements of institutional coherence in a habitat management program

Institutions in Policy Field	Relationship to Proposed Policy
Complying with CITES	The new policy, RA 9147, allows the country to comply with CITES, to which it is a signatory. This may help access international sources of support and diffuse criticism over other practices. This responds to international, not local, concerns.
Established local system of egg harvest and conservation	RA 9147 would remove up to 80% of family income in the Turtle Islands almost overnight. Aside from the income, this would also be a loss in a relatively low-conflict system of habitat management and potentially transform the system into an unmanaged open-access situation.
Centralization of DENR	The remoteness and insular nature of the Turtle Islands makes it almost impossible for the national government to implement RA 9147 effectively.
Local fishing industry	Fishing, as a livelihood, exists as family or small-scale enterprises meant for local consumption. Access to external markets is poor, and it is doubtful that fishing can make up for a significant portion of loss in egg-related revenue due to RA 9147.

would enter possible consequences of each of these (or all of these) areas of coherence — this last task essentially involves a large degree of speculation and/or prediction, and the analyst should note this.

Policy Application

The application of this mode of analysis would result in policy reports that would have a distinctly different look and format. The analysis would entail more local color, a greater attention to developing the case study and description of context, and practically, a greater amount of the researcher's time spent in the field. The reason is that the stronger focus of this type of analysis is not on classification, or, as in the case of utility theory, cardinally quantifiable classification, but on description.

The question that we must ask is, How do we link this type of analysis to policymaking? Often we can find analyses that include elements of that described herein in reports that might be called institutional analysis, capacity building, social impact evaluation, or other titles. As a simple rule, we might recommend that the analyst consider this type of methodology in any study that purports to be a policy analysis. The entire study might be a deep entry into institutional coherence, or it might simply be a section in a larger planning or policy study. The linkage can take the place of refinement of the proposed policy or focused public dialogue. However, the analysis can have its most powerful impact when there is a systematic effort to link its recommendations to action. The linkage can be spelled out in the analysis itself, as in the following diagram:

External institutions → Relationship to proposed policy → Response

In this case, we begin with the analysis of Table 10.2, wherein we assess how external institutions and practices either help or hamper the proposed policy, and we link this to a proposed response. The response may be, as in the case of supportive institutions, to propose ways to link the proposed program to these institutions. For example, strong local church groups can be linked to a health information campaign by engaging these groups and requesting their help in hosting and running health fairs. The response can also be an attempt to resolve the conflict between the external institution and the proposed policy. For example, suspicion of ethnic or other enclaves of externally imposed policies might call for an extended planning forum conducted within the community and the delegation of project management to residents of the place. The gist is that the analysis should point out areas for action so as to increase the coherence between the policy and the place of enactment.

Another important use of this type of analysis is that of revealing needed changes in the proposed policy itself. What might have been possible in the Turtle Islands case? The first thing we should note is that this type of analysis would directly lead to the questioning of the appropriateness of a regulatory model of policy action wherein standards are set from the seat of government and assumed to automatically blanket the policy field and change entire landscapes in each of the affected jurisdictions. Rather than impose an absolutist standard and a constraint to individual action, the policy might seek to enable progressive initiatives in the field. For example, the policy may create planning grants that a community might use to create forums for integrative deliberation (e.g., on how to wean the community away from dependence on the protected resource). The policy may have been adaptive in form, calling for each municipality to create a plan for incrementally reducing the harvest of turtle eggs over time. The plan could then be used as a basis to track the incremental adjustment of the community from egg harvesting to other modes of revenue collection. Or, if complete withdrawal from harvesting is impossible, then the plan could be used as the basis for a local partial-use regime that may even be identical with the established practice. This would not exactly be an "exception to the rule," but rather a move away from a sole focus on establishing rules and onto the task of establishing practices, i.e., institutions.

Coherence means paying close attention to conditions on the ground. In this return to the real and to the contextual, is there any room in the analysis for interpretation? The answer is that there necessarily is an interpretive component, but the more apt descriptive for the policy situation is a manifold, phenomenological reality. We do not posit that the reality to be studied is an objective phenomenon simply to be measured and recorded. Institutions and policies are experienced. In understanding institutions as experience, we subscribe to the phenomenological notion that while there is no way to distance ourselves from the reality of this experience, it is subject to a realization that is complex and irreducible to a unitary notion such as utility or text. The analysis of institutions as cohering in one time and place is not an exercise in simple interpretation. Rather, we recognize the undeniable yet multidimensional modes by which different practices and institutions coexist and, in many cases, support each other in a certain context. Coherence is not a matter of mere interpretation, any more than coordination among motorists through the alternating of green and red traffic lights is a matter of mere interpretation. This coordination is real, in physical and other terms. It is not simply enough to remark on the textuality or the intent of policy — rather, we insist on contextuality and multiplexity of analysis.

CHAPTER 11

Topology

Introduction

One of our foremost objectives is to formulate new analytics that allow us to better merge text with context. In chapters 9 and 10, we presented two such conceptual frameworks, each drawing from different bodies of theory to develop novel modes of analysis. We continue this in the present chapter and proceed to draw up the outlines of new theoretical constructs.

Part of the "ethic" of this chapter is to not insist that policy situations be translated into a single, unidimensional plane of analysis. Once we allow ourselves to think this way, however, we encounter context in all its utter complexity. One aspect of complexity has to do with dimensionality. That is, if we are to insist on bracketing an experience into categories, we then realize that, to be faithful to the experience, we have to admit many categories. The other recourse is to allow the phenomenon to remain in its gestalt — but experience, in its raw form, is ultimately not communicable. Policy is a communicative, public process, however, and somehow we need to bridge the span between experience, nature, context, field, object, and analysis, theory, text, center, and subject.

Related to the issue of multidimensionality is the multimodal nature of reasoning, cognition, perception, and understanding. The act of splitting out into components of reason is reminiscent, and possibly symptomatic, of Weber's account of disenchantment (Weber, 1864). Weber himself might say that this is a one-way process without recourse to reentering a new enchantment, so to speak. Perhaps this is true. But we can find ways to be cognizant of the different spheres of rationality and find ways to bring them together, not translated into a single plane of exchange but simply to account for the multiplexity of understanding. Thus, the first analytic task is that of simply increasing the dimensionality of the analysis. The first objective of this chapter is stated below.

> Objective: We need to broaden our analytic to consider multiple dimensions of experience and understanding.

The other facet of complexity that concerns us is that of the nonformal nature of policy phenomena, where we choose not to use the word informal because this is often associated with the ad hoc or provisional. In other words, when we treat policy situations as phenomena and approach them as they are, they begin to exceed, spill over, and contradict the formal models we put them in. By formal, we simply mean the form or concept that we impose on the phenomenon in our analysis of it. It is the penchant for the typological of which academics are the most guilty — the insistence on reducing complex phenomena to the rarified *lingua franca* of our categorical schema.

> Objective: We need to envision modes of analysis that overcome the stricture of typology. One way that we can do this is by linking analysis to the practice and phenomenon of policy situations.

An example of form is found in the organizational. A central concept that we use to portray collective action is that of organization. Oftentimes, we proceed to then depict the situation in the form of a structure — the most classic manifestation of this is the organizational chart, wherein we have levels of authority or centrality, and various sublevels in a hierarchical fashion. Membership in the organization means entering into this organizational structure.

But, as various writers have impressed on us, the logic of practice defies the formal. Returning to the example of organization, we realize that associations between individuals are not well bounded, and belonging to groups often involves gradations of membership (e.g., informal kinship circles or even less formal circles of friendships). Even when formal organizational boundaries and membership rules are rigid, the functional boundaries that delineate who is who, who does what, and numerous other elements of organization, can be very blurred. Tasks are done outside the formal pathways, and people's roles are more complex than they are supposed to be (i.e., take the example of an elementary school teacher who has to function also in the role of ersatz parent, guidance counselor, referee, judge, jury, troop leader, and pediatrician). If we are to understand what makes policies and institutions work or fail, then we need to enter into what these entities really are like, not just how they are formally laid out. Boundaries are blurred, flexible, evolutionary, and nonformal. Similarly, roles and identities are multiplex, shifting, evolutionary, and nonformal. These are not fixed categories, in reality, but rather, fluid phenomena.

By treating policy and institutions as phenomena, we need to increasingly be open to their fuzzy, boundary-spanning, dynamic, and hypermeaningful nature. Taking a cue from the critical realists, if reality consists in underlying generative mechanisms, then observable elements such as roles, boundaries, and structure are indeed phenomena (or, perhaps more accurately, epiphenomena) that arise from the action of these mechanisms. This brings us to the next objective of our analysis.

> Objective: We need to develop analytics that are not rigidly formal and that can allow us to be faithful to the multiplex and nonformal character of policy action.

Why is it necessary to account for nonformal aspects of policy? Most simply, it is because policy analysis is an applied discipline. If we are to intervene in the real world in effective ways, then we must be able to understand how it functions in a real sense. This means having the ability to go beyond the purely formal.

We realize that the action of context somehow resides in the nonformal. In the beginning of the book, we used the example of structural adjustment programs for developing nations. Why is it that this recondite set of prescriptions might have widely differing effects in different nations? Perhaps, it is precisely because the prescriptions begin, and end, in the formal. Undoubtedly, context affects the working of the policy in ways that go beyond the boundaries of the formal model. Real policy actors are not autonomous, atomistic, rational agents, at least not in the sense of the rational model. Real institutions are not simply rules and organizational structures, but intertwined with culture, histories, personalities, and other contingencies of context. In fact, not even the formal model that lies behind these prescriptions, that of the market, is true to real-world markets. Markets are made up of real people in real places, exhibiting their own contextuality and, in fact, embedded in the habitus of place (Granovetter, 1985). Used car dealerships in Hungary probably function in different ways than their counterparts in Los Angeles. Judiciaries vary widely from place to place, even within the same state system. Our most basic question should be whether, especially given the typologization of policy analysis, some of the most important elements that aid or undo a policy may lie embedded in context. The formal, in contrast, is inherently a universalist concept (e.g., recall Aristotle's concept of the pure forms or Kant's noumena). Just as important, the formal is also a wholly constructionist concept.

In this chapter, we chart some directions for moving beyond the formal. This involves creating modes of analysis in which we begin not with form but with the working of a policy or institution as such. By approaching policies and institutions from an almost phenomenological perspective, we can better choose forms by which to describe them or, even more significantly, create analytics that allow us to depart from the formal. We outline examples of these approaches in the hope of furthering this task from this point onward. The intent of this chapter is not so much to present finished models of analysis but to propose approaches by which we can construct (or, with a nod toward Weber, reconstruct) models and processes.

In the following section, we lay out a mode of description that begins with the need to go beyond the formal. We then use a case study to illustrate how these new analytics might be applied.

Theory: From Typology to Topology

In this section, we describe a new theory that portrays individuals and institutions in topological terms. By topological, we simply mean unbounded sets that can span multiple dimensions and overlap each other in a complex collection of sets. We could have used the less daunting term "multidimensional" instead. However, the notion of a topology evokes the image of multiple and overlapping memberships in different sets, which is useful for our theory. Terminology is not so important in this case.

We begin with the topology of rationality, concentrating on the modes of reasoning, action, and identity of the individual person. We discuss the need to extend our models of the individual as one possessing the skill to understand situations along different and multiple dimensions simultaneously and, moreover, to somehow integrate these differing aspects. The first topology that we speak of, in this case, is that of reason. We, in fact, would like to expand the idea of reasoning to include other ways of knowing and acting in the world.

We then use the notion of a topology to describe institutions. Specifically, we illustrate how we can formulate a model of institutions that responds more powerfully to practice than classic models (e.g., hierarchies or coalitions). We construct a model that is not rigidly formal and instead sees the institutions as emerging from the working and reworking of relationships. What is important in this model is neither structure nor agency but relationship. We formalize the model of care and end the chapter with an application to the Turtle Islands case study. How we assess policies and institutions immediately follows our model of knowledge and action. In the previous chapter, an ecological notion of institutions gave us a way to analyze policies in terms of coherence. Here, we depict institutions as products of relations (or care) and so analyze the effect of policies and institutions through this lens. In the following sections, what is most important is not the particular model that we develop, but the mode of theorizing that allows us to construct these alternative models.

Topologies of Rationality

The liberal model began with strong notions about who and what the person is (e.g., *res cogitans*) and proceeded to build a corresponding concept of reason (e.g., individual rationality) which has assumed a dominant place in policy thought. It is only fitting, then, that in order to build new frameworks for policy, we should push beyond these boundaries, to the extent that we can. In this section, we attempt to describe a less constricted notion of rationality. We will use the word "topology" to refer to this more expansive notion. When we talk of rationality as a topological concept, we simply mean that there are differing and multiple, perhaps infinite, planes of rationality. To use an analogy, imagine reason as the combined mapping that results when all of these modes of knowing are placed on top of each other. Returning to the example, in chapter 7, of the interviews done with residents who live beside the landfill, we recall the multiplicity of ways that people talked about the issue (see Figure 11.1). The point is that if we are to take people seriously in the way they talk, then this is not far from recognizing that we each employ, simultaneously and with seeming coherence, multiple modes of reasoning. Again, a geometric analogy may be helpful. Consider the topology as a multidimensional surface. As we have seen before, analytics most often work by reducing or projecting everything onto a single plane. In this manner, utility theory privileges one dimension of reasoning, which is that projected onto the plane of individual utility (or commensurable value). In contrast, we recognize the existence of multiple planes of knowing and, furthermore, that we posit (and this is a bold statement) that they do not exist simply as separate planes but, to a great extent, as one integrated whole. Our model for analysis is then this concept of knowing in an integrated, multidimensional fashion.

When we speak of rationality as topological, it pertains to the idea of multiple and overlapping generative norms of reason. Related to this is an understanding of universalist or particularist norms of rationality as dimensionalities of a higher-ordered, undifferentiated rationality. Using

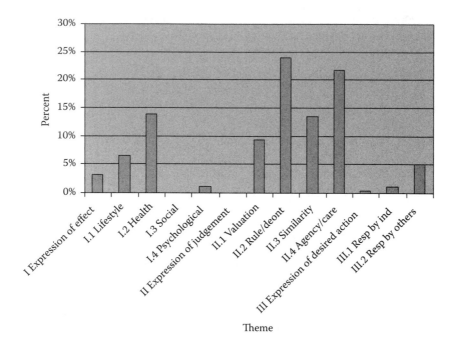

Fig. 11.1 Morphology of individual reasoning. (From Lejano, R. et al. New Methodologies for Describing the Phenomenology of Environmental Risk. Working Paper, 2005. University of California Toxic Substance Research and Teaching Program, Davis, CA.)

the same analogy employed in chapter 9, this is akin to the projection of a multiplex, undifferentiated object onto a subspace or simplifying plane. One might ask whether we can, by observation of a multitude of projections onto subspaces, piece together an understanding of the entire topology? Maybe not — that is, it is possible that we can only construct more complete descriptions, but we cannot completely reverse the reduction to lower-ordered spaces any more than, by inspection of the tail, can we reconstruct the entire pachyderm. Now, is it essential to reconstruct the entire topology? For argument's sake, I would say that we cannot and, generally, do not want to. Policy situations invariably emphasize some dimensions or elements of policy more than others, and, generally, some perspectives will suffice to allow us to act in a policy sense on the basis of these subspaces of particular understandings.

This brings us to the idea of coherence. Embedded in Figure 11.1 is the implicit assumption that though we distill different modes of reasoning, they are all employed by the individual as a coherent, integrated whole. Why would we need to presume that such exists, and, indeed, why presume that there is something expansive for distinct understandings to be embedded in? To begin to answer this, we (ironically) borrow epistemological notions from the liberal model. We encounter in society and, in fact, within each individual, distinct motivations, beliefs, impulses, feelings, allegiances, reasonings, and constructs. Within each individual, these differentiated phenomena seem to mingle and diverge, perhaps to contradict in a teleological and epistemological dialectic. Yet, these diffractions do come together and cohere — this phenomenon is none other than the concept of the *person*. However we construct the person, that is where coherence resides, as if the uncountable planes of understandings and conceptions all intersect in a finite embodied person. The concept of the person, in fact, can be considered a universal category and, at the same time, the situated integration of these directions, extensions, and infinitudes (Lejano, 2002). Unless we are willing to doubt the integrity of personhood and the very category of person or to reduce it to the particular, residual outcome of a dialectic of situated discourses.

However, unlike the liberal conceptualization, this person-space is embedded in a field of intersecting and diverging planes of reference. This questions our understanding of what autonomy is or how it is localized. It does not seem particularly helpful to conceive of the person as a simple bundle of thoughts, feelings, needs, motivations, and endowments, i.e., like an unassimilated *bricolage., r*. Rather, let us think of the person as an undifferentiated entity, extending continuously from experience to experience, without betraying or detracting from the integrity of self. Doubtless, some will argue the existence of the irrational, the subconscious, nature, or, interestingly, community, to question the integrity of the person, yet all these things project as surfaces from the topology of its undifferentiated origin. The person is the thick description of coherence. Neither is the person an incidental node in the discursive field because the person is its own topology. It can at least be argued, effectively, that we at least perceive and understand self as an undifferentiated whole and reject the contrary — how else would self-reflection be possible. Introspection shows that we each at least believe in the integrity of self. This is what we mean by a topology: a multiplex and integrated whole that exists as the coming together of diverse and multiple dimensions of action and being. Part of what makes the person is the social self, which is not just understood as being one among others.

Rather, the communities to which a person belongs are part of the dimensions that make up that person. The topological notion of personhood sees the person as extending beyond the unitary, atomistic self, and encompassing all of the associations, encounters, and affinities associated with the person. In short, the person is also a product or topology of the system of relationships in which she is involved. This suggests that we see the person as not simply a node in a web of relationships. Rather, person-hood is partly defined and constituted by relationships. That is, an important dimension of personhood is the integration and overlapping of these complex, possibly innumerable relationships with others.

In the next section, we extend the idea of the topological notion of the person and expand the topology to social groups and institutions. Later in the chapter, it will become clear why such an alternative framework should have profound policy implications.

Topologies of Institutions

Our main objective is to bring together text and context. This entails developing policy models that stretch beyond the rigidly formal. In the last section, we saw how an individual is the integrand of multiple rationalities and, moreover, the sum total of the person's extension into an entire system of relationships. In this section, we will see how this extends to the level of the institutions. Specifically, we will understand institutions to be the product of the unceasing working and reworking of relationships. To help us develop the new model, it will help to begin by considering two, more traditional, models and, then, painting a new contrast with the new model. Two dominant models of institutions strongly emphasize form, namely, that of *hierarchies* and *coalitions*. In this section, we develop an alternative mode of depicting institutions as *structures of care*. The three models are represented in Figures 11.2a, b, and c.

Hierarchical models are most often used in policy situations wherein the administrative state is a dominant actor. In this model, depicted in Figure 11.2a in the form of a classic "organizational chart," what is important is the assignment of functions to the different parts of the system. While the overall system, overseen by the seat of authority at the top of the chart, might have the welfare of the public as its overall objective, nodes lower down in the hierarchy can take on narrower concerns in a type of rationality that Weber termed *zwekrationalitat* (Weber, 1864) and, in fact, corresponds to the bureaucratic form of organization that Weber described so insightfully. This depiction of systems of administrative governance emphasizes the *formal*, where the dimensions of form are composed of structure, clear lines of authority, and routines. What matters is the positioning of actors in this overall network and the macroscopic configuration of the system.

In other policy situations, we find "big government" to be less dominant. One such case is the phenomenon of decentralization in which

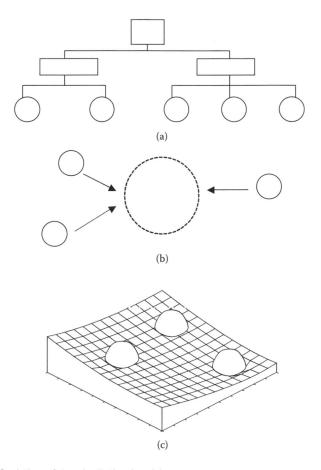

Fig. 11.2 Depictions of three institutional models.

responsibilities for governance shift from the central state and onto more local policy actors (Manor, 1999). These experiments in institution building revolve around attempts to construct modes of governance that are more inclusive, flexible, participative, and more conducive to public–private partnerships. One model that has been developed around less state-centered arrangements posits a group of policy actors (whether individuals or groups) who freely come into association and form a coalition of agents who cooperate to pursue a larger, public goal. In the model of the coalition (depicted in Figure 11.2b), rather than emphasize structural elements of the system, the formal is seen in the depiction of the policy actor as an autonomous agent. In other words, the model emphasizes *agency* rather than structure. As with the hierarchy, this model also emphasizes the formal, but it is embodied in the model of the rational actor and the set of outcomes or payoffs obtained from the coalition. The most dominant depiction of the rational agent is, as we saw in chapter 2, that of a utility maximizer who joins a coalition to increase personal utility (Olson, 1968; Taylor, 1987). In other models of the coalition, the collective is forged through commonalities of belief or professional training (e.g., see Haas, 1992; Sabatier, 1993). How we understand institutions to evolve and operate is bound up in this formal model of the actor and the "relentless workings" of individual interest. Self-interest binds the actors together in a cooperative arrangement formalized by *rule systems* (Ostrom, 1990). While *structure* characterizes hierarchy, coalitions emphasize *exchange.*

In this section, we propose an alternative model that allows us to depict institutions for collective action as *structures of care.* Rather than a macroscopic focus on system structure or a microscopic focus on the individual actor, we choose to build our model by focusing on what goes on in the social "space" between actors (depicted in Figure 11.2c). In this model, we use the truism that, as social actors, people cannot but help forming relations with others, so we find webs of relationships already present in any situation. We then use these relationships to explain the rules, practices, and roles that characterize the system of governance. It is a model that is less rigidly formal than the previous one and works well in explaining some real-world systems of governance. What makes the institutions function is not the setting of clear lines of authority or individual interest, but the coherence of actions with the web of relationships. What is important is not structure or individual rationality but the active working and reworking of relationships. In this model, structure and agency emerge as epiphenomena of relationship building. The model allows us a way to more richly describe decentralized modes of public management, especially when policy actors are embedded in extensive, long-standing cultural, socioecological ties (e.g., see Barrett et al., 2001 as an example). This model also responds to situations where practice clearly exceeds the boundaries of the formal (e.g., Bourdieu, 1990).

At this point, we should draw a distinction between the model of institutions as *structures of care* and that of *networks.* Networks are often defined as multinodal structures consisting of relationships, often informal, that cross formal organizational boundaries (Powell, 1991a; Mayntz, 1993). A general feature of most depictions of networks is the existence of relationships outside the traditional administrative state or market (Jones, Hesterly, and Borgatti, 1997; Keast et al., 2004), encompassing informal relationships and, in this regard, related to our notion of structures of care. These models have different points of emphasis however. The network, as a concept, is primarily a teleological one. Networks exist mainly to allow some function or task to be carried out, a notion closely related to the functionalist model of Mitrany (1975). Structures of care are ontological — they characterize any social situation, and we describe functions, roles, rules, and structure to merely emerge from the workings of relationships (or structures of care). Networks still invariably either emphasize structure (Powell, 1991a) or exchange (e.g., Miles and Snow, 1986), while structures of care focus on relation building as constitutive of policy actors.

The alternative model allows us to focus more closely on new aspects of institutions. In particular, the model of structures of care better characterizes systems of governance that rely less on formal bureaucratic structures of authority or on voluntary associations of atomistic actors, and more on transactive systems that exist in contexts where policy actors are inextricably bound together in rich relations of culture, history, kinship, and others. Moreover, we believe that the relational is another dimension to add to the various elements of policy design (e.g., Schneider and Ingram, 1997), that element of policy construction that occurs within relationship building. We lay out the model in more formal terms, before proceeding on to the case study.

A Formal Model of Structures of Care

We begin by returning to some of the phenomenologists discussed earlier, for whom one basic essence of existence was that of intentionality, or the ability of the person to form a relation with other beings and things in the world (see Brentano, 1874; Husserl, 1900; Heidegger, 1927). Another word for this being-in-the-world is care. The concept of care was given a more explicit formulation by Gilligan who wrote "… care is thus an activity of relationship, of seeing and responding to need, taking care of the world by sustaining the web of connection…" (Gilligan, 1982). An ethic of care emphasizes relation over juridical rulemaking. Whereas the traditional model creates formal-juridical lines of organization or hierarchy (e.g., organization charts, legal authorities), the model of care seeks to establish complex and active relationships between policy actors. The model is characterized with a set of principles, beginning with the following.

> Principle: In this model, we characterize institutions by describing active relationships between policy actors.

Institutions have traditionally been characterized by describing formal elements such as structures or rules. Let us instead describe an institution as a complex web of relationships among members of a community — what we will refer to as *structures of care*. Structures of care result from relationships that are constantly worked and reworked to maintain shared understandings and sustained relationships between individuals and groups. This gives us a notion of institutions as other than static systems of rules or structures, but patterns of relating that need to be nurtured and reworked. Thus, linkages between policy actors are not formal or juridical — they are, instead, transactive.

In the hierarchical, coalitional, and network models, what matters for an actor are position, payoff, and exchange, respectively. In contrast, with the model of care, what matters is the imperative to maintain relationships and to let the latter guide the actions of an individual or a group. When relationships are the primary generative mechanisms for social patterns and institutions, the following principle follows.

> Principle: Structure, agency, rules, roles, etc., are all epiphenomenal to relationship building. For this reason, these same elements, e.g., rules and roles, blur.

In many real-world situations, rule systems are either not followed or seem to be inordinately complex. A good example of this, as described in Stone (2000) is the institution of elder care. In this example, we can readily understand how care cannot be so simply understood (or codified) as a simple set of formal rules. Were such a complex set of rules to be written, it might quickly lose relevance as the condition of the person being cared for changed. In fact, caring involves an innumerable set of practices that basically involve responding to the needs, feelings, and desires of the care for. When we think of exemplars of care, we realize that these cannot be encompassed by describing formal elements — such care is too complex, dynamic, fluid, and responsive. However, situations that seem to be "exceptions to the rule" are comprehensible when we understand them as arising out of the pattern of relationships. Returning to the example of elder care, "caring" is best described as a complex relationship between persons. The second thing that we will find is a blurring of structure and role since relationships can be more open-ended and multiplex than a simple delineation of roles. Not bound by formal descriptions of rules and structures, we are now open to more indeterminate, transactive, and amorphous systems. Most significantly, it is easy to understand why rules, roles, structures, and other formal elements should seem blurry if we understand these same elements to be merely epiphenomena to the main generative mechanism — relationships.

This complicates what we understand as organization, which is also epiphenomenal. One classic model of the organization is again that of the coalition, which is simply an aggregate of the member individuals — a simple set operation, in geometric terms. In contrast, a differing notion of organization is found in the proposed model, one that is more akin to a topology, which simply means an overlapping, loosely bounded set of actors. In a topology, an individual can be a member of differing sets at the same time, and a set can be a member of a higher-order set, etc. Boundaries are open (or fuzzy), and linkages between individuals and groups are difficult to characterize formally and so are better described as multiple systems of relation. Organization, in this more complex model, is the sum total (or, in another manner of speaking, the density surface) of all of these interlocking, overlapping, and manifold associations all overlain onto each other. Figure 11.3 depicts this difference between a simple set operation and a topology.

Let us now formalize what we mean by a relationship. We define it as a set of "mappings" carried out along three dimensions. By mapping, we simply mean the constitution of identity of a policy actor as a set of characteristics or attitudes that the actor takes on as an individual and in relation to other actors. Because these mappings (or relationships) link a policy actor to numerous other actors and groups, the individual may belong to a large number of groups concurrently. We depict the relations established by a policy actor in three interrelated operations (as depicted in Figure 11.4):

Constitution of self: establishing one's own identity or position, in that particular context.

Constitution of self-to-other: establishing one's identity or position vis-à-vis, or in reaction to, another.

Constitution of self-and-other: establishing the identity or position of self-and-other, i.e., the union formed by the two policy actors taken as a group.

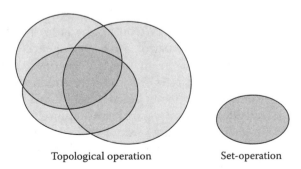

Topological operation   Set-operation

Fig. 11.3 Organization as set-operations and topologies.

Fig. 11.4 Mapping relationships.

The entire field of these relational mappings constitutes the structure of care. We illustrate how these mappings work in the case study below. Depicting institutions in terms of structures of care will help us understand more deeply what makes institutions work and how they work. The main tasks of the analyst are twofold:

1. To describe the nature and evolution of relationships in a system.
2. To describe how these relationships drive and structure the system of governance and how the system is sustained.

Case Study   In this section, we return to the Turtle Islands case study, first described in chapter 10, and illustrate how we can apply the model of care to analyze it. We elaborate on how the actual system deviated from and exceeded the formal hierarchical structure and set of rules. In describing how the system actually ran, members of the PCP (Pawikan Conservation Project) would recount practices that could not be captured by established rule systems. Take, as an example, how PCP members would patrol the islands to enforce the ban on egg poaching. As one PCP member recounted:

> (Some portions translated) "…We cannot be in the position of condoning poaching, but we patrol…so as not to encounter any poachers. For example, one of my favorite pastimes there was vocalizing (he then demonstrates)…I would vocalize until I heard echoes back from the other pocket beaches, till I heard three echoes…in the context of these negotiated relationships, they would know that I was coming, because I would project, and they could hide, so I would not see anyone when I passed the area.…I was telling them "hide," and I will not catch you, because if I do, as a law enforcement agency, we are supposed to apprehend you. If the

relationship were otherwise, then people may start bearing arms ...sometimes it's four of us and twenty of them...We would know when we were going to get hit...first, when we hear that there is an upcoming wedding, and you sometimes just need to turn a blind eye...and another is during the Hari Raya Puasa (involving the return to one's place of origin) when they need to find funds for travel...you learn to understand the culture, their dilemmas..."

In essence, what the program amounted to was a mode of "patrolling without patrolling." Through a continuous process of signaling, communicating, and negotiation, the PCP established a finely tuned relationship with the locals. We contrast this with the simple rule system in place, i.e., the directive banning the poaching of turtle eggs and penalties for those caught engaging in the activity. In fact, we found actual practice to go beyond and exceed, in terms of complexity, the formal set of rules and roles, along the following lines:

1. Enforcement of rules involved "patrolling without patrolling."
2. Punitive measures for violators were avoided in favor of counseling, worked through the violators' social circle, particularly elders of the clan.
3. Additional egg harvesting was allowed in times of emergency (e.g., following a death in a family of one of the locals).
4. Equity was an additional factor in egg permit allocation, and PCP staff sought out and favored elderly and infirm residents in allocating permits.
5. Marines, coast guards, and others assisted in enforcement and, later on, conservation education. At the same time, some of these people are thought to also be engaged in trawling.
6. PCP members monitored against trawler fishing around the islands and yet relied on these boats for transportation to and from Manila, for supplies, etc.
7. Local officials combined private encouragement with public censure in dealing with the PCP. While formally subordinate to the Department of Environment and Natural Resources (DENR), local government exerted authority over the PCP.
8. Rules evolved continually and actually would deviate considerably from any set parameters. For example, fishing restrictions were flexible (especially in rough seas).
9. Roles were multiplex, and policy actors normally took on multiple functions in the system. The PCP, for example, would be engaged in

such community activities as refurbishing the local school (in which the trawler companies also assisted), setting up a communications system, etc.

The complex patterns of behavior are best understood through a description of the relationships that were forged between the PCP and locals, which might be imagined as a kind of détente. Indeed, the PCP could not have managed open conflict because they were a small group of conservationists with few resources who had to deal with larger groups of locals, some of whom were better equipped and sometimes armed. It was a dynamic and evolving relationship, and the pattern of working and reworking of relationships was something that had to be established each time the PCP went out on patrol. The relationship also involved the evolution of mutual understanding. The locals came to understand the PCP's need to establish a formal management system and, at the same time, their need to do this without conflict. In turn, the PCP came to respect the role that turtles played in the lives of the residents. For some, the eggs had become a source of insurance to which they could turn when in an emergency or other need. It was understood by the PCP that poaching would increase some weeks before a wedding (where, among the Mapun, the institution of dowry is still practiced) or before the annual pilgrimage to one's birthplace (when some residents would need additional revenue to manage their trip).

An important point, as PCP members would remind us, is that these were not simply informal, unprofessional modes of action — these were, actually, the essence of the program, itself. *These practices, in fact, constituted the program.* The one time when the local wardens did actually apprehend a violator and turn him in, it was to test whether the formal process did actually function (which it did not).

The multiplicity of roles in the PCP program mirrored patterns in the larger society of the islands, in general, as the PCP observed: "...a Jama Mapun may be also a municipal fisherman, an egg collector, and a farmer. The Muslim religious leader may be also a Tausug and a business operator. A government official may be also a farmer and egg collector. They may be also related by kinship and ritual..." (PAWB, 2004).

People regularly departed from, and surpassed, the roles they were supposed to take on. These multiple roles exhibit many elements of irony. Taking the PCP as an example, it has always been an enigma — it represents the authority of the state and yet it was nothing more than an underfunded, makeshift unit within the DENR. To this day, it is recognized only as a project unit, funded out of soft monies on an annual basis. It began as an alien presence on the islands, but increasingly took root in the place.

The PCP is, in fact, partly staffed by personnel from Manila but also includes local wardens from the islands. The local wardens, in turn, are caught between their role as agents of the state and local residents. In this manner, we can understand how they maintain their role as strong proponents of conservation, and yet in some instances, a few of them have been suspected of assisting local residents in poaching.

Blurred positions abound in this system. For example, when the entire system fell apart in 2001, some marines took it upon themselves to attempt to encourage conservation in the absence of the PCP from the harvest areas. On the other hand, the same marines and coast guard who sometimes provide assistance to the PCP in enforcing rules against poaching and illegal trawl fishing, include in their ranks some who own a few of the illegal trawlers. While positioned against the illegal trawler activity around the islands, the PCP is nonetheless dependent on them for transport between the islands and Manila. While anomalous when seen within the formal parameters of the system, these roles emerge directly from the manner of integration of each of these policy actors into the web of relationships. In the following section, we use the model to explain why.

Mapping Relationships The thesis of this chapter is that, in many instances, we can draw much insight by depicting institutions as webs of relationships. This requires that we develop modes of description of relationship building. As explained previously, we characterize a relationship as the constitution of the policy actor along three dimensions. As illustrated in Figure 11.4, wherein we posit two policy actors, Actor A engages in these three operations in setting a relation with Actor B, and vice versa. Out of this congruence of mappings emerge perceivable rules, structures, and organization — it is in this sense that the latter can be thought to be epiphenomenal. To illustrate, let us take the relationship between the PCP and the poachers and attempt to reconstruct these operations for the PCP side of the equation. That is, we begin by reconstructing the constitution (i.e., the identity, characteristics, or attitude) of the PCP along these three dimensions.

Constitution of the PCP As evidenced in numerous interviews, the members of the PCP remain, essentially, conservationists, both in training and organizational mandate. At the same time, they are considered to be a group in the fringe of the larger organization, DENR. It is in this respect that the PCP perceives a need for legitimacy along organizational and personal dimensions. At the same time, the members we spoke to come across as socially progressive, each with a definite, personal focus on poverty alleviation.

At the same time, it is clear from the interviews that they also see themselves as particularly vulnerable. They understand their identity as new entrants into the islands with no long-standing networks or ties. The majority of the PCP are Christians from the Tagalog region of the Philippines, while the greater part of the resident population is composed of Muslims from Mindanao and Visayas. Moreover, the PCP controls few resources with which to establish itself, both financially and logistically. At the same time the members of the PCP are the representatives of the national government on the islands, they are also poorly equipped, vulnerable newcomers to the place. Their two most central motivations are fulfilling their mandate and the equally important objective of security, i.e., being able to do their work without threat of harm or other injury.

Constitution of the PCP-to-Other   In their stance vis-à-vis the poachers, the PCP understands itself to be, first and foremost, a regulator with an organizational mandate to patrol against poaching. At the same time, there is a relationship of dependence with the other island residents, including the poachers. This dependence stems from their need for active recognition, if not cooperation, from the locals — this translates to the need for the others to respect their territory and their need to meet their organizational mandates. Interviews with the PCP members also reveal an attitude of empathy taken toward the island residents, including the poachers. This attitude of empathy is essentially a decision on the PCP members' part to see the situation from the other's perspective. This translates into a position of, at least, latent support for the locals' strategies for survival. Thus, the position taken by the PCP vis-à-vis the other is both that of regulator and sympathizer.

Constitution of PCP-and-Other   Lastly, we want to depict how the PCP constitutes the joint identity of the PCP and poachers as a set, i.e., not one taken independently, but both parties taken together. As a unit, the two groups seem to have evolved into a pattern of coexistence or détente. That is, there is both a mutual recognition of the others' needs and a coordination of each others' actions. By coordination, we mean, among other things, the mutually nonconfrontational delimitation of each others' activities in some coherent way. The coordination has a physical dimension which, in this case, involves both groups being on the islands without directly encountering the other — something that needs coordination on the part of both parties. At the same time, through this same action, each party's identity is reinforced. Sustainability, in this situation, means preserving the PCP's conservation ethic along while, at the same time, preserving the poachers' survival ethic. Sustainability also includes maintaining the PCP's position as a unit within the DENR, as well as the poacher's membership in the larger community of the islands, along with their need for livelihood, respect, and safety.

How the Institution Emerges from the Field of Relationships Understanding these mappings allows us to understand how practices and structure evolve in a context. The links from relations to institutions is not a simple or determinative one. As a counterpoint, we should note that this model cannot give as strong a behavioral explanation as a simpler model such as rational choice. While rationality can at times allow one to solve for unique, optimal strategies, the model of care is not so deterministic. Part of the reason is that the cognitive operation we are talking about is not one of optimization but of coherence. That is, the way the PCP constitutes itself (along the three fields) needs to be coherent with the poachers' constitution, and both, in turn, have to lead to practices and organizational structures coherent with these constitutions. However, there is perhaps a gain in authenticity. For example, in trying to explain collective action within a rational choice framework, Olson had to posit a new type of utility which he called a solidary benefit (Olson, 1968). It is not at all clear that volunteerism of an extensive sort normally results from something like solidary benefit (e.g., Green and Shapiro, 1994; Whiteley, 1995). However, when we explain collective action through the model of care, we realize that such behavior is an outcome of the way a person constitutes self, self in relation to others, and self in union with others. That is, a person chooses to act for the greater good because such action is coherent with her notion of self-identity, i.e., someone who seeks the greater good or is motivated by moral concerns.

In the case of the Turtle Islands, we can use relationships to understand the practices that emerge in this situation. For example, the strategy of "patrolling without patrolling" can be seen to be coherent with the PCP's need to maintain their organizational mandate while, at the same time, survive in the place when survival means eschewing confrontations that they cannot handle. Moreover, such a strategy coheres with their ability to empathize with the locals. In the past, for example, PCP members were known to have taken eggs themselves to donate to locals after a loss of a family member. These strategies evolve from the attitude of détente that characterized the relations between PCP and poacher. This can help explain epiphenomenal structures that we can discern in this situation. For example, the widely cast structure that the PCP employs in censuring poachers encompasses the poacher's elders. This coheres with the PCP's need to regulate with empathy and to respect and find some level of fit with the culture, tradition, and social structures of the place. The hesitation to punish violators accords with their respect for the need of the locals, even the poacher, to maintain standing in their community (which, being insular, allows no one to leave the web of relationships). In return, the locals allow the PCP to fulfill their organizational mandate.

The Unraveling and Restoration of an Institution In a sense, the unraveling of the system underscores the power of the model in capturing this system of governance. In contrast to the careful, respectful manner by which the PCP began establishing and maintaining relationships in the early 1980s, RA 9147 came upon the scene as a completely alien intrusion (as described in chapter 10). Fashioned in a place far removed from the islands and without so much as an effort to consult the locals, the new statute threatened to take away the islanders' sense of ownership of their place. When the PCP first informed the mayor of the new statute, he tore the letter they brought from the DENR and began a verbal tirade on their program. It was evidently not even the fear of losing the income from the egg sales that was most threatening because by the authors' calculations, each family stood to lose the approximately $350 they received every three of four years from their egg allocations — not even 10% of their annual income. Rather, it seems to have touched on the very core of their identity. As we have pointed out, these systems are established on acts of constitution of self and others, i.e., the identity of the islanders themselves. An indication of how systems of care are built upon first, the very sense of identity of the locals, and second, their sense of the entire system as an integrated whole, is read in the following letter:

> Your Excellency, the newly enacted law will deprive us of our traditional livelihood which we have adopted since the time of our forefathers, that is, turtle egg collection.... Our life and living, therefore, revolve around turtle eggs as the natural adaptation of our ecosystem.... And our only hope and solid anchor for our living are the eggs that the Allah-given turtles produce.... This is a prayer that will define our life and death, demarcate the line between hunger and sustenance, and between living and dying. Your Excellency, our fervent prayer. Signed: Sarajul M. Jihim, Mayor
>
> Letter from Mayor Jihim to President Macapagal-Arroyo
> (Jihim, 2002)

In this system, the turtles were an integral part of their very lives and culture, and so the act of separating this component of the ecosystem is evidently tantamount to a threat to the entire society of the islands. As we have pointed out, these systems are necessarily relational and integrative — as a local warden would explain how they met visitors to Baguan Island (the only island where, pre-RA 9147, a sanctuary had been established):

> (Translated from Tagalog) When visitors first come to the island, I tell them: this is a sanctuary. Now, you should know that what this means is that you are part of the sanctuary. That's why you are welcome here. It is not you, and then, the sanctuary...no, you are part of it, and everything else.

Part of the threat was the thought that establishing sanctuaries on all the islands would completely alienate the residents, leading to their eventual exit from the islands altogether.

We also see how systems of care work in observing how efforts are presently being made to repair the broken system. In November 2004, the newly appointed director of the Protected Areas and Wildlife Bureau (the PAWB, under which the PCP is assigned) took an unprecedented visit to the islands. Seizing the opportunity when her schedule permitted the long circuitous trip to the Turtle Islands, she first traveled to Zamboanga on the Philippine mainland to seek out the mayor. They also made other visits to the vice-mayor, councilors, and other stakeholders. It was only on the way back that she realized that they had not arranged for the usual security contingent (and other arrangements) to accompany the team. What seems, on the surface, a haphazard visit was actually an important turning point in restoring the system. Just as RA 9147 had severed the systems of care that the PCP had established since the 1980s, these recent efforts should be seen as the active restoring of these same systems of care. Part of the director's agenda was to propose a five-year moratorium on imposing the conservation plan on the islands. This transition period speaks to the need to rebuild the system based on the main elements of care: time and presence. The moratorium should be seen as a proposal to rebuild and restore damaged relationships. As of last report, the PCP had again begun making plans to return to the islands and begin working anew with the locals. It is a period of renewed hope.

Reflection

The Turtle Island example is one illustration of how we might construct an alternative model that better accounts for the fuzzy, boundary-spanning nature of institutions. It is another perspective on what makes policies succeed or fail. The important point is not so much the particular model of care, but the method of theorizing that allows us to aspire toward greater dimensionality, i.e., topologies of description. The most essential element of this kind of theorizing is to first relax the rigid constraints from the formal. Whatever elements of form are introduced by extant policy models, we need to envisage alternatives beyond them. Having relaxed these formal constraints, we then reflect on what new elements come to the surface. In this chapter's particular model, this new element is that of the relational, but it might be something else, e.g., the cultural, the improvisational, the stochastic, or others. The point is to take these other dimensions more seriously and even analyze them rigorously.

In this chapter, we illustrated how we might generate a model that can, to some extent, capture the inherent multidimensionality of modes of understanding on the part of persons and groups, and a corresponding complexity in the forms and workings of institutions they create. In doing this, we also attempted to capture elements of knowing and organization that go beyond the strictly formal. This is not because of our rejection of the formal, but rather the purpose is to bring analysis closer to how things actually are and how they function in the real world. The intent is to escape the strictures of the typological, wherein analysis is confined to the dictates of particular (and self-contained) categorical schema. In so doing, perhaps we can find ways to reimagine how real institutions and policies are experienced in the real world. It is this task of reimagination that occupied us throughout this chapter, i.e., the aim of reclaiming the essence of policy situations that we lost when we enshrined the process of formalization. The following lays out this mode of analysis as a series of steps:

1. Coherence: Intepreting institutions as the outcome of the constant working and reworking of a system of relationships.
2. Topology: Seeking out elements of an institution that escape the strictures of formal description. This means that, rather than ignoring or rationalizing away "blurry" elements, we instead focus our attention directly at the blur and, inside it, find new ways to describe the situation.
3. Design: Relate the relational aspects of an institution to the larger administrative, regulatory, and political structure supporting (or threatening) it. This allows us to consider reforms to these institutions that might better nurture and maintain these active relationships rather than supplant them with more rigidly formal models of governance.

There is a phenomenological aspect to this, in that we do not simply construct models but begin with the discovery of institutions as they are experienced and practiced. We then seek better modes of description to capture these phenomena. We used the word topology to describe the tendency of institutions to transcend the boundaries of our formal models. We then began to describe one alternative, that of institutions as structures of care, that is both less rigidly formal and perhaps more adaptable to institutions, policies, and practices that are dynamic, amorphous, multiplex, and boundary spanning.

We have emphasized the necessary consideration of context in policy analysis. In the previous chapter, we spoke on the need for a policy to attain some degree of institutional coherence. The aspect of this that we have emphasized is that of a policy somehow fitting the particularities and contingencies of its context of application. This leads us to a related notion, which is that of *contextualization* — the process by which, as local actors get increasingly involved, the policy itself evolves and changes to adapt to a place. If a policy is not to be merely imposed upon a place, then, to some extent, it must evolve into it. The alternative, of course, is for the state (or other entity) to maintain the externally imposed policy through hegemonic action. This latter recourse can be both oppressive and resource intensive.

If contextualization is to occur, or in other words, for text and context to somehow come together, then we should expect the actions of local stakeholders to somehow have a transforming effect on the policy. For this reason, as we discuss in chapter 10, we should not simply expect to find institutional isomorphism all throughout the different contexts, but rather a dynamic process in which programs begin to differentiate away from each other. If policies are to fit their various contexts, then they should start to exhibit elements of differentiation.

The process of contextualization runs counter to the strictures of more formal models of policy. In the case of the Turtle Islands, we saw how the conservation program began to adapt to the actions of the conservation team, the island residents, poachers, and others. This can serve to blur formal boundaries of the policy model — in this case, the blurring was most evident in terms of organizational form and rule systems as the program began to be coursed through the web of relationships existing on the islands instead of the more formal, bureaucratic lines of authority. There are several lessons gained from this analysis. The first is the realization that if a policy is to be embraced by local actors, then it cannot be hegemonic — in this sense, contextualization is a necessary element of a sustainable program. We saw this in the unraveling of the conservation program, in almost overnight fashion, after the state began to impose its rigidly formal conservation statute onto the island community. The second is that contextualization can allow a policy to evolve into greater complexity. In the ideal, we might envision a program that exhibited a degree of adaptation to its context that somehow matched or coped with the inherent complexity of the policy situation. In the case of the Turtle Islands this led to a program that would eventually encompass the entire web of relationships on the islands. It allowed the program to exhibit a complexity in purpose, also, as it evolved to meet both the needs of the conservation community for preservation of the turtle population and the multiplex needs and motivations of the community of island residents, who had established long-standing relationships with place, the turtles, and the ecology. There are even more general lessons for policy formulation. Practices, institutions, and systems of governance can become unstable when we impose strongly formal or juridical notions of institutional design and push out the relational. To cite another instance of this, we return to the example of elder care, where we wonder about what it is that might be lost when we professionalize elder care, essentially taking it away from the realm of the family and giving it over to the professional providers. In a sense, this is a turning away from a mode of care that is strongly relational, characterized by virtues and practices associated with the bonds of family, and a turn towards the formal-juridical, where we attempt to encompass care in a set of rules, formal institutions, and contracts. Some authors have pointed to the possibility that this may result in the loss of essential aspects of caring (e.g., see Stone, 2000) that inheres in the loving relationship between family members. Generalizing this situation, we wonder whether formal models of institutions do, in fact, drive out the essence of what fuels some institutions — namely, relationships. Conversely, how can policies be formulated so as to be supportive of the complex and contextual web of relationships found in each place?

In this chapter, we developed a model that portrayed institutions as structures of care, i.e., outcomes of the working and reworking of relationships. The method we employed is a more general one, however. Essentially, what we have referred to as a topological framework of analysis begins with the complexity of the system or context being studied. We then construct analytics and descriptives to better capture the essence of these systems, beginning with the need to find modes of description that portray the elements of the program that exceed the boundaries of formal models. One truism about practice is that it always extends itself beyond the form in which an institution is cast. A topological framework involves attempts to somehow describe even the aformal aspects of practice — it responds to the phenomenology of an institution wherein policies are experienced, and analysis consists of attempting a faithful representation of such experience. The strategy can begin with a negative dialectic, in which we presume a formal model of policy, and then proceed to find elements of practice that blur these boundaries. This leads us to develop, hopefully, more powerful modes of description.

Lastly, we should note some parallel between these insights and those taken from the growing field of complexity theory (for an example of how complexity is treated from an institutional perspective, see Stacey, 1996 and Mitleton-Kelly, 2003). Complex systems are said to be dynamic, non-linear, evolutionary, and inherently difficult to capture within a formal, predictive model. For this reason, scholars in the area of management of complex systems point to the need for adaptive management schemes wherein learning, innovation, and adaptation are in the forefront of program design.The quality of being "adaptive" invariably involves what we have referred to as contextualization. That is, for a program to be able to be effective despite the unpredictable conditions found in a complex environment, its design or operation has to evolve to fit its context. Moreover, for the program to be responsive to uncertain and dynamic conditions, it cannot be captured by a static system of rules or organization — in other words, it has to go beyond the formal and into the realm of practice. The mode of analysis we developed in this chapter is one response to the growing need to evaluate complex systems.

As we discuss further in the final chapter, adaptation and contextualization require closer attention to practice and some escape from the strictures of typology.

CHAPTER 12

Conclusion

Let us retrace some of our steps. We began by examining the foundations of policy analysis, tracing it back to the influential model(s) of rationality that grew out of the Enlightenment (but, of course, traces its origins to much earlier Western and Eastern thought). By entering into its foundational elements in some depth, we began to see how its formalization of human cognition (and, by extension, what analysis means) led to a strongly positivist, authoritarian mode of inquiry. It is the construction of policy as a decision that, from that point onward, that has dominated the very way we go about policy analysis. It is, in many ways, a beautiful construct, and the problem really resides in the aspect of dominance.

We then proceeded to examine what might be described as a revolt against the strongly rational-purposive model of the Enlightenment in the form of various movements that, for lack of a better term, are sometimes lumped under the term postpositivist. In these diverse movements of thought, the analyst is urged to leave the idea of analysis as measurement and take on an alternative concept of analysis as interpretation. In this movement, we begin to see policy as a process of construction. Whether pluralist, poststructuralist, or agonistic, the discursive practices by which policies are constructed become the focus of these disciplines.

In all these frameworks, thus far, we found a residual hypostasis that reveals itself, in policy talk, as a strong tendency to separate text from context. It is this cognitive gap that we referred to in the beginning as the problem of mythology and that persists in our attempt to fit policy situations, and the world at large, into the mold of our cognitive framework. This volume speaks to a different mode of analysis, and that is by first entering into the context and seeing the policy situation itself as a phenomenon. We then attempt to give a faithful description of this situation using our various policy discourses, but always starting from an attitude of utter respect and openness for the situation itself. This reminds me of a Zen *koan* about the teacher, Tokusan.

> A monk came out of the congregation and proceeded to bow before Tokusan, as was customary for a disciple to do. But Tokusan struck him without even waiting for him to finish bowing. The monk naturally failed to understand and protested, "I am just beginning to bow before you, O master, and why did you strike me?" The master explained, "Because if I wait for your mouth to open it is already too late."

> Suzuki, 1962

Sometimes it seems that, to an economist, every problem in the world looks like a market failure, and to a political scientist, everything seems like a pluralistic power struggle. To begin and end with our policy constructs — that is the movement from which the gap between text and context emerges. The idea of policy as text runs through the entire history of policy thought, from the rationalist notions of the *summum bonum* to the strong postmodernist position of communication as paralogy. It speaks to the analyst's hubris and to the devolution of context, community, and place as merely inert targets for intervention (as pointed out by Schneider and Ingram, 1997).

I am reminded of a research project I had been working on some years ago. It involved the program evaluation of a new public–private partnership in municipal recycling. At one point, one of the collaborators turned to me and asked, "So, what do you think, is this program top-down or bottom-up?" I sat for a moment to think about it, and finally told him that I just could not decide one way or the other. The reason was not that the program was so very unique, but that the question was impossible to answer. Essentially, it required the reduction of a complex, many-faceted institution into a simple, dichotomous variable. I believe I said something about there being no arrows pointing us one way or the other in real life. That is, the real world is not ordered according to any categorical scheme, and we have difficulty judging what might be "top" from "bottom." On the other hand, the strength of these categorical systems is that they are easy to operationalize. They give us directions to proceed.

The theme of this chapter, and book, is that perhaps there are ways to be more respectful of the rich, inscrutable nature of real institutions, places, and practices while, at the same time, finding useful ways to proceed even in the midst of complexity. However, this requires that we open up our understanding to what *analysis* might mean. At times, the word will seem less like *problem solving* than *learning* or *discovery*. At other times, it might take on the color of *critique* or *description* or, as in this chapter, *reconstruction*. In every instance, analysis is, first and foremost, *understanding*. In Part III of this book, we sought to imagine analytics that emphasized, respectively, experience, context, and dimensionality. In so doing, we tried to open up new avenues, not by any means complete, for understanding. They give us new ways to begin discovering why some policies work and others fail. What does it mean to say that a policy "worked" in the first place? (There are answers to the last question, by the way, but the point is that such answers may not be so simple.)

Part of it is to free the analyst from the curse of methodology, i.e., the insistence on particular templates before reflecting on what the policy situation warrants. Different templates provide different perspectives on a situation. In general, our modes of analysis have to increasingly be multiplex. At least to some extent, understanding requires opening up methodology to the policy situation. At times, the analysis itself will take on a multimodal form. Other times, the analyst will find herself improvising fresh modes of reasoning and inquiry. We use method instead of having method use us.

The other requirement is to approach policy situations with utter respect. Always and invariably, the situations hold something ineffable from us. If there are fundamental uncertainties (e.g. the Heisenberg principle) even within the natural sciences, what more with the social? Someone should propose, sometime, an equivalent social Heisenberg principle. Policy studies is a multidisciplinary field — more than this, however, it is supradisciplinary, transcending scholarly categories (on a related note, see Stokols et al., 2003, for some discussion of how integrative, collaborative research might possibly lead to entirely new frameworks or *transdisciplines*). This calls for a fundamental respect for other disciplines and, moreover, for those who cross or bridge disciplinary boundaries. Contrary to fears that this may foster some sort of dilution of method and theory, the degree of analytical and theoretical rigor may, in fact, increase, with the increase in dimensionality because we are now to be judged not only according to the norms of the *a priori* analytic, but also that of authenticity. There is a decidedly pragmatist element to some of this discussion, but this inheres not in the analytics presented herein so much as in the entire field of policy studies itself. Policy begins, and ends, in the real.

But the real defies analysis. The social world is, to borrow a line from Gerard Manley Hopkins, full of "dappled things" and "all things counter, original, spare, strange; whatever is fickle, freckled (who knows how?) with swift, slow; sweet, sour; adazzle, dim" (Hopkins, 1918). Intervention in policy situations requires sophistication, a fundamental honesty, and openness to discovery. When some point out how we see the world through either pluralist or postmodern lenses, they may forget that there is much that we see together or that, invariably, we see. Authenticity requires that we admit that there are phenomena that we can understand together. Authenticity requires being open to deconstruction of whatever construct we favor, and even of deconstruction itself. We cannot let plurality or doubt take us away from our main analytical task, which is *to see, and to constantly see new things*. The aspect of seeing the new within the constant is crucial to analysis. People are complex. Institutions are a rich manifold of differences. Academic nominalism may not circumscribe the experience of things. Coffee drinkers know this. To see the new within the old. For the analyst, this may require a willingness to go beyond the strictures of method or discipline. At times, it may require us to focus away from the things that everybody else sees. In the previous chapter, we noted how some insights are arrived at only when we look into the blur of things. Some things become clear only when we look away from the center and into the periphery (for a particularly concrete illustration of this, see Ingram, Laney, and Gillilan, 1995, for an extended treatment of border regions).

I cannot help but end the book on a personal reflection. I am in the business of advising students, and I am reminded of some of my many conversations with them. Many seek advice from me on research involving some kind of program evaluation, and increasingly these students are curious about programs that have taken on more decentralized, participative forms. They typically go off and study an organization or program for some months, and then come back and report to me. The following is my attempt at reconstructing and condensing some of these conversations:

"So, tell me, how did your research go?"

"I think it went really well. I was able to enter into the organization and study it up close for three months. I used participant–observer techniques, and basically employed an ethnographic approach."

"Wonderful. So...what did you observe?"

"Well, they try and open up to community and make everything participative ..."

"Well, okay!"

"...But they don't do enough, you know. There's not enough participation."

"What does that mean?"

"Well, there should be more participation. They should do more to access local knowledge, to empower locals, and to do capacity building. There's not enough participation...there should be more participation, more empowerment."

A year or two later, I am approached by another student wanting to study a similar program. The student goes off and works, then comes back in a couple of months. I ask that student the same questions, and they tell me, well, it was all very interesting, but, you know, there was not enough participation. So now I make it a point at the beginning of a student's research to tell him or her: "Look, I will save you some work and write the first thing in your conclusion section for you, and it is this: 'There was not enough participation.'" Then, I tell them, you can go beyond it, and now go and do your research. Or, just substitute for the word, participation, whatever construct looms large in our minds at the moment (e.g., community, efficiency, power, etc.). The only point I want to make is a simple one. To aspire toward a policy analysis of some measure of authenticity, we need to somehow liberate ourselves from the hegemonic practice of typology. When our construct revolves so completely and single-mindedly around some overweening concept, often our policy prescriptions never get much beyond them (i.e., more community, more efficiency, etc.).

At any rate, as analysts we need to constantly remind ourselves that our models are never, *never*, quite authentic enough. And I should remind the reader of the same. We cannot forget that the foremost requirement of analysis is a capacity for wonder. Wonder overcomes the policymaker's hubris and the academic's myopia. It needs to be a ceaseless wondering in the hope of perhaps, someday, together, even stumbling upon some answers.

References

Adorno, Theodor. 1973. *Negative dialectics.* Trans. E. B. Ashton. New York: Seabury Press, [Reviewed by James Bradley, 1975. *Philosophical Quarterly* 25(October): 368–70].

Alinsky, Saul. 1972. *Rules for radicals.* New York: Vintage Books.

Argyris, Chris and Donald Schön. 1974. *Theory in practice: Increasing professional effectiveness.* San Francisco: Jossey-Bass.

———. 1996. *Organisational learning. II: Theory, method and practice.* Reading, MA: Addison Wesley.

Aristotle. 350 B.C. Nichomachean Ethics, Book II. Trans. W.D. Ross. Oxford: Clarendon.

Arrow, Kenneth. 1951. *Social choice and individual values.* New York: John Wiley & Sons.

Arrow, Kenneth and Gerard Debreu. 1954. Existence of an equilibrium for a competitive economy, *Econometrica* 22:265–90.

Atkinson, Scott and Tom Tietenberg. 1991. Market failure in incentive-based regulation: The case of emissions trading. *Journal of Environmental Economics and Management* 21:17–31.

Aumann, Robert J. and Lloyd S. Shapley. 1974. *Values of non-atomic games.* Princeton, NJ: Princeton University Press.

Bansal, S., S. Davis, C. Buntine, and B. Piazza. 1998. *Holding our breath: Environmental injustice exposed in southeast Los Angeles.* Huntington Park, CA: Communities for a Better Environment.

Barrett, C., K. Brandon, C. Gibson, and H. Gjertsen. 2001. Conserving tropical biodiversity amid weak institutions. *BioScience* 51:497–502.

Baudrillard, Jean. 1994. *Simulacra and simulations.* Trans. Sheila Glaser. Ann Arbor: University of Michigan Press.

Been, Vickie and Francis Gupta. 1997. Coming to the nuisance or going to the barrios? A longitudinal analysis of environmental justice claims. *Ecology Law Quarterly* 24:1–56.

Bentham, Jeremy. 1789. *An introduction to the principles of morals and legislation.* London: T. Payne.

———. 1838–1843. *The works of Jeremy Bentham.* 11 vols. Published under the Supervision of His Executor, John Bowring, Edinburgh: W. Tait.

Benvenisti, Eyal. 2002. *Sharing transboundary resources: International law and optimal resource use.* Cambridge: Cambridge University Press.

Berger, Peter and Thomas Luckmann. 1966. *The social construction of reality.* New York: Doubleday.

Bhaskar, Roy. 1979. *The possibility of naturalism.* Brighton: Havester.

Blumer, Herbert. 1969. *Symbolic interactionism: Perspective and method.* Englewood Cliffs, NJ: Prentice-Hall.

Boer, J. T., M. Pastor, J. L. Sadd, and L. D. Synder. 1997. Is there environmental racism? The demographics of hazardous waste in Los Angeles County. *Social Science Quarterly* 78(4):793–810.

Bourdieu, Pierre. 1977. *Outline of a theory of practice.* Cambridge: Cambridge University Press.

———. 1990. Structure, habitus, practice. In *The logic of practice.* Trans. Richard Nice. Palo Alto, CA: Stanford University Press.

Brentano, Franz Clemens. 1874. *Psychology from an empirical standpoint.* English trans. A. C. Rancurello, D. B. Terrell, and L. L. McAlister. London: Routledge.

Brown, S. and K. Eisenhardt. 1997. The art of continuous change: linking complexity theory and time-paced evolution in relentlessly shifting organizations. *Administrative Science Quarterly* 42(1):1–34.

Bunge, Mario. 1979. *Causality in modern science.* New York: Dover.

Cain, M. T. 1977. The economic activities of children in villages in Bangladesh. *Population and Development Review* 3:201–228.

Chambers, Robert. 1983. *Rural development: Putting the last first.* London: Longman Chambers.

Chang, Ruth. 1997. *Incommensurability, incomparability, and practical reason.* Cambridge: Harvard University Press.

CBE, Communities for a Better Environment. 2005. *Children's health and environment in SELA: A participatory research project.* Huntington Park, CA: Communities for a Better Environment.

Cooke B, and U. Kothari. 2002. *Participation: The new tyranny?* New York: St. Martin's Press.

Delfino R. J., H. Gong, Jr., and W. Linn. 2003. Children's health — Asthma symptoms in Hispanic children and day ambient exposures to toxic and criteria air pollutants. *Environmental Health Perspectives* 4(111):647–656.

Descartes, Rene. 1984. Meditations on first philosophy. In *The Philosophical Writings of Descartes, Volume II,* Trans. J. Cottingham, R. Stoothoff, and D. Murdoch, Cambridge: Cambridge University Press.

Dewey, John. 1925. *Experience and nature.* Chicago: Open Court.

DiMaggio, P. and W. Powell. 1991. The iron cage revisited: Institutional isomorphism and collective rationality in organization fields. In *The new institutionalism in organizational analysis,* eds. P. DiMaggio and W. Powell, Chicago: University of Chicago Press.

Dinar, Ariel, Aharon Ratner, and Dan Yaron. 1992. Evaluating cooperative game theory in water resources. *Theory and Decision* 32:1–20.

Etzioni, Amitai. 1993. *Public policy in a new key.* New Brunswick, NJ: Transaction.

Fair, Jo Ellen and Lisa Parks. 2001. Africa on camera: Television news coverage and aerial imaging of Rwandan refugees. *Africa Today* 48:35–57.

Festinger, L. 1954. A theory of social comparison processes. *Human Relations* 7:117–140.

Fischer, Frank. 2003. *Reframing public policy: Discursive politics and deliberative practices.* Oxford: Oxford University Press.

Fischer, Frank and John Forester. 1993. *The argumentative turn in policy analysis and planning.* Durham, NC: Duke University Press.

Fisher, Roger, William Ury, and Bruce Patton. 1991. *Getting to yes: Negotiating agreement without giving in*, 2nd ed. New York: Penguin Books.

Foucault, Michele. 1977. *Discipline and punish: the birth of the prison*. Trans. Alan Sheridan. New York: Pantheon.

Freire, Paolo. 1973. *Pedagogy of the oppressed*. New York: Seabury Press.

Freud, Sigmund. 1899. *The interpretation of dreams*. Leipzig-Wien, Die Traumdeutung.

Gadamer, Hans-Georg. 1960. *Truth and method*. Trans. G. Barden, 1975. New York: Continuum.

Geertz, Clifford. 1973. *The interpretation of cultures*. New York: Basic Books.

———. 1983. *Local knowledge: Further essays in interpretive anthropology*. New York: Basic Books.

Giddens, Anthony. 1984. *The constitution of society*. Berkeley: University of California Press.

Gillies, David. 1953. Some theorems on n-person games. Ph.D. diss., Department of Mathematics, Princeton University.

Gilligan, Carol. 1982. *In a different voice: Psychological theory and women's development*. Cambridge, MA: Harvard University Press.

Glaser, B. G. and A. Strauss. 1967. *The discovery of grounded theory; strategies for qualitative research*. Chicago: Aldine.

Goffman, Erving. 1958. *The presentation of self in everyday life*. Edinburgh: University of Edinburgh, Social Sciences Research Centre.

———. 1959. *The presentation of self in everyday life*. New York: Doubleday.

Granovetter, Mark. 1985. Economic action and social structure: The problem of embeddedness. *The American Journal of Sociology*, 91(3):481–510.

Green, Donald P. and Ian Shapiro. 1994. *Pathologies of rational choice theory: A critique of applications in political science*. New Haven: Yale University Press.

Haas, Peter. 1992. Introduction: Epistemic communities and international policy coordination. *International Organization* 46(1): 1–36.

Habermas, Jurgen. 1984. *The theory of communicative action. Volume 1. Reason and the rationalization of society*, Trans. T. McCarthy. Boston: Beacon Press.

———. 1987. An alternative way out of the philosophy of the subject: Communicative versus subject-centered reason, in *The philosophical discourse of modernity*. Cambridge, MA: MIT Press.

Hahn, Robert W. and Gordon L. Hester. 1989. Marketable permits: Lessons for theory and practice. *Ecology Law Quarterly* 16:361–406.

Hannan, Michael and John Freeman. 1977. The population ecology of organizations. *American Journal of Sociology* 82:929–64.

Hardie, W. 1981. *Aristotle's ethical theory*. Oxford: Oxford University.

Hardin, Garrett. 1969. Tragedy of the commons. *Science*, 162(3859): 1243–1248.

Harsanyi, John. 1966. A general theory of rational behavior in game situations, *Econometrica*, 34:613–634.

Harsanyi, John and Reinhard Selten. 1988. *A general theory of equilibrium selection in games*. Cambridge, MA: MIT Press.

Hayek, Friedrich A. 1948. *Individualism and economic order*. Chicago: University of Chicago Press.

Healey, Patsy. 1996. The communicative turn in planning theory and its implications for spatial strategy-making, *Environment and Planning B: Planning and Design* 23(2):217–34.

Heidegger, M. 1927/62. *Being and time*. Trans. J. Macquarrie and E. Robinson. New York: Harper & Row.

Herstein, I. N. and Milnor, J. 1953. An axiomatic approach to measurable utility. *Econometrica* 21:291–297.

Hobbes, Thomas. 1651. *Leviathan; or, The Matter, Forme, & Power of a Common-wealth Ecclesiasticall and Civill.* London: Andrew Crooke.

Hopkins, Gerard Manley. 1918. *Poems.* London: Humphrey Milford.

Horkheimer, M. and T. Adorno. 1972. *Dialectic of Enlightenment,* Trans. John Cumming. New York: Seabury.

Husserl, Edmund. 1900. *Logical Investigations,* Vol. 1, *Logische Untersuchungen,* English Trans. J. N. Findlay. New York: Routledge.

———. 1913/72. *Ideas: General introduction to pure phenomenology.* Trans. W. R. Boyce Gibson. New York: Collier.

Ingram, Helen, Nancy Laney, and David Gillilan. 1995. *Divided waters: Bridging the US-Mexico border.* Tucson: University of Arizona Press.

James, William. 1975. *Pragmatism.* Cambridge, MA: Harvard University Press.

Jihim, Sarajul. 2002. "Turtle eggs are Allah's gift to the people of Turtle Islands, deprive us not," Letter to President Macapagal-Arroyo, Office of the Mayor, Municipal Government of the Turtle Islands, Tawi-Tawi.

Johnson, S., and D. Pekelney. 1996. Economic assessment of the Regional Clean Air Incentives Market: a new emissions trading program for Los Angeles. *Land Economics* 72(3):277–97.

Jones, Candace, William Hesterly, and Stephen Borgatti. 1997. A general theory of network governance: Exchange conditions and social mechanisms. *The Academy of Management Review* 22:911–45.

Joyce, James. 1916. *The Dubliners.* Dublin: B. W. Huebsch.

Kahneman, Daniel and Amos Tversky. 1979. Prospect theory: an analysis of decision under risk. *Econometrica* 47:263–91.

Kalai, E. and M. Smorodinsky. 1975. Other solutions to Nash's bargaining problem. *Econometrica* 43: 513–18.

Kant, Immanuel. 1981. *The grounding for the metaphysics of morals.* trans. James Ellington. Indianapolis, IN: Hackett. Originally published 1785.

———. 1933. *Critique of pure reason,* trans. Norman Kemp Smith. London: Macmillan. Originally published 1787.

Keast, Robyn, Myrna Mandell, Kerry Brown, and Geoffrey Woolcock. 2004. Network structures: Working differently and changing expectations, *Public Administration Review* 64:363–71.

Kohlberg, Lawrence. 1981. *Essays on moral development,* Vol. II, *The psychology of moral development: The nature and validity of moral stages.* San Francisco: Harper & Rowe.

Last, Jerold, Wei-Min Sun, and Hanspeter Witschi. 1994. Ozone, NO, and NO_2: Oxidant air pollutants and more. *Environmental Health Perspectives* 102(supp. 10):179–84.

Laswell, Harold. 1970. The emerging conception of the policy sciences. *Policy Sciences* 1:13–4.

Latour, Bruno. 1987. *Science in action.* Cambridge, MA: Harvard University Press.

Lejano, Raul. 2002. Toward a topological concept of rationality. *BUDHI* 6(2,3):245–55.

Lejano, Raul and Climis Davos. 1995. Cost allocation of multi-agency water resource projects. *Water Resources Research* 31(5):1387–93.

Lejano, Raul and Climis Davos. 2002. Fair share: siting noxious facilities as a risk distribution game under nontransferable utility. *Journal of Environmental Economics and Management* 43:251–266.

Lejano, Raul, Bill Piazza, and Douglas Houston. 2002. Rationality as social justice and the spatial-distributional analysis of risk. Environment and Planning C: Government Policy 20:871–888.

Lejano, Raul and Hirose Rei. 2005. Testing the assumptions behind emissions trading in non-market goods: The RECLAIM program in southern California. *Environmental Science & Policy* 8:367–77.

Lejano, Raul and Alma Ocampo-Salvador. Context and differentiation: Comparative analysis of two community-based fishers' organizations, *Marine Policy* (forthcoming).

Lejano, Raul and C. Scott Smith. 2006. Incompatible land uses and the topology of cumulative risk. *Environmental Management* (forthcoming).

Lejano, Raul, Daniel Stokols, Toby Warden, and Hannah Aoyagi. 2005. New methodologies for describing the phenomenology of environmental risk. Working Paper.

Levinas, Emmanuel. 1961. *Totality and infinity.* Pittsburgh, PA: Dusquense.

Levi-Strauss, Claude. 1968. *Structural anthropology.* London: Allen Lane.

Lyotard, Jean-Francois. 1979. *The postmodern condition: A report on knowledge.* (12th Printing, 1999), Minneapolis: University of Minnesota.

Manor, James. 1999. *The political economy of democratic decentralization.* Washington, D.C.: IBRD.

Marcuse, Herbert. 1964. *One-dimensional man.* Boston: Beacon Press (2nd ed. 1991).

Marx, Karl. 1887. *Capital (Das Kapital).* Moscow: Progress Publishers.

Mayntz, Renate. 1993. Modernisation and the logic of interorganisational networks. *Knowledge and Policy: The International Journal of Knowledge Transfer and Utilization* 6:13–6.

MacIntyre, Alasdair. 1983. *Whose justice? Which Rationality?* Notre Dame: Notre Dame University Press.

Mead, George Herbert. 1934. *Mind, self and society.* Chicago: University of Chicago Press.

Mercer, R., D. Costa, and J. Crapo. 1995. Effects of prolonged exposure to low doses of nitric oxide or nitrogen dioxide on the alveolar septa of the adult rat lung. *Laboratory Investigations* 73:20–8.

Miles, R. and C. Snow. 1986. Organizations: New concepts for new forms. *California Management Review* 28:62–73.

Mill, John Stuart. 1863. *Utilitarianism.* London: Parker, Son, & Bourn.

Mitleton-Kelly. 2003. *Complex systems and evolutionary perspectives on organisations: the application of complexity theory to organisations.* Oxford. Pergamon.

Mitrany, David. 1975. *The Functional Theory of Politics.* London: Martin Robertson.

Morello-Frosch R., M. Pastor, C. Porras, and J. Sadd. 2002. Environmental justice and regional inequality in southern California: Implications for future research. *Environmental Health Perspectives* 110:149–54.

Morrow, R. A. 1994. *Critical theory and methodology.* London: Sage.

Mosse, David. 2004. Is good policy unimplementable? Reflections on the ethnography of aid policy and practice. *Development and Change* 35(4):639–71.

Nash, John. 1950. The bargaining problem. *Econometrica* 18:155–62.

Nash, John. 1951. Non-cooperative games. *Annals of Mathematics* 54:286–95.

Nietzsche, Friedrich Wilhelm. 1901. *Der Wille zur Macht* (English trans. *The Will to Power,* 1910).

———. 1967/1989. *Zur Genealogie der Moral* (*On the genealogy of morals.* Trans. Walter Kaufmann and R. J. Hollingdale. *Ecce homo.* Trans.and ed. Walter Kaufmann; with commentary by Walter Kaufmann). New York: Vintage Books.

North, Douglass. 1990. *Institutions, institutional change, and economic performance.* New York: Cambridge University Press.

Olson, Mancur. 1965. *The logic of collective action.* New York: Shocken Books.

Ostrom, Elinor. 1990. *Governing the commons.* Cambridge: Cambridge University Press.

———— 1994. *Rules, games, and common-pool resources*, with Roy Gardner and James Walker. Ann Arbor: University of Michigan Press.

Palmer, K., W. Oates, and P. Portney. 1995. Tightening environmental standards: The benefit-cost or the no-cost paradigm? *Journal of Economic Perspectives* 9:119–32.

PAWB, Protected Areas and Wildlife Bureau. 2004. *Situational analysis on the Turtle Islands*. Quezon City: PAWB.

Peirce, Charles. 1905. What pragmatism is. *The Monist* 15:2(April):161–81.

Piaget, Jean. 1929. *The child's conception of the world*. New York: Harcourt, Brace Jovanovich.

Portney, Paul R. 1990. Economics and the Clean Air Act. *Journal of Economic Perspectives* 4:173–81.

Powell, Walter. 1991a. Neither market nor hierarchy: Network forms of organisation. *Research in Organizational Behaviour* 12:295–336.

————. 1991b. Expanding the scope of institutional analysis. In *The new institutionalism in organizational analysis*, eds. Walter Powell and Paul DiMaggio. Chicago: University of Chicago Press.

Pressman, J. and A. Wildavsky. 1979. *Implementation: how great expectations in Washington are dashed in Oakland: or, why it's amazing that Federal programs work at all, this being a saga of the Economic Development Administration as told by two sympathetic observers who seek to build morals on a foundation of ruined hopes*. Berkeley: University of California Press.

Rapley, John. 1996. *Understanding development: Theory and practice in the Third World*. Boulder, CO: Lynne Rienner

Rawls, John. 1971. *A theory of justice*. Cambridge, MA: Belknap Press of Harvard University Press.

Ricoeur, Paul. 1971. The model of the text: Meaningful action considered as a text. *Social Research* 38:536–62.

————. 1981. *Hermeneutics and the human sciences: Essays on language, action, and interpretation* (Paris: Editions de la Maison des sciences de l'homme). New York: Cambridge University Press.

————. 1991. *From text to action — Essays in hermeneutics. II*. London: Athlone Press.

Roe, E. 1994. *Narrative policy analysis: Theory and practice*. Durham, NC: Duke University Press.

Rorty, Richard. 1980. *Philosophy and the mirror of nature*. Oxford: Oxford University Press.

Rose-Ackerman, S. 1999. *Corruption and government: causes, consequences and reform*. New York: Cambridge University Press.

Ryle, Gilbert. 1971. *Collected Papers*. New York: Barnes & Noble.

Sabatier, Paul A. and Hank C. Jenkins-Smith. 1993. *Policy change and learning: An advocacy coalition approach*. Boulder, CO: Westview Press.

Said, Edward. 1993. *Culture and imperialism*. New York: Random House.

Savage, L.J. 1954. *The foundations of statistics*. New York: Wiley.

SCAQMD (South Coast Air Quality Management District). 1993. RECLAIM Volume III: Socioeconomic and Environmental Assessment. Diamond Bar, CA: SCAQMD.

Scheler, Max. 1957. *Gesammelte Werke* (Collected Works), Berne: Francke Verlag.

Schneider, Anne and Helen Ingram. 1997. *Policy design for democracy*. Lawrence: University of Kansas.

Schön, Donald. 1983. *The reflective practitioner: How professionals think in action*. New York: Basic Books.

Schön, Donald and Martin Rein. 1995. *Frame reflection: Toward the resolution of intractable policy controversies*. Cambridge, MA: MIT Press.

Selten, Reinhard. 1975. Reexamination of the perfectness concept for equilibrium in extensive games. *International Journal of Game Theory* 4:25–55.

Sen, Amartya Kumar. 1970. *Collective choice and social welfare.* San Francisco: Holden-Day.

Shapley, Lloyd S. 1952. Notes on the N-Person Game III: Some Variants of the von-Neumann-Morgenstern Definition of Solution. Rand Corporation research memorandum, RM-817.

———. 1953. A value for n-person games. In *Contributions to the theory of games,* vol. 2, eds. H. Kuhn and W. Tucker. Princeton: Princeton University Press.

Simon, Herbert. 1957. *Models of man,* New York: Wiley.

Smith, Adam. 1776. *The wealth of nations.* Edinburgh: Glasgow.

Stacey, Ralph. 1996. *Complexity and creativity in organizations.* San Francisco: Berrtt-Koehler.

Stavins, Robert. 1995. Transactions costs and tradable permits. *Journal of Environmental Economics and Management* 29:133–49.

Stokols, D., Fuqua, J., Gress, J., Harvey, R., Phillips, K., Baezconde-Garbanati, L., Unger, J., Palmer, P., Clark, M., Colby, S., Morgan, G., & Trochim, W. 2003. Evaluating transdisciplinary science. *Nicotine & Tobacco Research* 5:S-1,S21-S39.

Stone, Deborah A. 1988. *Policy paradox and political reason.* Glenview, IL; Boston, MA; London: Scott, Foresman.

Stone, Deborah. 1997. *Policy paradox: The art of political decision-making.* New York: Norton.

Stone, Deborah. 2000. Caring by the book: How work rules thwart good care, In Harrington-Meyer, M. ed., *Care Work: Gender, Labor, and Welfare States.* New York: Routledge.

Susskind, Lawrence, Jennifer Thomas-Larmer, and Sarah McKearnen. 1999. *The consensus building handbook: A comprehensive guide to reaching agreement.* Thousand Oaks, CA: Sage.

Suzuki, Daisetz. 1973. *The essentials of Zen Buddhism: Selected from the writings of Daisetz T. Suzuki,* ed. B. Phillips. Westport, CN: Greenwood. First published 1962.

Szasz, Andrew, Michael Meuser, Hal Aronson, and Hiroshi Fukurai. 1993. *Demographics of proximity to toxic pollution: The case of Los Angeles County.* Santa Cruz: University of California, Sociology Board.

Taylor, Michael. 1987. *The possibility of cooperation.* Cambridge: Cambridge University.

Tiebout, Charles. 1956. A pure theory of local expenditures. *Journal of Political Economy* 64:416–424.

Tsebelis, George. 1990. Penalty has no impact on crime: A game theoretic analysis. *Rationality and Society* 2:255–86.

UCC (United Church of Christ). 1987. *Toxic wastes and race in the United States: A national report on the racial and socio-economic characteristics with hazardous waste sites.* New York: UCC Commission for Racial Justice.

USEPA (U.S. Environmental Protection Agency). 2002. Framework for Cumulative Risk Assessment. Washington, D.C: Risk Assessment Forum.

USGAO (U.S. General Accounting Office). 1983. Siting of Hazardous Waste Landfills and Their Correlation with Racial and Economic Status of Surrounding Communities. Washington: DC.

von Neumann, John and Oskar Morgenstern. 1944. *Theory of games and economic behavior.* Princeton, NJ: Princeton University Press.

Waldrop, M. Michael. 1992. *Chaos: The emerging science at the edge of order and chaos.* New York: Touchstone.

Walzer, Michael. 1990. The communitarian critique of liberalism, *Political Theory* 18:1:6–23.

Weber, Max. 1958. *The protestant ethic and the spirit of capitalism.* New York: Charles Scribner (first published in German 1904).

———— 1978. *Economy and society* (translation), eds. B. Roth and C. Wittich. Berkeley: University of California Press. Originally published in German 1864.

Weiss, Carol. 1998. *Evaluation.* 2nd ed. Upper Saddle River, NJ: Prentice Hall.

Whiteley, Paul. 1995. Rational choice and political participation. Evaluating the debate. *Political Research Quarterly* 48:1:211–33.

Wittgenstein, Ludwig. c1922/1961. *Tractatus Logico-Philosophicus; Suivi De Investigations Philosophiques.* Paris: Librairie Gallimard.

Yanow, Dvora. 2001. *Conducting interpretive policy analysis.* Thousand Oaks, CA: Sage.

Young, Lawrence. 1997. *Rational choice theory and religion: Summary and assessment.* New York: Routledge.

Young, Lawrence, W. Peyton, N. Okada, and T. Hashimoto. 1982. Cost allocation in water resources development. *Water Resources Research* 18:361–73.

Index